WARTIME CUMBRIA, 1939-1945

Aspects of Life and Work

WARTIME CUMBRIA, 1939-1945

Aspects of Life and Work

Patricia & Robert Malcolmson

CUMBERLAND AND WESTMORLAND
Antiquarian and Archaeological Society
2017

Cumberland and Westmorland
Antiquarian and Archaeological Society
Hon. General Editor
Professor Colin Richards

Wartime Cumbria, 1939-1945

Aspects of Life and Work

EXTRA SERIES NO. 46

ISBN 978 1 873124 75 8

Printed by
Titus Wilson & Son, Kendal
2017

'...we search for the relations of things, one to another, as this young man searches for a warm light in his wife's eyes and that one for the hot warmth of fighting.'

(John Steinbeck, *Sea of Cortez*, 20 March 1940)

'...historians must and ought to be exact, truthful, and absolutely free of passions....'

(Miguel de Cervantes, *Don Quixote*,
First Part, Chap. IX)

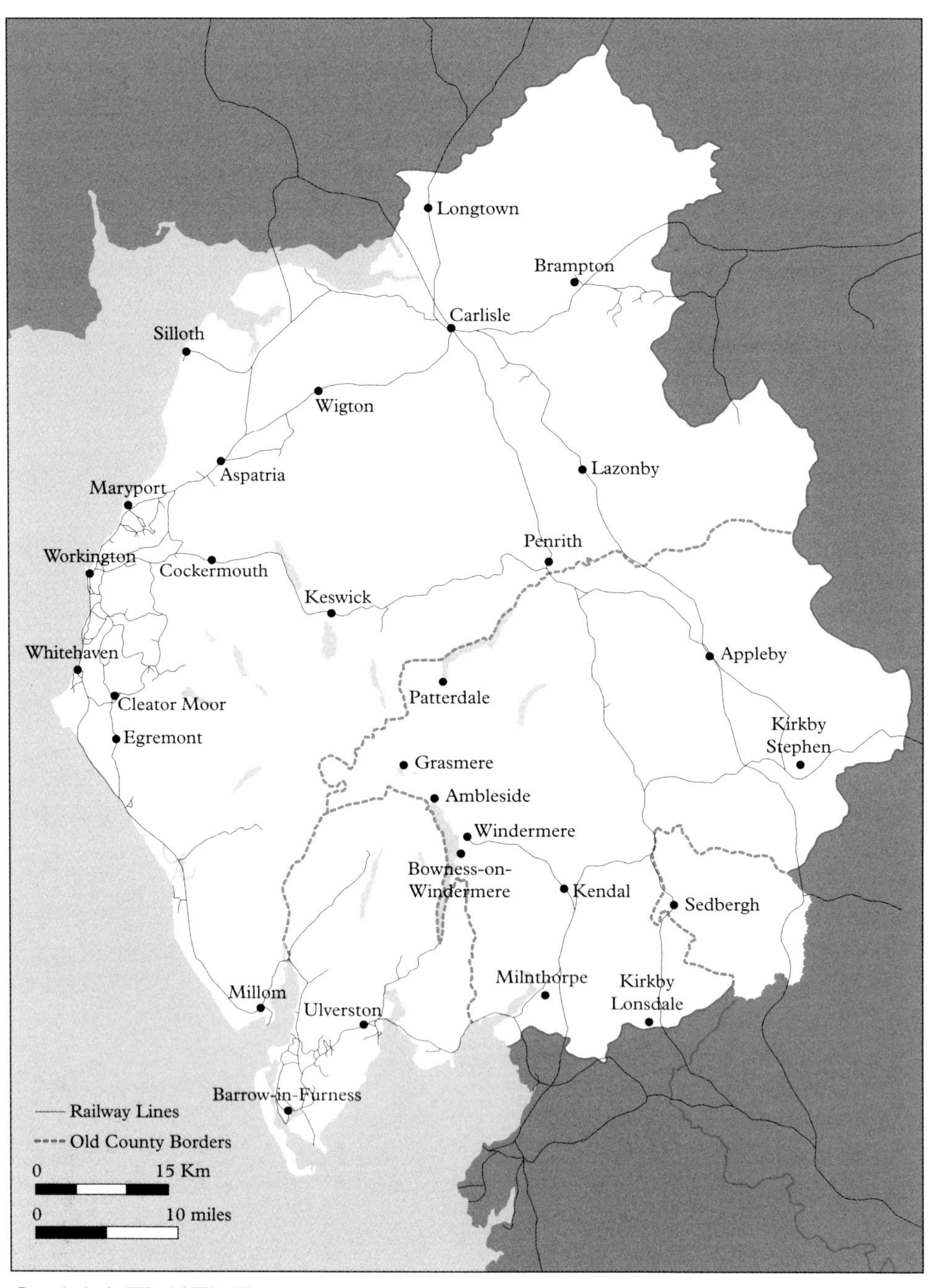

Cumbria in World War Two.

Contents

List of Figures

Acknowledgements

Our main debts in producing this book have been to the excellent archivists and librarians in Cumbria. They have helped us on many occasions and in all sorts of ways, with references, practical support, and useful information, both when we were working in Cumbria and when we were working from home in Canada. We have depended on them to a remarkable degree. We worked in all four county archive centres (in Carlisle, Whitehaven, Barrow and Kendal) and in four libraries (in Carlisle, Penrith, Kendal, and Workington) and invariably had productive experiences. Sometimes the help we were given came from persons whose names we did not know (or have forgotten), but we do wish to mention those who stand out in our memories. These include Susan Benson at the Barrow Archive Centre, the late Lorraine Harper at the Workington Library, and in particular Stephen White at the Carlisle Library, who was very generous with his advice and always prompt in responding informatively to our various enquiries. During the several weeks we lived in Cumbria in 2015 and 2016, mostly in Kendal, we often worked in the Local Studies Collection at the Kendal Library, our main base for research in Cumbria. Initially we were much helped by Jackie Fay, who gave us some valuable guidance, and, after her retirement, by Sylvia Kelly and Kate Holliday, both of whom took pains to ensure that our work would be as successful as possible. We have a high regard for the staff and services at the Kendal Library.

Our friend Ann Stephenson kindly worked for a day on our behalf in the Tyne and Wear Archives. We have benefitted as well from the assistance of Bryan Harper at Titus Wilson & Son Printers and of Corinna Peniston-Bird at Lancaster University.

One fruitful contact from our work in Cumbria was a fortuitous consequence of a Sunday afternoon walk in May 2016 along Garth Row, outside Kendal. There we met Lisa Bell, walking near her home, and our conversation revealed that she had in her possession the wartime correspondence between her mother in Bowness and her father abroad in the army. She subsequently showed us some of these letters and allowed us to quote liberally from several of them. For this we are most grateful, and we do hope that in due course this impressive collection finds a publisher.

One member of the Cumberland and Westmorland Antiquarian and Archaeological Society has given us invaluable advice and support. Colin Richards, General Editor of the Society, helped us to navigate the sometimes perilous journey from manuscript to publication. We are also grateful for his careful reading of the text, which led to our correcting numerous errors, and his editorial comments and suggestions for changes. This book is better than it would otherwise have been as a result of his many thoughtful and constructive observations.

Nelson, British Columbia

January 2017

Preface

Each county in Britain lived its own distinctive World War Two. The same might be said for every town and city and village. While there were experiences that could be seen as national, others were very much locally distinctive or at least much more prominent in one place than another. Any social history of one region of wartime Britain is likely to include references *both* to practices that were found everywhere (rationing, the blackout, civil defence, transportation restrictions, listening to the wireless) and to activities that, while virtually absent in some districts, loomed large in others. This is a book that is written mostly from the ground up – and any social landscape is particular. The land and inhabitants of the far North West and its Lake District are to be distinguished in important respects from the land and inhabitants of, say, Kent or Hampshire or Oxfordshire.[1] Wartime realities varied. Certain directives from London had more impact in some places than in others. Our main concern is to portray the locally-documented experiences of the some 450,000 people who were then living in what is now the modern county (since 1974) of Cumbria, which comprises the old counties of Cumberland and Westmorland, the Furness portion of Lancashire, and a section of the West Riding of Yorkshire centred on Sedbergh.[2]

Cumbria is now the third largest county in England in terms of area, but it was and still is one of the most sparsely populated counties. Its peoples were very scattered. Its population density was (and remains) low; at the beginning of the war Carlisle, the largest town, was home to no more than some 60,000 people. Much of the county is hilly or mountainous – it includes every peak in England in excess of 3,000 feet. It also has a long coastline. Its Lake District was a prominent and already famous attraction for sightseers and walkers, though only around ten percent of the county's population permanently lived there. The economy was marked by a striking diversity: widespread sheep-farming in upland regions, fishing in a few coastal towns, tourism, dairy farming, several major manufacturers (e.g. Carr's Biscuits in Carlisle), the great shipyard in Barrow, important districts of coal- and mineral-mining and arable agriculture. Outsiders probably thought of Cumbria as a bit detached from the rest of England, with Scotland and the Solway Firth to the north, the Irish Sea to the west, Morecambe Bay to the south-west, and the Pennines to the east. It was certainly remote – by most English standards. While already a tourist destination, many outsiders did little more than go through it by train en route to Glasgow. And while its natural beauties were indisputable and connections to great poetry impressive,[3] anyone seeking a university education had to leave the county prior to the early twenty-first century.

* * * *

Some time ago, when one of us was asked what we were working on, her answer was followed by another question: 'Did Cumbria *have* a war?'. No doubt the questioner was thinking of civilian deaths and destruction from bombing. In that sense Cumbria was let off lightly. The fatalities in Cumberland and Westmorland from German aerial offensives were barely in the double digits. Neither ancient county offered attractive targets for the Luftwaffe. Of the some 62,000 people killed on the British home front by enemy attacks, only a little over 100 of these deaths occurred in Cumbria, the great majority of them during four weeks in 1941 in Barrow-in-Furness, then in Lancashire. Coventry's population was about half of Cumbria's: five times as many people were killed there in one night in mid-November 1940 as were killed by bombs in all of Cumbria during all of the war. No Briton, of course, was entirely safe, and the prospect of invasion persisted as a widespread concern until late 1942. But relatively out-of-the-way Cumbria was about as safe a place as anywhere to live in wartime England. Thus its experiences of war were dramatically different from those of, say, Surrey or Warwickshire or industrial south Lancashire.[4]

One consequence of this relative safety and distance from large cities was that Cumbria served as an important reception area for evacuees, and this is a major and recurrent theme of this book. Evacuees arrived in several waves, mainly on at least three occasions in 1939-1941 and again in the summer of 1944, though many soon returned home, perhaps after just a few weeks or a few months. Some evacuees, especially schoolchildren, stayed much longer. The presence of thousands of evacuees was a key distinguishing feature of wartime Cumbria. It was not, however, the only one. Places accustomed to being off the beaten track were exposed to strangers and to unprecedented pressures and intrusions from outside. These were usually irresistible, a function of military and security demands and diktats from London. Local independence was seriously eroded, as it was virtually everywhere in the nation. Labour and consumption were no longer governed primarily by market forces. Longstanding social norms were forced to change. World War Two was bound to absorb, in some way or other, almost everybody. Detachment was impossible. Constraints were inescapable – and new opportunities were also not uncommon, especially for women and teenagers. This is a book that depicts how and with what various consequences Cumbrians *did* have a war. Some of these ways were to a degree distinctive; others were akin to those in many south-western and eastern parts of England, notably districts that were distant from large cities.

While this is in a sense an academic book, with notes and other conventions of scholarship, we have tried to make it as lively and readable as possible. Historical writing should not be stiff or stuffy or ponderous. It should be both supported by evidence and speak to a wide range of readers – readers who are curious about a vital part of their country's recent past and would like to appreciate it more fully. This past was made up of the diverse experiences of tens of thousands of men, women and children who, while living through extraordinary times, often led their everyday lives in ways that were fairly routine, though of course they were coloured by the peculiar demands and difficulties of wartime. Mundane realities often intersected with wartime urgencies. Everyday life was felt as both normal and abnormal. Unexpected and once unfamiliar events and startling episodes became almost commonplace.

We have written what we see as a sort of portrait of society, covering a broad canvass and embracing many aspects of life and work. And we have tried to be attentive both to the individualities and the commonalities of Cumbrian lives. Some experiences were widely shared; others were confined to a particular place, group, association, or family. Chronology, too, is vital. What can be said about social life and conditions in, say, 1944 is usually significantly different from how they can be represented in 1940 or 1941. The details of everyday experience are important. We have tried always to be sensitive to these details and to be cautious about generalizations that tend to lump lots of people together, so obscuring their diversity. Diversity, indeed, is a central theme of this book.

⋆ ⋆ ⋆ ⋆

Life in wartime Cumbria is revealed by an impressive variety of sources, and this is a major reason why we embarked on this project. From past research we were aware of some fine archival sources relating to the county. Two of these deserve special mention. The first is the remarkable collection of papers produced by the Women's Voluntary Services in Westmorland, which is held in the Kendal Archive Centre. These are the richest holdings of WVS material anywhere in England outside of the central WVS (now RVS) Heritage Centre in Devizes and are a tribute to the county's hard-working and very capable organiser, the Honourable Mary Hornyold-Strickland of Sizergh Castle, near Kendal. The collection has been of major importance in writing this book.[5] The second notable collection is the Mass Observation Archive at the University of Sussex, housed in The Keep, adjacent to the University. Here, for Cumbria's history, there is a singular source of distinction – the wartime diary of housewife Nella Last, born in 1889, who lived at 9 Ilkley Road in Barrow-in-Furness. Selections from her massive – she may have written on average a third of a million words a year – observant and spirited diary have now been edited and published in four volumes, two of which cover the war. This compelling diary, much of it still unpublished, is one of the most detailed and wide-ranging personal documents from anywhere in England that relate to life on the home front.*

In due course we learned more about the rich variety of sources concerning wartime Cumbria, and this knowledge helped to nudge us to write this book. First, there are, unusually, four archive centres in the county – at Barrow-in-Furness, Kendal, Carlisle, and Whitehaven – and this virtually guarantees more abundant and more diverse evidence than found in many counties. Second, a lot of newspapers were published in wartime Cumbria – a reflection of its robust civic life, despite the absence of any large city. Barrow, Kendal, Penrith, Workington, Whitehaven, Cockermouth, and Carlisle each had at least one weekly or twice-weekly paper and Barrow had a daily as well, the *North-Western Evening Mail.* These papers are held in the local history collections of four of the county's main public libraries, at Kendal, Penrith, Workington and Carlisle, while the *Whitehaven News* is held in the Whitehaven branch of the Cumbrian archives and the Barrow newspapers in the Barrow branch. Local newspapers have been of the first importance in constructing this book, for, although they were subject to censorship, many everyday matters could be and were reported on, with no or minimal restriction. The third category of sources – and we learned of these only later – comprises various works by local historians, some recording oral recollections. Most have been published since around 1990. They both document topics of importance and help others to find further details about events and issues that otherwise they probably would not have encountered. Two or three of these local case studies appear prominently in this book.

The chapters in *Wartime Cumbria* are sometimes mainly chronological, sometimes mainly thematic. The first three are primarily chronological, covering the first two years of the war, for there was a lot of dramatic change, mainly related to air raids and fear of raids, much of it episodic, during relatively short periods of time. The same applies both to Chapter 7, which focuses on the third quarter of 1944, and to parts of the final chapter. The other chapters (especially 4, 5 and 6) examine most of the wartime years, usually highlighting late 1940 through to mid-1944, when, except for the months up to May 1941, blitzes in England were infrequent or even non-existent and thus evacuation receded in importance. These chapters deal

---

* During the five weeks from 11 April to 16 May 1941, which include the blitz on Barrow, Nella Last wrote 179 pages, an average of almost 36 pages per week. Selections from her diary were first edited by R. Broad and S. Fleming as *Nella Last's War: The Second World War Diaries of 'Housewife, 49'* (London, 2006; first published 1981). Three later volumes of her writing, also published by Profile books and edited by us, are *Nella Last's Peace* (2008), *Nella Last in the 1950s* (2010), and *The Diaries of Nella Last: Writing in War and Peace* (2012).

with persisting aspects of wartime experience – work, leisure, welfare, social relations – that certainly altered but usually gradually, in undramatic ways, at least for most of the population. Individuals and families, of course, often did experience change as abrupt, disruptive and unsettling, perhaps even lethal. While such personal struggles are revealed in all chapters, they are centre stage in Chapter 8.

The challenges of war in Britain confronted the political nation and private households and all forms of association in between. *Wartime Cumbria* strives to take account of the many diverse vantage points from which these challenges, in one county, can be observed, described, and appropriately appreciated and understood.

Notes and References

The two archival sources most frequently drawn upon are the diary of Nella Last and the large collection of papers of Westmorland's Women's Voluntary Services held in the Kendal Archive Centre (WDSO 92/1-2). The latter are organized chronologically, from 1940 to 1945, the first file relating to the county, the second to Kendal. The majority of these documents are monthly reports ('Narrative Reports'), some very detailed, on local WVS activities. Almost all the passages cited or quoted from this collection are identified in the text with reference to the date when a document in WDSO 92/1-2 was produced (thus, for example, 'Westmorland WVS, NR June 1943', or 'Kendal WVS, NR September 1944'). All WVS evidence that is not footnoted or endnoted can be assumed to be found in this collection. The few documents available from the WRVS (now RVS) Archive in Devizes, mostly concerning Cumberland, are distinguished by their own footnote references.

As for Nella Last, the writer of diary no. 5353 in the Mass Observation Archive, all quotations from or citations to her diary are dated in the text and linked to one of the following three sources: *Nella Last's War* (*NLW*, 2006), *The Diaries of Nella Last* (*DONL*, 2012), or, when her words have not yet been published, the Mass Observation Archive (MOA). We have occasionally made minor alterations or additions to passages quoted from the two books, notably when her handwritten manuscript is more revealing than a published selection.

All other sources that we draw upon, such as newspapers and local histories, are identified through individual notes.

1 One recent county history highlights experiences that were, in many respects, vastly different from those in Cumbria: P. Rusieki, *Under Fire: Essex and the Second World War 1939-1945* (Hatfield, 2015). Another wartime county history is M. Graham, *Oxfordshire at War* (Stroud, 1994).

2 The best general account of the nation's home front is J. Gardiner, *Wartime: Britain 1939-1945* (London, 2004).

3 Not only Wordsworth. In the famous 1936 film, *Night Mail*, the scenes shot near the border between Cumbria and Scotland are accompanied by verse composed by W.H. Auden.

4 P. and R. Malcolmson, eds., *Warriors at Home 1940-1942: Three Surrey Diarists* (Surrey 2012); N. Longmate, *Air Raid: The Bombing of Coventry* (London, 1976); G. Phythian, *Blitz Britain: Manchester and Salford* (Stroud, 2015).

5 Because of this material, Westmorland is prominent in our *Women at the Ready: The Remarkable Story of the Women's Voluntary Services on the Home Front* (London, 2013; paperback 2014).

Chapter 1
On Alert

> 'The repercussions of war in civil life might be likened to hurling a spanner into the works of an internal combustion engine.' (*Westmorland Gazette*, 9 September 1939, p.5.)

The first two days of September 1939 witnessed dramatic events in many parts of Cumberland and Westmorland and other regions that were distant from large cities: the arrival of thousands of evacuees, most of them children (Fig.1). This was a movement of people unprecedented in regional or national history. Most major British cities had been designated as areas at risk from German bombing, which might (it was thought) occur at any moment; many predominantly rural counties had been declared reception areas for these endangered city-dwellers, who were eligible to make use of the government's plan for evacuation to safer districts. With a European war looming menacingly and then being officially declared on 3 September, towns and villages in Westmorland and Cumberland were suddenly confronted with trainloads and busloads of newcomers, who had to be housed, taught – the school year was just beginning – and their welfare overseen, though it was unclear specifically what all this might mean. These encounters between (mainly) young visitors and hosts were happening in scores of places nationwide.

The numbers were substantial. Westmorland, with a normal permanent population of around 65,000, was expecting at least 10,000 evacuees; Cumberland, home to around 265,000 people, was preparing at the beginning of September to receive almost 40,000 evacuees (though not that many actually turned up: commonly many fewer evacuees arrived at a reception destination than were expected).[1] Approximately 1,340 evacuated children, all or almost all from Newcastle upon Tyne, arrived in Wigton on Friday, 1 September and another 1,410 were expected the following day.[2] Aspatria received 756 evacuees during these two days, many of whom were billeted in parishes nearby.[3] Carlisle received 3,900 evacuees on 1 September with hundreds more to follow; there were 5,000 evacuees in the city by the end of the first week of September.[4] On 2 September 750 school children arrived in Egremont, and over 600 in Whitehaven; the former were distributed among nineteen parishes in the Ennerdale Rural District. West Cumberland as whole received some 10,000 evacuees in early September.[5] London's Mill Hill School was evacuated to St. Bees and its 300 students (plus others) needed accommodation; there was a sudden increase in St. Bees' population by about 33 per cent.[6] The arrival of evacuees in Kendal in the first fortnight of September may have enlarged the town's population, roughly 16,000 to 17,000, by as much as 20 per cent. Almost all these official evacuees came from the North East, principally Newcastle and South Shields, which had a combined population of a little over 400,000. The majority of the evacuees – almost certainly the great majority – were from working-class families.

Initial newspaper reports were extensive – these, after all, were extraordinary events – and they were mainly intent on celebrating how efficiently the evacuations were carried out, purportedly with few glitches. These reports had an upbeat, cheer-leading tone, consistent with the (understandable) priority of sustaining morale at a time of national emergency. Critical reporting was not a priority. On Friday, 1 September over 500 schoolboys from the Royal Grammar School in Newcastle arrived by train in Penrith, 'half a minute before its scheduled time'. They were received on the platform by local officials (most were named, some lauded); dispersed to two schools, where they were fed; and then despatched to their billets. According to the *Cumberland and Westmorland Herald* the following day (p. 1), 'It was a cheery, smiling crowd of boys who poured from the train on to the station platform. All carried rucksacks or kit bags, and gas masks in their cardboard containers were conspicuous. There was not a sad face among them to reflect the tragedy which brought them from their homes to seek refuge from the horror of a possible air invasion, but to the onlooker there was something very pathetic about it all. Each boy had in his lapel a strip of coloured material – yellow, blue or red – and according to their colours they were directed to their respective group, indicated by standards. Two by two they left the station, followed by a number of their teachers, and were very soon assembled to leave.' Hundreds more evacuees arrived later that day, including 'some 430 mothers and children under school age from Newcastle' and 675 school children for billeting in the Penrith Rural District.

These were very busy days in normally quiet places. On Friday 1 September Keswick received around '325 mothers with young children, expectant mothers and blind people' and another 925 were expected on Saturday, for billeting in both the town and rural area. Appleby and the surrounding countryside were said to be in the process of planning to receive some 750 evacuees, Kirkby Stephen around 220. According to this journalist's account, those responsible for making the necessary arrangements in Penrith 'have been hard at work for many weeks, and the efficiency of the organisation was reflected in the smoothness with which it all worked'.[7] The 2 September issue of the *Westmorland Gazette* (p. 9), published in Kendal, wrote at length about how well prepared the town was for dealing with the anticipated reception of 4,500 evacuees. In a long and wide-ranging story, the *West Cumberland Times*,

2 September 1939 (p. 12) was similarly enthusiastic about the arrangements for handling evacuees the previous day in Keswick, Cockermouth, Wigton, Maryport, Workington, and Whitehaven. It was said that the locals almost everywhere welcomed the Tynesiders warmly, and in Whitehaven 'Housewives discussed the news [about the evacuees' expected arrival] in excited groups, while many more made haste to prepare spare rooms and air bedding'.[8]

With evacuation underway at the beginning of September, Kendal and other towns became activity-filled places. The *Westmorland Gazette* for Saturday, 9 September 1939 headed its main account of these memorable events with the words: 'Westmorland's Warm Reception for East Coast Evacuees – Smooth and Expeditious Billeting Arrangements'. Nearly 2,000 were billeted 'to strange homes' in Kendal and 2,380 to houses in villages in the South Westmorland Rural District – and at least 1,000 more were expected to be housed in Kendal that weekend. Praise was largely unstinting. These Westmorland hosts 'are maintaining their reputation of being cool, calm and collected in troublous times, and, if anything, this week has seen an increase in that jovial spirit for which the county is noted. Never has Westmorland's hospitality been put to such a severe test, but people of all classes have combined in making the new life of the evacuees as comfortable and as happy as possible'. Some 700 children and mothers arrived at Windermere and were housed there and in the local area, including Ambleside, Grasmere, Patterdale, Langdale, and Troutbeck. At Sedbergh, then in the West Riding of Yorkshire, the evacuated children came from Bradford. 'Some of the children were taken to the Dent and Garsdale districts. Local people have supplied toys.' The press almost everywhere praised the handling of the emergency,[9] partly in the hope that citizens would be reassured. Not all Cumbrians were having to make sacrifices, for, with all these newcomers, many local shopkeepers were doing a brisker trade than they had enjoyed for years.

Large numbers of evacuees were also arriving in Cumberland, and there too, much was made of the hearty welcome they received, the hospitable conduct of the county's residents, and the indications, explicit or imagined, of the evacuees' gratitude, contentment and relief. On the afternoon of Saturday, 2 September in Maryport 'women out shopping were proudly introducing their "families" to their friends and traders are reporting better and brisker business from these new "mothers", who are buying their children more clothes'.[10] (A similar point was made a few days later about Cleator and Cleator Moor: the newcomers 'brought a good amount of money into the area, and tradesmen of all kinds have had a busy time in attending to the requirements of their numerous customers'.)[11] The concluding words of this six-column story of 6 September were that 'Evacuees, mothers and children with whom a *West Cumberland Times* reporter has had conversation express their perfect happiness in their new homes'. The arrangements in

Kingstown, two miles north of the centre of Carlisle, were accorded high praise: 'Determined to house their quota of evacuees, the local officials secured the use of no fewer than five condemned cottages in the villages, and rapidly furnished them for their new occupants.' Sixty children and forty mothers were accommodated over two days. 'To safeguard against any unforeseen influx of evacuees, personal calls had been made among the residents in order to ensure additional accommodation.' One man who owned an empty house made it available for two families and several others 'gave the use of cottages ready equipped and furnished for the exclusive use of the evacuees'.[12]

A few reports were sensitive to the darker side of the children's experiences. One observer in Whitehaven thought that 'Some of the children [from South Shields] presented a pathetic sight. Tired by their long journey, hungry, some with reddened eyes and tear-streaked cheeks, they tried bravely to smile cheerfully at their new friends. A good meal in the school dining-room soon cheered them and they were rushed off to their temporary homes by the fleet of voluntary car-owners'.[13] Seeing individual distress eye-to-eye seems in this case to have dampened a bit the desire to highlight organisational efficiencies. While officials in Carlisle were full of praise for how the evacuation had been handled, one alderman was less impressed – given the thousands of incidents that occurred in only a few days, some differing perceptions were surely inevitable. 'He (Mr. Cant) had seen children being dragged very late at night to houses at which application was being made for them to be taken in. He had heard mothers say, "Please take us"..... The thing had been more like a slave market.' His was an atypical view, though it was probably based on direct observation. Another alderman spoke of the refusal of some residents to take children in.[14] The children evacuated during these early September days had mixed experiences and emotions: this was the case of those sent from Leeds to safer districts (often in Lincolnshire), and the children arriving in Cumbria were unlikely to have been different.[15]

Not all was sweetness and light, as the *Carlisle Journal* for 5 September 1939 (p. 2) pointed out. It praised the warmth of the reception in most places for most of the evacuated children, and the 'generosity of spirit' on display: 'many homes have accepted more children than they originally agreed to take'. But there was another side to this positive picture. 'There were some persons who flatly refused to redeem their promise to help those in need of succour. This sad facet to the story was, unfortunately, very prominent in the case of the reception of expectant mothers, some of whom, heartbroken and distressed at the cold shoulder they received, wended their weary way, as best they could, back to Newcastle and beyond. For such who meted such inhumane treatment to their fellow countrywomen, there can be little comfort in the voice of their conscience.' Compulsory billeting was rarely if ever resorted to, though on occasion it was contemplated, as in Wigton in November, according to a local billeting officer. 'The authorities know that some householders, who are well able to care for evacuees, have refused to do so.'[16] This was the beginning of a pattern of behaviour (remarked on throughout the war, in Cumbria and elsewhere) in which the residents of larger houses displayed more reluctance to receive evacuees than the residents of poorer houses.[17]

Cumbrians wanted to see themselves, and be seen by others, in a good light – this was hardly surprising – and thus there was the tendency to choose for publication certain kinds of evidence. '"Cumberland is so cheerful", a Newcastle woman on a weekend's visit to her children billeted in different parts of the county told me at the weekend (writes our Maryport representative). "Things seem to be going on as if nothing had happened and a stranger coming into the country would hardly guess the country was at war." The woman said she had left her home wondering all the time how her children were getting along in their billets and whether they were being properly looked after.' She found a cheerful, can-do attitude in all four reception areas she visited. 'She said she was going back to tell her friends, whose children are billeted here also, how happy and well looked after the children are.' She apparently contrasted this happiness with the grimness of Newcastle, the loneliness women felt with their children gone, and diminished diversions with the cinemas still closed (they would soon re-open).[18] The chief billeting officer at Workington, after hinting at a lack of cooperation by some of the town's more affluent citizens, was quoted as saying that 'The working people have been splendid – practically a hundred percent have taken on their responsibilities without the slightest demur'.[19] By mid-September almost all the government-sponsored evacuation into Westmorland and Cumberland was completed. Overall it appears that the total number of schoolchildren, teachers, mothers with children under school age, and infirm people then living as official evacuees in different parts of Westmorland was at least 9,000, perhaps closer to 10,000, almost 6,000 of whom were schoolchildren; the total for Cumberland was probably in the range of 22,500 (Fig. 2).[20]

* * * *

An immediate issue was commonly clothing, for many children from the impoverished North East arrived with few clothes, or at least few that were serviceable. In Workington the chairman of the Education Committee was within days of the evacuees' arrival acknowledging some of their 'urgent need for footwear' and appealing for 'discarded garments or footwear to be sent to the Committee, which voluntary helpers will fix or remodel'.[21] An advice bureau there appealed for gifts 'of all descriptions, particularly boots and shoes for boys'.[22] (The need for footwear was to persist for years.) It was said of the children who arrived in Kendal on Saturday, 9 September that the householders 'did everything possible to make the evacuees happy and comfortable, and in some cases the kiddies were wearing new clothing outfits within an hour. This generous spirit has also prevailed in the country districts of the county, and ill-clothed children of all ages have been fitted with new outfits'.[23] In Windermere there was 'an urgent appeal' for clothing for evacuees, along with blankets, sheets, and towels, since some householders did not have enough of these to provide for their guests.[24]

The sudden encounter en masse between town and country generated commentary and a few complaints. On 6 September fastidious housewife Nella Last remarked on what she had heard about the dirtiness of the children from Manchester and Salford who had been billeted on some of the country people north of Barrow-in-Furness (then in Lancashire). 'There is a run on Keating's and disinfectant and soap,' she wrote (*NLW*, p. 5), 'while children who arrived with a crop of curls look like shorn lambs – but have stopped scratching!' (She probably depended on others for this 'information'.) Two 'problem families' of evacuees in West Cumberland were deliberately billeted together in an empty country cottage – they soon asked to be sent home.[25] The Cumberland Public Assistance Committee in Carlisle, meeting on 8 September, was already unhappy that some children from Tyneside were arriving poorly clad, and so threatening to place a financial burden on the county. One member, Mr. J. Douglas of Aspatria, 'declared that many of the parents of the evacuees were earning good money' and were irresponsible in not proving adequately for their offspring. '"Some of these children," he thought, "are a disgrace to civilisation. It is not the fault of the children but of the parents."'[26] Similar grumbles were heard in following weeks.[27] Grievances were again reported from people in Aspatria, who had received around 350 evacuees: many residents 'had themselves been unemployed for considerable periods' and yet in numerous cases still 'had to rig the children out with clothing'.[28] There were debates in numerous places in October and November as to who would – or, more accurately, should – pay to properly clothe ill-clad evacuees.

One essayist wrote sympathetically about some of the challenges facing these city children, around fifty of whom had been billeted in his village. 'Some of these small exiles have gathered rowan berries under the impression these were hazel nuts. Of course, any country boy or girl will soon tell them that "hen drunks" or "cock drunks", as the fruit of the mountain ash is known in different parts of Cumberland, are supposed to possess the property of intoxicating fowls and are poisonous to human beings.' He recommended 'practical lessons of nature study' for the newcomers. 'Until they learn to discriminate they would be well advised to eat no wild fruit or berry before bringing it to the people with whom they are lodging.' Farmers, he added, had legitimate concerns about 'the increased dangers of fire, for one knows how serious farm conflagrations have been caused by children playing with matches near barns and stack-yards, and [were] not a little worried at the possibility of gates being left open, hedges broken down and tools going astray', all of which could happen innocently, at the hands of children who knew no better. Thus (he thought) the need for appropriate teaching about country life.[29]

Another plausible account of the social strains ensuing from evacuation was printed in the *Cumberland Evening Star*, 15 September 1939 (p. 1). 'Some of the evacuees from the North-East Coast to whom Workington is now acting as host appear to be very rough diamonds', it was said, 'especially certain of the adults. There are some who think that because the householder is receiving what is, in many cases, a nominal sum for their keep that they need not do a stroke of work and can demand what they like. There are householders, too, who are heart-broken by the treatment their cherished furniture is receiving.' (Alarming stories about disruptive behaviour easily found believers and circulated readily in reception areas.) But this was not the whole picture. 'On the other hand, there are people who are treating the evacuees billeted on them with cold indifference. These are all, we hope, isolated cases.' The writer called for an appropriate system of supervision and monitoring, 'so that grievances may be investigated and those taking advantage of the situation brought to more exact understanding of what their conduct ought to be'. As for the children, perhaps now that they 'are in such close proximity to the Lake District they should be given the opportunity of seeing it. To many, brought up among bricks and mortar, it will be a revelation and perhaps an inspiration for life'. By contrast, another writer imagined how much these children would likely be missed by their parents: 'The vacant chairs, the unusual quietness of the home, will be even harder to bear than the fears of the home front.'[30]

Strained relations between residents and newcomers were evident in Alston Moor, Cumberland, which, it was reported, 'is facing the problems of making its evacuees comfortable and at home. Unfortunately, some of the mothers received in the district have not yet realised the fact that there is actually a war on, and some of them fail to realise that it is not a holiday that they have come for, but that they have been evacuated from danger zones for the sole purpose of safeguarding their children. Some mothers are undoubtedly very grateful, but others drift about from place to place declaring that they do not like the country and are not going to stick it. Several mothers have already returned to Newcastle, taking their children with them. ...One hears on all sides the statement: "It is not the children who are making all the work and upset but the mothers."' The writer concluded by acknowledging that some of the women had in fact settled well and, despite talk about returning home, few had yet done so.[31]

A report by a resident in a village in the Penrith Rural District was typically upbeat but not undiscriminating (*Penrith Observer*, 12 September 1939, p. 6). She stressed the positives – the adaptability of the evacuated children, their pleasures in encountering the wonders of nature, the satisfaction expressed by their hosts and hostesses. The children, she said, 'have been very well-behaved and the tiny tots, especially', – she allowed that the older children were more liable to home-sickness[32] – 'have soon endeared themselves to their foster-parents, breaking down the wall of native Cumbrian reserve as if it had not existed'. (Some readers might find in these words a certain 'honeymoon-outlook'.) Still, there were limits to happiness. 'The children just love the countryside but some of the grown-ups, brought up in the town, have been unable to curb their longing for Tyneside and have returned home. The mothers who found the country too quiet for them have gone back – in some cases leaving boys and girls behind them – and now a new problem has arisen. In some cases where married women have come away to find refuge, lonely husbands left at home have complained of the impossibility of keeping two houses going. Besides that they have found the task of rising early and preparing their own meals almost more than they can manage – and so the wife has had to return, too.'[33]

These disruptions of traditional family life were inherent in evacuation. The vicar of Millom, Cumberland – he was also the billeting officer – was well acquainted with the people in his parish, and saw both sides. Evacuees were not leaving for home because they had been received indifferently, he argued in a public statement. To the contrary, 'except in a few odd cases, which I can count on the fingers of one hand, the people of Millom have done their very best to welcome the strangers and to make them feel at home, sometimes at great inconvenience to themselves and under great difficulties'. The evacuated women, he thought, experienced the understandable strains of feeling uprooted and homesick. 'Then there has come upon them the knowledge that their husbands, left alone at home, need looking after. In many cases these husbands have written and described their helpless condition. Very naturally the wives have been torn in two. The knowledge that there have been as yet no air raids has strengthened their wish to return home. They have found a little country town dull after the great cities. So they have departed, in many cases taking their school children away with them as well as their babies.' This is probably as fair-minded a portrayal of aspects of September's evacuation as you are likely to find – and it avoided finger-pointing. He concluded by remarking on the very different circumstances of children on their own. 'They have settled down most comfortably, and are in the great majority of cases extremely happy and well. They will soon be full members of our family circle. We shall go on doing our best for them, and we are confident that they will never regret having come to Millom.'[34]

Recollections more than half a century after the fact need to be handled with care, but at least two have the ring of accuracy. 'I can remember the children [from the North East] arriving with a few belongings – gas masks, bags of clothing and favourite toys,' said a woman from the village of Melmerby in the Eden Valley. They were gathered in the village school, names checked and then billeted out to various homes in the surrounding area. They had bewildered expressions on their little faces – some cried – others just stared into space.' (Her further words were sunnier, for she went on to observe that 'the majority of the children soon adapted to the village way of life and made lots of friends'.)[35] Another woman, a teenager or young adult in 1939 in Lanercost, near Brampton, Cumberland, remembered the cancellation on 2 September of both the Women's Institute's annual flower and produce show and a village dance. Then there was another abrupt occurrence. 'Suddenly there was pandemonium as three coachloads of very pregnant ladies arrived from the North East as evacuees and the vicar's wife took on the unenviable task of trying to find billets for them with rather reluctant hosts. ...It must have been a very traumatic experience for the women,' she later (in the early 1990s) thought, 'some of them placed in farmhouses with an earth privy down the garden, no electricity, and far from city lights and amenities. Most of them only stayed a few days and to put it politely their habits and manners were very different from ours and caused a few upsets. One villager remembers a group of them sitting on a farmhouse wall the day after they arrived anxiously waiting for the coach to take them to their Tyneside terraces because they couldn't visualise living without a picture house, and fish and chip shop nearby'.[36]

Evidence from subsequent weeks in the autumn of 1939 suggests a mixed picture of individual experiences – and this, surely, was inevitable, given the uncharted territory involved, with strangers being thrown together under the same roof, many unwelcome surprises, and local authorities displaying a wide range of competencies in dealing with the challenges. In some places, no doubt, children settled in fairly happily and found themselves in caring and responsible households, with lots of interesting new things to see and do. It was said that on Saturday, 5 November many children in Workington, evacuees among them, 'surprised their parents and "adopted" parents by taking home large quantities of herrings, many of them still alive. The herrings had been driven in by the porpoises. Such "landings" are not infrequent, and sometimes as many as several hundred fish are left upon the shore'.[37] These were the sorts of situations that were not likely to generate written commentary, though stories did appear to publicise the kindnesses of strangers, for example, to evacuated children who were initially unwanted.[38] There were no 'typical' stories. Moreover, the voices heard from September 1939 are almost entirely those of adults; the candid words of children were rarely heard, their voices often mute, so their actual feelings are not usually knowable – at least not until perhaps decades later, when hindsight and subsequent experience can readily mislead.

No mention has yet been made of private evacuations. An unknown number of people self-evacuated to Cumbria or arranged for their children to move there and be accommodated with (as a rule) friends or kin. No count was kept of these movements; there are only impressions. Since Carlisle, which received around 5,000 official evacuees, was thought to be safe from raids, there were also, it was said, many 'unofficial' evacuees 'staying with relatives or friends in the city. They come from London and many other parts of the country and there are in fact so many of them that the number of children in these parties is providing a problem for the education authorities in planning the re-opening of schools'.[39] It was observed that in Penrith in early September there was, in addition to official evacuees, a significant 'influx of people from large centres of population, many staying with relatives'.[40] Such arrangements absorbed some of the accommodation that the local authorities had counted on for official evacuees.[41] Private visitors usually had the money to get (within reason) whatever they wanted and thus strained the resources wanted for government-sanctioned evacuees – or at least fuelled local price rises.

* * * *

The other major and even more widespread set of changes in daily life resulted from the blackout. As soon as war had been declared, it was reported that ARP wardens in Cockermouth, 'detailed to see the carrying-out of black-out instructions, are diligently patrolling the streets after dark warning residents of overlooked chinks of light through imperfectly-screened windows, which may prove an attraction to the enemy bombers which everybody should be prepared for, even if they do not expect them'.[42] Almost everyone was in some way caught up in the blackout's constraints, both at home and in public places. People walking in the dark tripped over dustbins and kerbs, crashed into lamp-posts, stumbled on uneven pavements, bumped into one another, and sometimes had trouble finding their own houses. Indeed, all pedestrians became much more at risk from falls and stumbles and other such mishaps, and from being struck down by vehicles that couldn't see them. One suggestion was that a person's cardboard carton for carrying a gas mask should be painted white and a small red reflector pinned on the side.[43] Pedestrian fatalities increased significantly during the first months of the war. At a council meeting in Whitehaven on 11 October, one alderman asked that something be done 'to alleviate the lighting conditions in the town. ...The conditions were positively dangerous. He suggested a dimmed light at each street corner' – he worked at the docks and presumably walked there.[44] The

Whitehaven harbour had already been closed to the public, in part because of the hazard of walking near it at night.[45] Later, in early 1943, two men, after a few evening pints in dockside pubs, fell into these black and unprotected waters and were quickly drowned (the tide was in).[46] They were certainly not the first or only victims of the blackout on the Cumbrian coast.

Animals were also at risk. Dog-walkers were warned to take care, and to tie a white handkerchief around their animal's neck.[47] There were reports from Whitehaven of dogs and cats getting badly injured or killed; 'owners are requested not to let them roam the streets, as they are a danger to themselves and the people who have to get about in the darkness'.[48]

The blackout was a concern for everyone. Street lights were extinguished, car lights had to be dimmed to near nothing, railway carriages were poorly lit if they were lit at all. Evening activities were constrained as their sponsors and organisers knew that most people resisted putting themselves at risk by travelling about in the dark. They spent more time stuck at home. This could be stifling,[49] though it must have bolstered the role of the BBC in people's lives. Churches abandoned evening services, sometimes holding them in the afternoon. Restricted evening-bus services to rural areas made it difficult for country people to get to town for the cinema and other recreations. In early 1940 there was speculation that maternal mortality in Cumberland had increased partly because the blackout made it more difficult to move urgent cases to hospital.[50] Cows driven on a road at night, it was said, should be accompanied by lights.[51] And as the police moved to enforce blackout restrictions in later 1939 and early 1940, some householders and trades people found themselves in court facing charges, and often fines, for their negligence in allowing lights to be seen.

War meant not only sustained but heightened commitments to other aspects of Air Raid Precautions (ARP). Bombs, it was widely felt, could fall at any time, and citizens had to be properly prepared to deal with this threat. Fires would have to be put out; first aid posts would be needed. Knowing of the casualties of the Great War, gas attack was especially feared. The prospect of enemy attack was taken seriously and training in defensive measures had been underway for weeks or even months in several towns.[52] Air raid wardens were recruited in all towns and citizens were issued with gas masks. On 31 August in Whitehaven the ARP offices were 'hard pressed … to cope with the anxious mothers arriving in large numbers to test the special gas helmets which are to be issued for children under two years of age', and at the police station, 'a very important telephone centre', preparations began 'to fortify the outside of the building against possible damage from high explosives'.[53] That same day a list of 'Hints for Householders' on how to prepare for, and respond to, an enemy attack was printed in the Kendal press.[54] In Penrith on the morning of Sunday, 3 September, council workmen were busy sandbagging 'barricades against important points in the town', and were helped in this work during the afternoon and evening by over a hundred volunteers – war had been declared at 11.00 that morning. The sand was bagged at a local quarry and then taken by lorries to sites in the town.[55]

Standing on guard – this was what people were told to expect of themselves and others. Immediately after war was declared, residents of Cockermouth could hear at intervals the sound of planes patrolling to the west and on September 4th 'the roar of occasional bombers and fighters flying low over the town itself gave an air of grim reality to the situation and perhaps provided the strongest incentive to the completion of air raid preparations'.[56] There were many inducements to *appear* to be well prepared for self-defence, and most town authorities were keen to show a commendable alertness. This meant, among other novelties, efforts to enlist the work of women. The mayor of Carlisle made such an appeal in a speech to a public meeting on 31 March 1939. 'The Women's Voluntary Services', he declared – the WVS had just been established, with a special mission initially to help with ARP – 'would be of great value to the community, and it was of the utmost importance that everyone should undertake to stimulate and maintain the interest of the women in all branches of National Service.'[57] People of wealth started to step forward in support of national defence: in November 1939 an anonymous donor from Windermere sent a cheque for £500 to the Westmorland County Council to purchase a second ambulance for ARP purposes; a fortnight earlier the first ambulance had been purchased for the county by a woman in Temple Sowerby.[58]

Finally, war brought changes or even curtailment to a number of customary practices and expectations. Activities that had so recently been taken for granted no longer could be. In Workington the Ramblers' Association first suspended activities due to lack of transport, and later were 'carrying on as best they can' (it was acknowledged that new members would be hard to find).[59] Owing to the war, the Carlisle Opera Society's plans for a production of *Wild Violets* to play in December were abandoned and contracts terminated.[60] It was reported that most Ullswater packs of staghounds and harriers would not be hunting, and that some hounds had been destroyed because of the difficulty of feeding a large pack.[61] As men were called up for service, sporting events sometimes could not be held. The Rugby Union announced that all fixtures arranged for the 1939-40 season 'shall be considered as cancelled until further notice. It is hoped that games will be played which do not interfere with national duties or Government regulations'.[62] The planned tour of the New Zealand rugby team, which was to have included matches in Cumberland, was cancelled and the players returned home.[63] The time-consuming nuisance of putting up and removing blackout every day meant that many householders simply chose to inhabit less space when it was dark.

A proper primary education was harder to deliver, partly because classroom hours had to be shortened when a school building was shared between local children (attending, say, in the morning) and evacuees (attending in the afternoon). A few children may have received little or no schooling at all.

But all this did not add up to a compelling scenario of wartime losses. Active conflict for Britons was restricted mainly to the seas. Casualties were minuscule, sacrifices modest, and well-founded threats to personal security few and far between. As early as 30 September Nella Last was noticing how little interest there was in war news (MOA) – 'Perhaps it's because all is so "quiet on the Western Front"'. (Poland, of course, was different: it had already gone under.) 'War seems to be so far away,' she wrote later, on 24 February 1940 (MOA). The most widely-experienced stresses during this half-year were probably related to the brutal winter weather in January and February.[64] As for ARP, which certainly consumed much time and energy and perhaps fostered useful solidarities, some people did realise that Cumberland and Westmorland were unlikely to be priorities for German bombers – though admittedly, who could be sure what was on Hitler's mind? Evacuees, the most visible testimonies in the North West to the anticipated threats to national security, were soon returning home in large numbers – all over the country, in fact[65] – some of them not long after they had arrived.[66] Those who stayed into 1940, certainly a minority, were thus more readily accommodated by their Cumbrian hosts. For most people war only became objectively 'real' and its implications frighteningly immediate from May of 1940.

Notes and References

1 *Westmorland Gazette*, 2 September 1939, 9; *Penrith Observer*, 10 October 1939, 5; *West Cumberland Times*, 2 September 1939, 12.
2 *Wigton Advertiser*, 2 September 1939, 3.
3 *Cumberland News*, 9 September 1939, 7.
4 *Carlisle Journal*, 5 September 1939, 2; *Cumberland News*, 9 September 1939, 7.
5 *Whitehaven News*, 7 September 1939, 2.
6 *Whitehaven News*, 7 September 1939, 5.
7 *Cumberland and Westmorland Herald*, 2 September 1939, 1.
8 Also *Penrith Observer*, 29 August 1939, 5. Internal documents show that these evacuations were carefully planned, with close attention to details concerning transportation, feeding, distribution of evacuees, and the like (Kendal Archives, WC/C9, Bag 3). The classic account of this evacuation nationwide endorsed the view that, administratively, the work was well done (R.Titmuss *Problems of Social Policy* [London, 1950], 106).
9 For example, *Kendal News*, 7 September 1939, 1 and *Penrith Observer*, 12 September 1939, 3.
10 *West Cumberland Times*, 6 September 1939, 3. This report was realistic enough to go on to observe that some of these women could not afford to be so generous – this was not a prosperous district – and 'as the children are in some cases urgently in need, those people who have suitable clothes they have no further use for would be doing a great service by handing them to the needful children'.

11 *West Cumberland Times*, 13 September 1939, 4.
12 *Carlisle Journal*, 5 September 1939, 2.
13 *West Cumberland Times*, 13 September 1939, 4.
14 *Cumberland News*, 16 September 1939, 5.
15 R. Boud, *The Great Exodus: The evacuation of Leeds schoolchildren, 1939-1945* (Leeds, 2000), 70-80, 83-84, and 89-93. This is one of the most detailed studies available on evacuation.
16 *Wigton Advertiser*, 11 November 1939, 2.
17 Evidence on this issue from other counties is presented in T Crosby, *The Impact of Civilian Evacuation in the Second World War* (London, 1986), 46-51 and 56.
18 *West Cumberland Times*, 16 September 1939, 3.
19 *Workington Star*, 8 September 1939, 3.
20 *Westmorland Gazette*, 16 September 1939, 7; *Cumberland and Westmorland Herald*, 30 September 1939, 1; R.Titmuss, *Problems of Social Policy* (London, 1950), 553. Cockermouth was probably fairly typical: with almost 600 evacuees remaining in mid-October, the town's population had been enlarged by a little over ten per cent (Whitehaven Archives, SUDC1/3/202). There is some inconsistency in the statistical estimates for Cumbria from various sources; the numbers cited in all sources should be regarded as approximate and, even if accurate, perhaps accurate for only a few days.
21 *Workington Star*, 8 September 1939, 1.
22 *West Cumberland Times*, 9 September 1939, 3. In South Shields there was actually a charity named the 'Shoeless Children's Fund' (*Carlisle Journal*, 24 November 1939, 7). Evacuated Leeds children were also frequently in need of proper footwear: Boud, *Great Exodus*, 115-16.
23 *Westmorland Gazette*, 16 September 1939, 7.
24 *Westmorland Gazette*, 9 September 1939, 6.
25 N.Longmate, *How We Lived Then: A History of Everyday life during the Second World War* (London, 2002; first publ. 1971), 60.
26 *Cumberland and Westmorland Herald*, 9 September 1939, 1. The matter was put in the hands of the public assistance officer to sort out (*Cumberland Evening Star* 12 September 1939, 2). By contrast, an account of the arrival on 8 September in Penrith of 260 children was much more generous in outlook. 'One big sister led her little brother by the hand and it was evident that, although the children had come from the poorer homes of South Shields, the parents had done their utmost to see that they entered their new homes clean and cared for. Two little eight-year-old girls came from the station entrance proud with their identical coats and hats, two little boys marched like men with their newly-purchased ruck-sacks on their backs' (*Penrith Observer*, 12 September 1939, 4).
27 *West Cumberland Times*, 21 October 1939, 16, from Workington.
28 There may, too, have been quality to consider when struggling parents did send clothes for their evacuated children. On 3 December 1939 Nella Last expressed the opinion that 'Parents send things – pitiful shoddy things from Marks & Spencer or similar shops – things which look all right but are done in no time'.
29 *Cumberland and Westmorland Herald*, 9 September 1939, 4.
30 *Westmorland Gazette*, 9 September 1939, 6.
31 *Cumberland and Westmorland Herald*, 9 September 1939, 6.
32 Before the middle of September two homesick Newcastle girls billeted in St. Bees had already twice tried to return by train to Newcastle (*West Cumberland Times*, 13 September 1939, 4).
33 Similar reasons for women returning home were reported from Warwick and Rockliffe in Cumberland (*Carlisle Journal*, 12 September 1939, 2).
34 *Whitehaven News*, 5 October 1939, 2. This letter first appeared in the parish's church magazine.

35 Cumbria Federation of Women's Institutes, *Cumbria within Living Memory* (Newbury, 1994), 184. A report on the evacuees in Carlisle was explicit about the children coming 'from slum homes' (*Cumberland News*, 9 September 1939, 7).
36 Ibid., 185-86.
37 *West Cumberland Times*, 9 November 1939, 2.
38 *West Cumberland Times*, 16 September 1939, 3.
39 *Cumberland News*, 16 September 1939, 8.
40 *Cumberland and Westmorland Gazette*, 9 September 1939, 1.
41 *Penrith Observer*, 5 September 1939, 8; and for Kendal, *Westmorland Gazette*, 16 September 1939, 7.
42 *West Cumberland Times*, 6 September 1939, 3.
43 *West Cumberland Times*, 16 September 1939, 3.
44 *Cumberland Evening News*, 12 October 1939, 1.
45 *Whitehaven News*, 7 September 1939, 4.
46 *Whitehaven News*, 14 January 1943, 3.
47 *Kendal News*, 28 September 1939, 2.
48 *Whitehaven News*, 5 October 1939, 2.
49 *Kendal News*, 28 September 1939, 1 and 12 October 1939, 1.
50 *Cumberland News*, 10 February 1940, 10.
51 *Westmorland Gazette*, 2 December 1939, 2.
52 G. Edwards, *The War Years: Life in Cockermouth and at Moota POW Camp* (Cockermouth, 2009), 12-17; R. Freethy, *Cumbria at War, 1939-1945* (Newbury, 2009), 40-46; *Cumberland News*, 15 April 1939, 6, 29 April 1939, 21 and 13 May 1939, 3; *Cumberland and Westmorland Herald*, 15 July 1939, 5 and 29 July 1939, 1 and *Penrith Observer*, 29 August 1939, 4 (on Penrith); Carlisle Archives, SUDP1/2M/1 (on Penrith); *Westmorland Gazette*, 22 July 1939, 9 (on Sedbergh) and 2 September 1939, 9. The *Penrith Observer*, 29 August 1939, on page 2 offered specific advice as to how to deal in an emergency with domestic pets, since they would not be permitted in public shelters or allowed to accompany government-sponsored evacuees.
53 *West Cumberland Times*, 2 September 1939, 12.
54 *Kendal News*, 31 August 1939, 3.
55 *Penrith Observer*, 5 September 1939, 5.
56 *West Cumberland Times*, 6 September 1939, 3.
57 *Cumberland News*, 1 April 1939, 6.
58 *Westmorland Gazette*, 25 November 1939, 7.
59 *Workington Star*, 8 September 1939, 8 and 10 November 1939, 6.
60 *Cumberland News*, 30 September 1939, 4.
61 *Westmorland Gazette*, 23 September 1939, 6.
62 *Cumberland Evening Star*, 15 September 1939, 1.
63 *Whitehaven News*, 14 September 1939, 6.
64 See for example B. Trescatheric, *A Shipyard Town: The Story of Barrow in the 20th Century* (Barrow-in-Furness, 2007), 40.
65 Malcolmson and Malcolmson, *Women at the Ready*, 38-40.
66 *Whitehaven News*, 14 September 1939, 2. Only nine of the thirty-nine children evacuated to Arlecdon, not far from Whitehaven, were still there in November (*Whitehaven News*, 23 November 1939, 4). Almost half of the evacuees in the Border Rural District had returned home by mid-October (*Carlisle Journal*, 17 October 1939, 1). In most towns and villages by the end of the year, expectant mothers and women with young children were much more likely to back at home than still in Cumbria. By contrast, larger bodies of evacuated schoolchildren (e.g., grammar schools) became more rooted in their new Cumbrian homes and stayed much longer, such as those in Penrith and Carlisle. The

Newcastle Central High School for Girls was said to 'form by far the larger part of the evacuee children at Keswick' (*Cumberland News*, 23 March 1940, 4). 'A lot of evacuated children are leaving the district', Nella Last wrote on 15 October 1939 (MOA), 'some because now winter is coming and petrol short the weekly chara[banc] trips will stop running from the Manchester district and the mothers will not be able to see them for a while'.

Chapter 2
Buckling Down

> 'In these desperate days there is a part for everyone to play, and there is no finer way by which we can enter upon the year 1941 than by making a firm resolve that if we have been neglectful of our obligations in the past we are not going to be from now onwards.' (*Barrow Guardian*, 4 January 1941, p. 2.)

If September 1939 was a month in the limelight, the last weeks of 1939 and early months of 1940 in Cumbria were much more low key – this was common in England during the 'phoney war'. Certainly the possibility of air raids and invasion was, at least intermittently, on people's minds, and matters of civil defence were regularly in the news. These included debates and initiatives related to bomb shelters.[1] Whitehaven prominently publicised the opening in December of its air raid shelters. They were designed to accommodate 1,700 people and 'are amongst the finest in the country'. The town enjoyed some historic advantages. 'Years ago when Whitehaven was one of Britain's most famous ports, the town was honeycombed with cellars for the safe housing of the rare wines, tobacco, and other goods brought by wooden ships from the four quarters of the globe'; and these cellars had now been reinforced and provided with lighting and suitable amenities in order to have them serve as bomb shelters.[2] Cumberland invested over £50,000 in ARP, of which public shelters were the largest single cost.[3] Air raid shelters were constructed in Carlisle, 'at considerable expense', according to the mayor in January 1940, but, being open at all times in case of need, some had been vandalised. 'Lamps and meters have been damaged, wiring pulled down, and fittings torn from the wall.' These and other acts of destruction were committed under cover of the blackout. The mayor urged citizens to report any suspicious incidents to the police.[4] (While some people championed the merits of public shelters, despite their cost, others argued that sheltering at home would usually offer just as good protection.)[5] Possible threats to animals also came up for discussion – though not until later: a meeting in Carlisle in July focused on how to deal with casualties to farm animals – and Cumbria had plenty of them – in the event of air raids.[6]

The blackout, for various other reasons, many of them related to serious, sometimes fatal, accidents, continued to get lots of attention. Numerous pedestrians, cyclists, and motorists came to grief, largely because of the treacherous conditions created by the blackout. Precautions were urged upon all, including those in rural districts. Cows were not to be driven on the road without lights, and one farm labourer who did so was summoned to Sedbergh police court.[7] Horses, too, were to carry lights after dark.[8] Some thefts were attributed to blackout conditions.[9] The blackout was for almost everyone an inescapably intrusive and oppressive new fact of life; and when infractions occurred – and many were committed, often fairly innocently – normally law-abiding citizens could find themselves in court.

But the harshest facts of war were still kept at a distance. Life for most people could be, and was, carried on more or less normally, barring the blackout, and in unthreatened ways. While there were undoubtedly changes beneath the surface, they weren't remarkable enough to attract much attention in the press. Rationing began at the start of 1940 but imposed only modest constraints. Fuel restrictions were still minimal. Recruitment drives by the forces were underway but not much discussed in public. While conscientious objectors were suddenly in the news as tribunals met to consider individual cases, this was not a particularly heated issue. Alarming incidents were rare. People were carrying on, albeit many more of them in uniform. The war – to the extent that there was actual combat – was far away and probably not discussed all that often. The Russian-Finnish War, starting in November 1939 and ending in March 1940, was the most prominent topic of active military news. Otherwise in many respects these were months of little movement, of treading water, and they felt like that.

* * * *

The spectacular German triumphs of April through June 1940 transformed both the stage of battle and domestic society. Britain and its dominions in the Empire were by mid-1940 fighting alone. The continent, with the exception of a handful of neutral states, was firmly in Hitler's grip. Invasion certainly then seemed possible and perhaps likely. A new national coalition government in Westminster was ruling the country, headed by an inspiring prime minister and armed with extraordinary dictatorial powers (though they were rarely used). The rescue from Dunkirk in late May and early June 1940 was a morale-boosting triumph of a sort, though it barely disguised the raw facts of a major retreat by the British Expeditionary Force and the massive losses of materiel. The news of the day was, in most households, followed very closely.

In Cumbria and virtually everywhere else in Britain there was a new mood of urgency. One consequence of these stark threats was a reversal of the exodus of evacuees from Cumbria just a few months before. Evacuation efforts, both private and government-sponsored, were actively renewed, and the sorts of movements of people that had been observed at the start of the war were re-enacted, only now over a longer period of time and episodically, not in one large surge. In June some people were already speaking of 'the infiltration of people' into the Penrith area and saying that 'houses were gradually filling up with people who would have evacuated themselves'.[10] Taking official and private evacuees together, it is probable that the total numbers continued to rise until the third quarter of 1941, when they plateaued and then again declined. The great majority of the evacuees in Cumberland and Westmorland in the summer of 1941 had arrived at various times during the preceding twelve to fourteen months.

There are many references to these movements – or expected movements – of people. The log book of Victoria Jubilee School in Newcastle recorded that on Sunday, 7 July 1940 sixty-four children were evacuated to Kirkby Stephen accompanied by six teachers, and more may have been sent to Westmorland later that summer.[11] In June 1940 the Cockermouth Rural District was facing the prospect of having to accommodate 900 school children from South Shields, in the event of further evacuation.[12] The South Westmorland Rural District Council was warned that it might have to accept from the North East up to 1,000 children; the Lakes Urban Council had been allotted 304, of whom half were to go to Ambleside.[13] In early July some 800 schoolchildren from Tyneside arrived in Carlisle and were billeted throughout the city – some were returnees from the first evacuation; almost 1,000 unaccompanied children were received in the Border Rural District and billeted in around 40 different villages and small towns.[14] At this time some 650 children plus 70 teachers and helpers arrived in Penrith (about two-thirds were distributed in rural districts), and around 950 in Workington.[15] In later August Cockermouth was facing the prospect of having to find billets for as many as 500 child evacuees, Keswick as many as 400.[16] A 1943 report estimated that some 2,560 unaccompanied school children were in fact officially evacuated from Newcastle and South Shields to Westmorland in July 1940.[17] Cumberland as a whole in July received some 7,500 school children from Newcastle.[18] These figures suggest that a total of some 10,000 children were officially evacuated to Cumberland and Westmorland in July and August 1940, almost all of them in school groups; they were accompanied by teachers and helpers, numbering perhaps 1,000 or so.

From June 1940 a major player in wartime welfare in Cumbria was the Women's Voluntary Services, established in 1938 specifically to assist with civil defence. In Kendal and Westmorland it was headed by an exceptionally capable and hard-working organiser, Mary Hornyold-Strickland, from a leading county family. Her conscientiousness is revealed in the thorough and detailed reports she made of her own work and that of others in the WVS. These documents, remarkable in their thoughtfulness and sensitivity to particulars, are invaluable in shedding light on many of Westmorland's wartime activities and are often cited in this and subsequent chapters.*

---

* Kendal Archives, WDSO 92/1-2; see p. xvii above for our method of referencing this material. A portrait of Mrs Hornyold-Strickland is found on page 55 of the National Trust's 2001 booklet on Sizergh Castle; an undated photograph of her is in K. Shepherd, *Lakeland Fifty Years Ago, Volume II* (Kendal, 1991), unpaginated, about three-quarters through the book.

At the end of 1940, when Lady Reading, who headed the WVS nationally, spoke in Kendal's town hall, hundreds of members from Cumberland and Westmorland were there to hear her, at what was described in the press as a 'mass meeting'. The membership of Westmorland alone, which had a population about the same as Barrow's, was said to be nearly 2,000.[19] Here, then, was an organisation, recently formed, that was to play a major role on the home front.

* * * *

First, though, it is important to acknowledge the certainly numerous but uncounted privately-arranged evacuations to Cumbria, often of children, and usually to the homes of relatives or friends. All this was occurring as the possibility of invasion and the safety of their children were much on parents' minds. In early June 1940 one woman wrote from Boothy, Brampton, Cumberland to another woman, probably her sister, whose four children had been evacuated there. 'Write, please, what you would like about where to send them in case of invasion. No place is really safe, though I should think this was as good as any.' A few days later she elaborated on this matter of trying to make the best choice possible in such dangerous circumstances – she mentioned German parachutists and the prospects of resisting invasion in the Carlisle region. 'Wherever one goes may be wrong' – there was talk about sending the children to Canada – 'and if one stays put one at least has food and the ordinary surroundings for the children.'[20] It is likely (though the evidence is far from clear) that these private evacuations were often relatively successful. One woman recalled her evacuation, at the age of six, from London to a farm in West Cumberland; her happy experiences there were rooted in the fact that she was evacuated with her younger sister and capable grandmother, so family relations were substantially maintained.[21] In 1940 a boy of eight was evacuated by his parents from Coventry to live with his aunt and uncle in Kendal, sharing a bed with his younger cousin; he had happy memories of his years living in this 'extremely friendly' town.[22] In such instances children were not thrown into the arms of strangers.

In the summer of 1940, the Women's Voluntary Services in Kendal was getting off the ground and expecting soon to receive 'British refugees' from towns bombed or expected to be bombed. In her report for September 1940, the town's WVS organiser wrote of just this happening – the flow of people into the town had actually been going on throughout the summer. 'The problem of evacuees and refugees is becoming very difficult,' she wrote. 'Kendal is already so overcrowded with self-evacuated people. More arrive every day and we still have the prospect of finding accommodation for the Government-evacuated North-East Coast children.' During the weeks of September, 'owing to the flood of self-evacuated people from bombed areas [the London blitz began on 7 September], we were besieged with enquiries as to lodgings, and have been able to help a number of people by getting lists from our country branches of farms, etc. willing to take in lodgers. My Deputy in Kendal, Mrs Pennington, is wonderful in her knowledge of local homes and able to squeeze in an extra mother and baby at a moment's notice!'

The WVS continued to be actively involved in helping to settle evacuees. The billeting officer sometimes sought their help with difficult cases, 'and we have usually been able to find the necessary billet.... We have also found quite a number of billets for unofficial evacuees'. A small social centre had been set up for evacuated mothers and their children to spend time in during most days, 'thus relieving the local hostesses for a couple of hours, and taking the children off the streets if the mothers wish to shop. Tea is provided by the WVS.' (Kendal NR, October 1940.) The following month evacuation was 'still the biggest problem'. By then Kendal had received almost 3,500 evacuees, which represented about a 20 percent increase in the town's pre-war population. Evacuees continued to arrive at the rate of about 100 per week. One result of these pressures was the resort to compulsory billeting, 'and this has meant', wrote Mrs Hornyold-Strickland in her report for January 1941, 'a lot of tact on the part of WVS members, especially our Deputy Organiser, Mrs Pennington, as the Billeting Officer is not always wise or tactful, either with the choice of billets or billetees.[23] Mrs Pennington has been able to smooth out various difficulties and has persuaded some people to share houses in order to make room for other evacuees.' Adding to the pressures, soldiers were being billeted on some households, as the army did not want troops in the area to have to spend the winter in tents.[24]

Since evacuees in 1940-41 came and left, the numbers in place were always changing. Aside from Kendal, those settled in South Westmorland in November 1940, both children and adults, were said to amount to 1,512; these may have been only the official evacuees, for a few weeks later it was reported that South Westmorland had a total of 3,153 evacuees, of whom 1,425 were being billeted with allowances to those putting them up (which meant they had been officially evacuated).[25] Evacuees in the North Westmorland Rural District numbered 980, plus 173 in Appleby. Windermere had around 1,000 official evacuees, 2,000 private evacuees, 500 students in private schools, and 200 in hotels. The total number of evacuees in late 1940 for the county as a whole was fairly stable at around 13,000 (Westmorland WVS, NR November 1940). It was said of the following month (Westmorland NR, December 1940, written 4 January 1941) that the greatest number of evacuees 'still come from London, but Kendal have had some from Manchester and Liverpool. On the other hand a great many of the Newcastle and South Shields children returned home for their holidays, and this has caused a certain amount of bad feeling as householders are naturally inclined to say that if it is safe for the children to go home for a month at Xmas it is obvious that they are just being used as a cheap form of boarding school for the rest of the year. It will be interesting to see how many of these children actually do return next week when some of the schools reopen.' She reported in January 1941 that about 90 percent of these school children had returned to Kendal, but only 75 percent to South Westmorland. By April 1941 large numbers of elementary-school children who had been officially evacuated were no longer in the county.[26]

This was by no means the end of Westmorland's evacuees. There were more in March 1941, 'a good many from Wallasey, some from Glasgow, all needing help and advice' (Westmorland WVS, NR March 1941). Major raids on Tyneside on 25 April and 3/4 May 1941 killed at least 220 people[27] and prompted some of the survivors in the region to evacuate. A large number of schoolchildren arrived from Barrow in later May and a smaller number in September (see Chapter 3). These months probably marked the peak numbers of post-1939 evacuees. Over half of the 183 school children in Burneside in April were evacuees.[28] In September 1941 almost half of the 310 children enrolled at Staveley School were evacuees – 80 from Barrow, 59 from Tyneside, and 8 privately evacuated.[29]

According to a letter of 15 March 1941 from the chief billeting officer in Penrith, the town's normal population was 9,300 'and we now have upwards of 4,000 evacuees, 3,000 odd of whom are privately billeted in the town'.[30] A local newspaper had acknowledged this reality almost a half year before. The original Tynesiders were then being augmented by families fleeing from their homes in the south. 'As a result the majority of local homes are now housing at least two families while in addition many parents are also acting as foster parents to the children evacuated to the town and district under the Government's Voluntary Scheme.'[31] Some of the newcomers in and near Penrith were war workers and the wives of soldiers. Wherever they came from, by the spring of 1941 Cumbria was packed with evacuees, some of whom, such as the boys of the Royal Newcastle Grammar School in Penrith, would remain until at least 1944, while others would return to their homes after the bombing subsided.

Many child evacuees were comfortably billeted with local families, and probably settled in well or reasonably well. Others struggled – though there is no evidence that allows more than rather vague generalizations. Some local householders were welcoming of the newcomers; others were not, and some did their best to resist housing any evacuee, since for the most part the programme was voluntary in practice even though the billeting officials had powers of compulsion, if they chose to use them – they preferred not to. A lot depended on particulars: the personalities of the evacuees, including how adaptable and manageable they were; the flexibility and sympathy, or lack thereof, of the billetors and how well their houses were suited to accommodate visitors.

One thoughtful perspective on the evacuation scheme was offered by a woman who wrote a letter to the *Kendal News*, 1 August 1940 (p. 2). She was, it seems, not reluctant to do her bit. But she wanted more attentiveness to individual circumstances. She thought that most women in Kendal were 'prepared to make some sacrifice in this direction, but there is widespread unrest and dissatisfaction on account of the dictatorial methods of the local authorities, and the undeniable inequality of sacrifice demanded'. She offered the view, 'as a practical housewife', that 'any woman who works single-handed in a household of four (including herself) is rendering a service to the full extent of her energy and ability. And most certainly does this apply in houses where there are no modern conveniences to lessen the work, and there are still many such houses in Kendal.' It was astonishing, she felt, that 'many people who lack these modern conveniences are being allocated more children, because they possess three bedrooms instead of two'. What seemed to matter to the higher-ups 'is space, and not a woman's capacity to look after children'.

The happiness of the evacuated children depended, she argued, first and foremost on 'a happy Foster Mother, and this is impossible if a woman's body and nerves are worn out with over-work and worry. Surely the authorities concerned must realise that 90 per cent of their troubles last September [1939] were due to the harassed women who cracked up under the strain'. Old and unwell people, she thought, should not have to take child evacuees at all; and larger families should not be required to take more than one, especially when some smaller families were allocated only one. The well-being of a woman's family should be the key consideration, and this well-being would be imperilled if her energies were over-stretched. The writer noted that the Ministry of Labour acknowledged the problems stemming from long hours and over-strain in the munitions industry, and had adopted ameliorative measures. 'If the women in the home were organised,' she concluded, 'the local authorities would be compelled to emulate this wise move.' Others shared her concern. A WVS recruiting meeting in Windermere in early October 1940 acknowledged the need 'to assist housewives, who were over-worked and harassed under the evacuation scheme', and there was a proposal to set up weekend play centres for children, supervised by WVS members, 'and so relieve the housewives'.[32] (If the post-August 1940 reports of Kendal's WVS are to be believed, over time greater sensitivity was exercised in arranging billets, and with happier results.)[33]

Billeting was rarely a black and white issue. Blame was not necessarily applicable in any particular case. Circumstances of living varied so greatly. Consider one Keswick householder's letter of 3 February 1942 asking that at the end of the school term he be relieved of the responsibility of billeting a child he had had one for almost a year. He put his case calmly. 'As Deputy Chief Warden', he argued, 'I have made during the last 3½ years, and am still making, some contribution to the Town's Civil Defence Services. Under the new regulations these duties are likely to become heavier than lighter.' There was more he had done. 'I took two Newcastle ladies and their three children into the Torebar Cottage in July 1940, letting it to them at the old rent. I regarded this as a War Service, and as our assistance to the Billeting Officer, who in those days might have had difficulty in fresh billets for these evacuees.' One of these women with her two children was still in the cottage. Then there was his personal situation to consider. 'I have my own business in Penrith to attend to, which is a heavy responsibility. And finally my Sister and myself have to run this house, as well as we can; and we have no domestic help.' All these pressures, he said, made it hard to continue to accommodate a billeted child. Here was a case that revealed the sort of concrete realities that could affect (quite understandably) how a householder liable to billeting might construe his or her wartime duties to the nation. [34]

* * * *

Evacuees had needs that wanted to be addressed, and the WVS's reports and other records are full of information about actions taken or intended to be helpful. There were two hostels (at least) in Westmorland for evacuated children, one at Appleby, another at Arnside accommodating forty children.[35] A WVS report of 17 June 1940 in the Kendal Archive Centre provides some background as to how this latter hostel came to exist. Some residents of Arnside agreed to rent a large house for these forty evacuees. 'They have begged the furniture and equipment and they think it can be run on the billeting allowance, plus the 5s a week that the people who would otherwise have the children in their houses' were prepared to give to maintain the hostel.[36] It was said of Milnthorpe in September (Westmorland WVS NR) that 'Self-evacuated refugees are crowding the district, chiefly from Merseyside. WVS continue their help to Hincaster House Hostel. ...Work parties are collecting and renovating clothing for refugees'.[37] In Holme 'Evacuees keep everyone busy' (Westmorland NR, October 1940). In Windermere this month there was a 'huge Sunday party for evacuated children; one hostel for evacuees already working, another planned'. In November six dozen pairs of boots were sent to Windermere for evacuees, and the WVS was 'still trying to arrange for the cobbling of shoes for evacuated children in the Lake District' (Westmorland NR).[38] A county clothing fund dispensed supplies from various sources, especially the American Red Cross.[39] Gifts of clothing were sought out for evacuees; one newspaper reported in September that 'Boots and shoes and underclothing for boys and girls are in particular demand'.[40] A social centre for evacuated mothers was functioning every afternoon in Kendal, though in Windermere the WVS 'had to give up their Sunday afternoon tea party for children' because of 'opposition from clergy' and difficulty finding suitable space (Westmorland WVS, NR November 1940).

These welfare initiatives and activities in aid of evacuees, and sometimes others as well, continued into 1941. Nursery centres were opened in several communities; many hands were kept busy knitting, mending and sewing; Westmorland's WVS was 'inundated with requests to clothe necessitous children, these requests mostly reaching us through the billeting officers' (NR February 1941); blankets were distributed; and work was well underway in Kendal to establish a British Restaurant (It opened in June and was highly successful: see below, Chapter 5.). The WVS also dealt with lots of instances of individual distress. In March 1941 (Westmorland NR) a 'pathetic case of a medical student, who had been invalided out of the army after Dunkirk and still seemed to have no pension, was clothed, together with a woman and three children dependent on him. They were specially sent to Kendal by the London County Council. A local mother too frightened to take her child to the doctor was persuaded to do so. It was a very bad case of spinal meningitis, and the child is now having proper treatment.' The previous month in Kendal (February NR) the deputy organiser helped at least five refugees from the continent and 'a slightly mental boy that she found in an unsuitable home where the woman was going mental, so she got the boy removed at once, and a terribly dirty child rescued out of an undesirable home'.

Stress was widely felt among those who had been uprooted and dislodged from their homes, especially, perhaps, those who had recently endured air raids. It was said in April 1941 (Kendal NR) that 'many of the children who have returned from the North East Coast after their holidays ... are worn out from sleeping in shelters. One child who returned home was killed there. Mothers with young children coming from the badly bombed areas are noticeably over-strung and very difficult to settle in any billets. We persuaded one mother with five children to go into the country to a farm.' Air raids on the North-East coast spiked in later April and early May of 1941, forcing many out of their beds at night and leaving around 150 dead in the Tyneside area.* One consequence was the movement of more evacuees to Cumbria (Westmorland WVS, NR June and July 1941).

* * * *

---

* Starting in late June 1940, the log book of a junior school in a working-class district of Newcastle reveals the extent of the residents' sleep disturbances and mental strain in 1940-41, even if warnings far outnumbered actual raids. Owing to the many alerts and a few raids, the children's education was repeatedly disrupted; on some days the school did not open at all or, if open, received only a handful of students. Between 13 March and 12 May 1941 there was probably a raid or warning almost every second day; it was recorded on 28 April that the school was closed all day – 'Due to enemy action it has been used as an Emergency Rest and Feeding Centre since midnight on Friday, 25 April'. (Tyne & Wear Archives, E.NC60/1/2.) We are very grateful to our friend, Ann Stephenson, for reading this source, reporting on its contents, and suggesting how it might be used.

One well-publicised evacuation was of children in little need of charity. In late August 1940 the exclusive Roedean School moved from Brighton, a recently declared danger area, to the Lake District, where it was quartered in the Keswick Hotel, with its 100 bedrooms, which had been emptied of paying guests. Plans were for the 220 girls with their 30 schoolmistresses to be transferred to Keswick on 5 September, and, with the school being an elite institution, the press took an interest in its arrival. 'Thirteen pianos (of the school's 53) are also being transferred, and for the last month dozens of door-to-door rail removal vans have brought furniture to the hotel. The schoolmistresses, who arrived on Monday, will put the school's library in order, sort out text and exercise books, arrange classrooms for the girls, whose parents pay £189 a year in fees to educate them at Roedean' – this sum was roughly equivalent to the annual income of millions of working-class families. In the Keswick Hotel 'classrooms will be held in the lounges, smaller classes in large bedrooms. Some lessons will be given in rooms over Keswick Railway Station, where desks have now been put in rows. Art lessons will be in the Art Gallery, shared with girls from an evacuated Liverpool school.' The girls' sports would be accommodated at the local football club's grounds, pavilions, and two small playing fields. The headmistress's words were quoted. 'Parents are delighted at the move. We shall be happy at Keswick. Though we have much less room for games, we shall encourage the girls to walk in the Lake District, and though our swimming pool at Roedean must be left behind we shall swim in the lakes.'[41]

Lots of private evacuees in the second half of 1940 were not children but adults. Appleby was said by local officials to have 'many private evacuees'; the Windermere area was reported to be 'abnormally full of self-evacuated visitors from the Eastern Counties and elsewhere'.[42] Many of the numerous hotels and boarding houses in the Lake District were full of them. Mrs Hornyold-Strickland once had harsh word for some of these people – she was trying to recruit women for hospital service (Westmorland NR, January 1941): 'There are still a number of lazy evacuee women in the best hotels in the Lake District, but they are the type that will never be much use in any job!' Almost all these people had money, unlike most of the official evacuees, who were overwhelmingly working class, some from very poor families. The presence of these private evacuees and their privileges were often resented, particularly when profiteering was suspected. At the end of the war Nella Last took a day trip to Bowness-on-Windermere and her thoughts turned to 'the hordes of self-evacuated folk – over-dressed and too well fed "city" people, many Jewish looking'. (MOA, 16 July 1945.) It is virtually certain that many other local residents felt the same way.

In October 1940 the *Cumberland and Westmorland Herald* wrote about these private evacuees. 'Many people who can afford to do so have moved to the Lake District,' it noted on 12 October (p. 3), 'and their presence is causing some embarrassment to billeting officers', who were struggling to find quarters for official evacuees. Some officials claimed that it was now impossible to find space for any additional evacuees who the Ministry of Health might dispatch to their district. One billeting officer in the Kendal district told a reporter that 'the householders who have assisted the billeting authorities by taking official evacuees are indignant that those who have refused to co-operate are now "making a good thing" out of people who are prepared to pay virtually anything for a room. From £2 to £4 a week, he said, was being charged for any kind of single room, and board and attendance were extras'. By contrast, those billeting officially evacuated children were paid 10s 6d or 8s 6d per child per week, board included. 'Places which were glad to take people on walking holidays for 3s 6d for bed and breakfast were now getting 12s 6d.' The towns were thronged with these people, he said, to the disadvantage of others. But at least these throngs did *not* include masses of evacuated civil servants, who were so prominent from 1940-41 in Harrogate and other inland leisure towns, and in seaside towns in the North West, notably Blackpool and Morecambe (where many Post Office employees were relocated from London). Unlike Cumbria, these places had substantial hotels, suitable for requisitioning for government offices.

On 19 October 1940 the *Cumberland and Westmorland Herald* (p. 1) returned to the issue of the 'extraordinary prices for rooms. There has been a process of bidding up, the worst feature of which has been the attempt to get landladies to give a week's notice to refugees already established and accept higher-paying guests. This has happened in Keswick, and so far as can be ascertained such offers have been rejected with scorn.' By this account, the landladies warranted sympathy, for the private refugees were said to be sometimes difficult and demanding, and the money paid to landladies helped to compensate them for revenue lost from the normal tourist season. This, it was suggested, was not really 'profiteering'.[43] While the writer tried to see both sides and acknowledged the value to these visitors of a temporary respite from the strains of nightly bombing, he wondered about their numbers: 'one cannot go anywhere here, in Keswick, Grasmere, Ambleside, Penrith, without being struck by the number of people who look fit enough to have something better to do'. Class consciousness was at the root of these critiques. Was it fair, it was asked, that wealth should buy safety for some and assure good money for others while 'the plebs' were obliged to do whatever the government told them to do? Class privilege was almost certainly a factor in some billeting. This is what members of the Labour Party in Appleby thought three years later when, at the time of the war's last major movement of evacuees, they complained of 'the methods adopted in the past of approaching working-class homes first for the billeting of evacuees', leaving larger homes untroubled.[44]

Similar complaints were registered elsewhere, including Oxfordshire.[45]

* * * *

The months that are the focus of this chapter saw significant changes in farming (Chapter 4) and the emergence and expansion of welfare practices and provisions, many of which were to remain prominent throughout the war. Canteens of one sort or another were established, to satisfy the needs of many people away from their homes. Members of the forces were often moving about, on leave, travelling to base, or driving vehicles, and facilities were being provided for them to rest, take refreshment, and sometimes get a night's sleep.[46] First aid training was supplied by the Red Cross. Civil defence exercises continued in most towns. Comforts were knitted for the troops. Care packages were put together for servicemen in hospital or stationed at isolated posts (cigarettes figured prominently, along, sometimes, with chocolate, toffee and sardines).[47] Efforts were made to meet some of the needs of the relatives of the hundred or so men from Westmorland who were prisoners of war in Germany (Westmorland WVS, NR October 1940). In Maryport the National ARP for Animals Committee was at work to ensure the best for animals in the event of a raid, including the proper care of those injured.[48] Savings groups were widely established to encourage investment in the war effort, and the many charities actively supporting some aspect of wartime welfare were constantly at work raising funds through flag days, whist drives, dances, auctions, and the like. Philanthropic initiatives in aid of the war effort were much applauded and well publicised, and the press was kept busy reporting to its readers on all the fine work that was being done – as indeed was true. Wartime volunteering was already impressively widespread.

In the spring of 1941 there was a significant new development. For the first time a town in the far North West, Barrow-in-Furness, was heavily bombed. As a result, personal experiences of dislocation, destruction, and recovery were brought directly to the region. These are the subjects of the following chapter.

Notes and References

1 B. Trescatheric, *The Barrow Blitz* (Barrow-in-Furness, 2009), 3-5; G. Edwards, *The War Years: Life in Cockermouth and at Moota POW Camp* (Cockermouth, 2009), 17. In early 1941 Whitehaven, with a population of no more than 25,000, had nearly 1,000 civil defence workers (*Whitehaven News*, 13 February 1941, 2). Most would have been part-time and unpaid.

2 *Whitehaven News*, 7 December 1939, 5.

3 *Cumberland News*, 9 March 1940, 9.

4 *Cumberland News*, 20 January 1940, 7.

5 For example, *Kendal News*, 20 June 1940, 2 and 4 July 1940, 1 and 3; and *Cumberland and Westmorland Herald*, 10 August 1940, 1.

6 *Carlisle Journal*, 2 August 1940, 3.
7 *Westmorland Gazette*, 2 December 1939, 2.
8 *Cumberland News*, 27 January 1940, 2.
9 *Cumberland News*, 9 March 1940, 8.
10 *Cumberland and Westmorland Herald*, 29 June 1940, 1.
11 Tyne & Wear Archives, E.NC60/1/2. The following summer another party of the school's children was evacuated to Keswick, on 21 July. We are grateful to Ann Stephenson for her research in Tyneside on our behalf.
12 *West Cumberland Times*, 1 June 1940, 4. 'To arrange accommodation in private billets for so large a number is no easy task', the report observed, 'but we are fortunate in having an excellent band of parish billeting officers, local committees and other voluntary workers'.
13 *Westmorland Gazette*, 22 June 1940, 2 and 29 June 1940, 6.
14 *Carlisle Journal*, 9 July 1940, 1.
15 *Cumberland and Westmorland Herald*, 13 July 1940, 1.
16 *West Cumberland Times*, 21 August 1940, 2 and 1.
17 Dow and Brown, *Evacuation in Westmorland*, p. 10. A contemporary newspaper account put the figure at 2,700 (*Westmorland Gazette*, 13 July 1940, 7).
18 *West Cumberland Times*, 13 July 1940, 4.
19 *Westmorland Gazette*, 14 December 1940, 12.
20 Carlisle Archives, DX/1690/8/1/1.
21 Imperial War Museum, Private Papers of Mrs T.M. Mooney, Documents no. 96/31/1.
22 Kendal Library, Kendal Oral History Group, Interview no. 0142, 4.
23 Her report for Kendal in March 1941 added that a dozen WVS members had been appointed billeting officers for different parts of the town. 'It is a most unenviable job', but she was hoping that they would make a valuable contribution. 'The officials had been making some bad mistakes, putting the wrong people into the wrong billets etc., and we feel sure that our women will make a much better job of it, though it won't make WVS popular in the town!' In Keswick, too, around this time, billets for evacuees under the voluntary system were getting harder to find ('some hostesses [were] refusing to take back school children evacuees after the holidays, saying that others who have had none should do their turn') and there was talk of introducing compulsion (*Penrith Observer*, 8 April 1941, 2).
24 *Penrith Observer*, 17 September 1940, 2.
25 *Westmorland Gazette*, 18 January 1941, 7.
26 *Westmorland Gazette*, 3 May 1941, 5.
27 www.ne-diary.bpears.org.uk
28 *Westmorland Gazette*, 26 April 1941, 5.
29 J. Scott, ed., *A Lakeland Valley Through Time: A History of Staveley, Kentmere and Ings* (Kendal, 1995), 112.
30 Carlisle Archives, SUDP/1A/Box 16. Two months earlier a newspaper put the number of evacuees in Penrith at 4,800; accommodation, it was said, might have to be found for 200 more if Newcastle were bombed (*Cumberland and Westmorland Gazette*, 25 January 1941, 1).
31 *Penrith Observer*, 8 October 1940, 2.
32 *Westmorland Gazette*, 5 October 1940, 10.
33 A resident of Burton-in-Kendal was prosecuted for her refusal in late September 1940 to billet evacuated twins, and the press report of her trial revealed the difficulties the billeting officer had encountered and the many refusals he had already met with – nearly twenty, he said – in trying to accommodate these five-year-old boys. The case was pursued, at least in part, to set an example and encourage better cooperation with billeting requests in the future. (*Westmorland Gazette*, 7 December 1940, 12.) Billeting encounters were bound to lead to some disputes, for tact was not always employed, people could be rude

or lose their temper, mixed messages might be conveyed, and householders were liable to misunderstand their responsibilities and the process of appeal available to them.

34 Carlisle Archives, SUDK/1/3/1/82, E2 (a). Housewives, notably well-off ones, no longer had easy lives. It was remarked in Westmorland's WVS Narrative Report for October 1942 that 'Few WVS now have maids, and they have to get their husbands' breakfasts, and in several instances send evacuees off to school also'.

35 *Westmorland Gazette*, 14 December 1940, 12.

36 This sounds like a tactic by some well-to-do people to avoid having to take evacuees under their own roofs. By contrast, it was stated in the WVS's September 1940 report on Arnside that 'Self-evacuated people from the bombed areas are being found billets with the cooperation of landladies and private householders.' These were probably mostly people who could pay, more or less readily, for what they were offered.

37 The *Westmorland Gazette*, 9 November 1940, 10 published a posed photograph of a 'happy group of Tyneside evacuees at Hincaster House'. Press reports of evacuees' lives were usually upbeat, whatever the evidence (which was almost certainly mixed).

38 Inadequate footwear was a persistent problem throughout the war, especially for evacuated children from poor families. A letter of 13 March 1940 from Burneside described circumstances that would be often repeated. Two evacuated brothers from South Shields, it was said, 'have suffered very much during the present winter through having no proper footwear [and] are again absent from school on this account, the elder boy being ill in bed'. The parents had been written to and footwear promised, but nothing had arrived. 'It is only a few days ago that the foster parents were compelled to purchase a new pair of trousers for the elder boy as his others were beyond repair and exposed him in a manner which prevented him from coming up to school.' (Kendal Archives, WC/C9, Evacuation Bags, File 1/1.) The WVS was routinely concerned with these matters. In January 1942 Kendal's WVS reported that 'A larger supply of clogs are urgently needed, as this form of footwear seems to be the only solution for the bigger and rougher boys. The Canadian Free Gift Wellingtons are very good, but not strong enough to stand the rough treatment they get from the South Shields and Newcastle schoolchildren. Arrangements have been made with the Education Authorities of Barrow, South Shields and Newcastle allowing us to buy a large quantity of strong wool, suitable for making into good wearing stockings to be worn with clogs.'

39 *Westmorland Gazette*, 14 December 1940, 12.

40 *Kendal News*, 5 September 1940, 2.

41 *Cumberland and Westmorland Herald*, 31 August 1940, 1. See also the Appendix.

42 *Cumberland and Westmorland Herald*, 10 August 1940, 4; *Westmorland Gazette*, 13 July 1940, 7.

43 Accusations of profiteering by landlords – 'robbing the refugees', it was called – were reported from Workington a few weeks later (*West Cumberland Times*, 11 January 1941, 9).

44 *Cumberland and Westmorland Herald*, 22 July 1944, 1.

45 M. Graham, *Oxfordshire at War* (Stroud, Gloucestershire, 1994), 47.

46 *Cumberland News*, 27 July 1940, 7; *Westmorland Gazette*, 28 December 1940, 2.

47 *Cumberland News*, 6 July 1940, 7.

48 *West Cumberland Times*, 26 October 1940, 4.

Chapter 3
Bombs on Barrow

> 'I often wonder whatever *would* happen if we got a blitz. I think we have stayed *too* safe and secure and a general feeling that we are "too out of the way" prevails.' (Nella Last, 31 March 1941 [*DONL*, p. 47].)

In 1941 the Easter weekend in Barrow-in-Furness was marked by a tangle of emotions. Yes, it was a holiday time, a break from work and routine. Spring was arriving. But many people were anxious about the prospect of air raids, which had been causing havoc in numerous British cities since August 1940. Virtually every major city had been pummeled – at least once. Big raids had happened recently: in Portsmouth, Merseyside, Hull, Clydebank, Bristol, Plymouth, Coventry, Birmingham, and of course London.[1] While most of the Furness district of Lancashire was rural and thus, like Cumberland and Westmorland, unlikely to be targeted by German bombers, Barrow, with a population of some 65,000 to 70,000, was an exception. It was a major shipbuilding town, heavily involved in producing vessels for the navy. The enemy would have good reason to raid Barrow's shipyards, easily the town's dominant industry.

Barrovians had for months been preparing for raids, and in early 1941 they were witness to various defensive precautions. Barrage balloons were dotting the sky; many householders had built their own outdoor shelters or devised interior shelters, or were actively planning to do so; and some public shelters were by now in place. RAF aerial activity and gun practices on Morecambe Bay had increased. There had already been a number of bombing alerts and a few actual, though only very small, raids, including ones on 13 March and 7 April.[2] Many personal connections existed with recently-blitzed Plymouth, another naval centre, and reports about the death and destruction there, while not detailed in the press, were still widely known. The enemy was manifestly at the door. When, some residents asked, would Barrow's turn come to be bombed? It was reasonable to fear that the sort of carnage that had been heard about elsewhere could and would someday engulf Barrow. A teenage diarist in Barrow, Nora Bainbridge, knew that on 2 January 1941 there had been a raid at Millom, not far away, in which five had been killed.[3] Since then deaths had been confined to relatively distant places, but nerves were on edge and foreboding was widespread, though mixed with complacency. Those convinced that the war would not last much longer included the Helms, neighbours of Nella Last on Ilkley Road. 'Mrs Helm was SO SURE that war would be overcome by this September that they have had a big greenhouse erected instead of an air-raid shelter' (MOA, 14 April 1941).

* * * *

Nella Last is a vigorous voice from wartime Barrow, and her diary offers an unusually probing account of living through a blitz – more probing, perhaps, and more revealing, than virtually any other personal account from anywhere in wartime England. On Good Friday, 11 April 1941, she wrote in her diary (*NLW*, p. 116 and MOA) how she felt shut in: 'everything so dark and depressing it might have been modelled on the first Good Friday'. Wartime privations had already made life seem bleaker – and constricted. So after lunch she and her husband, Will, a joiner, set out for a drive in the countryside – he was able to get petrol in order to carry on his joinery business. Nella was bearing a prized cake that she had 'been longing and yet dreading to cut into… I made it about last June when butter was more plentiful.' She took pride in her cleverness in preparing food, but knew that the times were against her. 'I expect it's the last good cake we will ever have – at least for years – and I do so love baking cakes and watching people enjoy them… When I saw my husband's enjoyment and heard his praise of it, I reflected it has taken a war to make him appreciate the toil and thought and planning behind a well cooked meal – and an economical one at that.'

Nella and Will were intending an outing to Morecambe. However, considering the dull weather, they thought of turning back. Then they encountered by the roadside 'a very dejected couple' and offered them a lift. The couple, an airman and his sister-in-law, had just visited in a nearby TB sanatorium the man's failing wife, who had in fact died that day. The couple could not afford a taxi back. After delivering them to a Lancaster bus stand, and with this reminder that everyday tragedy did not stop for wartime, an upset Nella tried her best to conceal her feelings. When her husband – not quite buying into her stoicism – asked "Is there anything you would like at all?" Nella replied, without thinking, '"Yes, an orange!" So silly a thing to say. It made us both laugh.' 'I felt a bit dim and came to bed early', were her words just before ending this almost seven-page diary entry. She then pondered the perils of a clear night, so favourable to the enemy. 'All is so quiet and still and a mist is over all. I wish it was a mile thick over England and nowhere did the moon shine brightly this full moon weekend.' (*DONL*, pp. 47-48.)

The following day featured practical issues of wartime sustenance, as the Lasts visited a poultry farm. She ordered 12 new chicks for her own garden hen run, to be delivered in 10 days, and pondered at length how she would house and feed them, including sharing her cornflakes with them until she could obtain the right feed, and how she would store the eggs they would (she hoped) produce. Easter Sunday, 13 April, opened with mildly amusing 'blind leading the blind' attempts to fashion a chicken coop with scraps from Will's shop. He came up the stairs 'and said in a stately *aloof* voice, "if you want your coopie you had better give me the directions!"' For 'festive' fare there was a joint of 'half a pound of shin – not even a bone for stockpot', and only the daffodils from her garden 'hinted at Easter day at all' (MOA). Later they drove to Coniston via Bowness, where 'every possible parking place was full of cars' with pleasure-seekers from south Lancashire, who were intent on enjoying themselves. For her part, Nella was thinking ahead to how she might redecorate her house. 'If I live to see the end of war, I will have my cream walls again – or at least a plain pastel paper.' Then she chided herself. 'It's no use grizzling over little things. "There'll come another day".'

This other day would be a long way off, and the holiday weekend ended with a nasty jolt. 'Last night', wrote Nella on Easter Monday, 14 April (*NLW*, pp 117-18), 'a noise like the crack of Doom sounded, and brought us springing from our beds to rush downstairs.' Her husband crossly declared the noise a false alarm. 'Just then the alert sounded' and they were alarmed by the sound of a plane flying so low 'that we feared for our housetops'. In response 'Our guns fired one volley, then stopped. There was a frightful bang bang-crack-bang, the rattle of machine guns and the sound of chaser planes. The noise was terrifying – all so near and low down.' The following day brought lots of work for Will and 'all the men he could collect to board up shop windows. There was only one stick of bombs but the destruction from the two they *have* found is unbelievable. One big commercial hotel got one [Fig. 4] and a "little" street the other and the former and four houses of the other are just piles of rubble and no one saved from them' (MOA). Other damaged property included Christchurch, now with gaping holes in the roof, which housed the hospital supply depot where Nella regularly volunteered. 'I could not have believed so few bombs could have done so much damage and it made me sick to think of what *two* airplanes and about four bombs could do to our town.'[4]

She spoke of the raid's aftermath: the 'Bulging walls, gaping windows, hundreds of broken panes of glass in big house windows and shops, crazily leaning chimneys, flying ambulances, dirty and tired Home Guard and wardens, ordinary citizens in demolition gangs working like men possessed.' Some 'dazed looking men ... were piling mattresses on hand carts where people had been ordered to evacuate'. And 'crowds of quiet white-faced spectators ... wanted to see but not to linger over sight of destruction.' She and Mrs. Atkinson, her next door neighbour, queued to buy cigarettes, which they distributed to some of the men at work. 'The look on those tired faces was a thing to remember and we passed the word round where we got them and both men and women rushed to the shop, got packets of cigs and passed them over rope to any man in uniform. I said to a policeman "Have any arrangements been made for tea for these men?" and he said "Yes, madam, don't worry about that, for all the people in the damaged homes have made tea and sandwiches at different intervals" and went on to say that the "town" had sent sandwiches too.'

The day's events got the Lasts thinking more deeply about matters of personal security. After Will's work of helping to clear up various messes, they drove to the coast road 'and filled the remainder of sand bags I had made. I'll go on making them from any strong bits of material I can piece together. They would do for others if we did not want them.' Then the Lasts revisited the question of a shelter at home, about which they had still taken no action. 'My husband said "I think we will order an indoor shelter after all". We have talked and talked about [one] and wondered if we should spend the £12 or save it in war certificates. It looked so dreadful to see the doll-eyed brick shelter standing by wrecked houses and to think that if people had been able to get to them they would have been still living. We have no shelters at all in our neighbourhood except the school shelter at top of road and it has to serve for children in the day and for a good many streets at night.'

Barrow had further raids to contend with the following two nights. Nella felt 'terrified'; Will regretted not having ordered an indoor shelter when she had first suggested one. The centre of town was heavily damaged, 'a church, printing office and public baths gone and such a lot of houses and shops uninhabitable, cinemas roped off and no shops opened'. (*NLW*, 16 April, p. 120.) Roads were closed off, traffic was diverted, and an eerie quiet hinted (she thought) at fears of future disasters. On Wednesday 16 April, schoolgirl Nora Bainbridge (aged 16), at 37 Derby Street, reported in her diary: 'Coliseum, Baptist Church demolished, baths partly also.[5] Thousands of windows broken. Tom [her father and head of the fire service] was out at a fire in Union Street, etc. 18 killed. Co-op shut through damage. Windows broken in Dalton Road – Cooks, Winders etc. damaged. What a mess! There's hardly a big window left in the town.' The next day she heard from one of the merchants on Dalton Road that 'he had lost thousands of pounds worth of goods in the raid. His night-watchman was buried in 3 feet of broken glass and crockery etc. Many shops were shut yesterday but I didn't go out today so I don't know about that.' When she did venture out the following day (18 April) she found a few areas roped off but most shops open, many with defiant signs: 'Business as Usual', 'Come in by the door – Hitler came in by the window', 'Hitler or no Hitler, business as usual'. One merchant was selling off damaged goods. She bought a record of Tchaikovsky.

This was the end of Barrow's first exposure to serious air raids. The bombs fell mainly in working-class neighbourhoods and killed some forty people.[6] The following days were relatively calm, as more barrage balloons were launched and as citizens strove to restore some normalcy in their lives. They were also worried about their collective futures. Nella reported one further alarming incident that month, early in the morning of Saturday, 26 April (MOA). 'A stick of delayed action bombs were dropped and 500 people were hurriedly evacuated until they were made safe. It is odd', Nella thought, 'how we are "picked out" by odd raiders, like a cat and mouse. One good thing – it's made people "shelter wise". After the raid a week ago and the "push" to carry gas masks, I noticed that shipyard office workers were carrying their gas masks. For quite six or eight months after war [was declared] *everyone* had to carry them or they did not get into Yard at all. It was a kind of passport at gate.'

* * * *

On Friday, 2 May Nella was preoccupied with her new chicks (*NLW*, pp. 128-29) – 'it's a while since I've had such a thrill over anything like I have over my new chicks! I've been on the run all day with little saucers of food – brown breadcrumbs and hard boiled eggs is their favourite, although they love cornflakes and this week I'm giving them my packet from the grocer's.' Exciting and distracting though these admirable efforts at food self-sufficiency might have been, larger worries were rarely absent. 'I do so dread these next few nights till the full moon, and tonight, with a slim crescent, it was clear and bright and some poor city will suffer.' And so one did. It was a disturbed night in Barrow, for 'the guns and bombs were so bad on Merseyside [about fifty miles away] that our windows and doors rattled!' The following night brought a direct assault on Barrow. Nora Bainbridge wrote in her diary for Saturday, 3 May: 'Siren at 11.45pm. BLITZ. A mine dropped in the council houses 100 yards away from where I was standing at the front door – blew my hat off and made a mess of the house. Lewis came down straight away and took me to the Sacred Heart shelter [at her school], so I spent the night there. Bombs all over the place. Searchlights were going and *guns*.' Then an all clear, followed by sirens again, and at last another all clear.

This was, for Mrs Last, 'a night of terror', and she described in detail the aftermath of these overnight raids (4 May, *NLW*, pp. 130-33). 'There are few windows left in the district – or roof tiles! Land mines, incendiaries and explosives were dropped and we cowered thankfully under indoor shelter [acquired after the April raids]. I've been so dreadfully sick all day and I'm sure it's sheer fright for last night I really thought our end had come.' She, a meticulous housewife, surveyed 'my loved little house' in dismay. It 'will never be the same again,' she felt. 'Windows are nearly all out and metal frames strained and ceilings down and walls cracked and garage roof showing four inches of daylight where it joins the wall. Doors splintered and off and the *dirt* from the blast that swept down chimney. The house rocked and then the kitchenette door careened down hall and plaster showered on to shelter.' She was struck by her own peculiar mental reactions. 'I'll never forget my odd sensations – one a calm acceptance "of the end" and the other a feeling of regret I'd not opened a tin of fruit salad to tea – and now it was too late!'

Later, she was able to get out and about and survey the damage. 'There are a number of people round here killed and houses flat. A dog whose master was killed and whose mistress was frantic with fear and grief ran over half a mile, climbed fourteen steps and crawled under a bed – and both its back legs were broken and it had internal injuries. A lady saw it and called a vet,' who put it down. It was still too early for anyone to assess the extent of the losses that night. 'I keep wondering and wondering how many killed and injured there are. It's only a little town and does not need a big blitz to wipe it out,' she feared. At bedtime she wrote more in her diary. Will had worked a very long day on shop repairs; she heard that 'whole districts [were] roped off' because of the damage done. 'Many I know are killed in different parts of the town.' The following day she was wondering if she should have her dog put down.

Nora Bainbridge spent Sunday, 4 May 'clearing away broken glass, soot, etc. and making the house a little more respectable' and then spent the night in an aunt's shelter, taking refuge from a blitz that seemed even larger than that of the previous night. To come through it, said Nella, 'and keep calm is a good test of nerves alright – *and* heart.' She thought that both of hers 'must be stronger than I think' (*NLW*, pp. 133-35). She reported the sounds of the night. 'Screaming bombs, planes we did not hear until the bombs dropped, dog fights overhead and machine gunning rattling and spattering – so dreadful, so frightening.' She was vomiting a lot. She was worried about 'desperate' mothers and their young children,[7] and about the head of Barrow's WVS who lived in a large house on a hill. Destruction seemed to be everywhere. 'Mr. Hemingway was killed last night,' wrote teenager Nora Bainbridge. 'Houses demolished in Hill Road, Hollow Lane (Aunty Mollie and Peggy bombed out), Salthouse Road, Suffolk Street, etc. Central railway station is a wreck.' (The Post Office was also badly damaged.) 'There are unexploded bombs everywhere,' wrote Nella, 'and long detours have to be taken by all traffic'. The following day (5 May) Nora Bainbridge found that 'All the people in our street living nearer the bomb than us are evacuating themselves. ...All our neighbours on the bomb side are leaving.[8] Found a lot of shrapnel in the garden.'

After a two-day lull, the aerial attacks resumed on the nights of 7/8 and 8/9 May (*NLW*, pp. 139-42 and *DONL*, pp. 50-52). 'The shipyard got a "plastering",' according to Nella (8 May), 'and there is to be no more night shifts – two day shifts of 6 till 2 and 2 till 10 at night.* As it is there will be several thousands out of work I hear.'** She went out during the day to visit and survey the damage to the houses of women she knew. 'Mrs. Boorman's home' – she was 'out of town with her husband; he has had a bad nervous breakdown' (5 May) – 'and the two next are a horror and five were killed in the shelter when a landmine took all gardens away and left a crater like a quarry. The Regional Commissioner came down and after looking round said "Barrow is blitzed as badly as any place in England, London or Bristol included, according to its size".' The following night, 8/9 May (Thursday/Friday), the shipyard was again attacked. 'Thank God the men are not on a night shift under the areas of glass roof.'

Later on 9 May Nella was seeing her younger son off at the station. People were fleeing to safety (they hoped). 'Hundreds of people jostled and milled to get into the train... The poor things with bundles and bedding were only going one or two stations out and there should have been a "local", and a *free* one, even if only made up of wagons. It was so pitiful to see their looks of terror at being left, for so many lived round the steel works and the Yard.' On the positive side, some public services were quickly restored. 'The damage to station was bad but order was coming out of chaos and tidy piles of planks and pieces of iron were about everywhere on platform.' It was a day of much improvising. 'When we came home I learned with pleasure that the service busses were all running free after a certain hour to take anyone out to nearby districts. They have been sleeping in hedges and fields all round outside town. No one has *any* faith in shelters for after first small attacks when people died in bed and amid their ruined homes and the shelters stood up unharmed, practically all deaths have been in shelters when houses crashed on them. In the centre of town last night it was dreadful for after the bombs started to fall and crash the poor things rushed from the little box-like back street shelters into their houses and then out into street, frantic with fear and not knowing where to go.[9] We have no really decent shelters. I don't think our Council ever really thought we would "get it". I don't really think many people did.'[10]

The major industrial assets in Barrow, including the shipyard, escaped serious damage. However, as a result of these April/May raids more than 100

---

* With double summer time, it would still be light when this shift ended and thus before any bombing was likely to begin.

** She had been told the day before that 'there is trouble brewing in the Yard for all lights are turned off and the men ordered into shelter [when an alert sounded] and now they don't pay them as they formerly did and four to six hours are knocked off night's pay'. This meant a big cut to the wages of the men who worked that shift. It was said that they 'think they should have tin hats and shelters by "machines" to crouch under, as in other places'.

houses were completely destroyed and some 500 others were so damaged that they were later demolished. Residential districts certainly suffered the most. Near the docks one row of houses called Aureol Terrace was obliterated by a land mine.[11] A further 2,000 houses received lesser damage. After surveying some of bombed neighbourhoods on 15 May, Nella lamented the 'wanton *useless* destruction everywhere'. The human toll was high. Officially, 79 civilians in Barrow were killed by German bombing in 1941, all or almost all of them during these four weeks (there were only four further Barrovian deaths from raids during the remaining four years of the war).[12] Other estimates suggest that 83 (or even as many as around 90) people were killed and 330 injured.[13] Some fatalities left few bodily remains. A formal 'Notice of Certification of Death due to War Operations' (a printed form), dated 10 May 1941, tersely states: 'Male, unidentifiable remains of human body', and under identifying features are the words 'One Pair of Black Boots, Large, Flat-footed'.[14] We do not know how his mangled body parts were disposed of or whether anyone claimed them.

* * * *

There are other things to be said about Barrovians' responses to the bombings. First, many left town. This had happened after other blitzes: the Chislehurst caves in Kent served as a temporary refuge for some people in East London; Plymouth's victims of raids self-evacuated to nearby communities.[15] For the middle class, flight could usually be exercised with a relative ease not available to many working-class people 'All neighbours who have cars and friends in country have fled,' according to Nella on Sunday, 4 May. This did not sit well with her. 'A woman opposite brought [her] key and said "Keep an eye on things, please!" I said "*No*. You must do it yourself. You have no right to expect me or anyone else to do it for you. You are strong and well and no children to think of. I'd not put out an incendiary if I saw it strike your house – unless I thought the flame would be a danger to others.' Nella surprised herself with this forthrightness. 'I think I'm a little mad today. I'd never have spoken so plainly until now.' The Helms, the family in the house attached to hers, 'were off to sleep out of town, like many hundreds more' (MOA, 5 May). Nella was advised by Mrs. Helm to do the same; it was easy, she said, to "run the car into a barn and sleep". Nella replied: 'No, I cannot do that – and why should I. Why do you think we got a shelter if we intended to run away!' Nella was committed to standing her ground, just as other women had. Her younger son also advised evacuating (6 May, *NLW*, p 136). "I said firmly NO. Not while I've a roof and my nerves can possibly stand it. Do you think I'd feel shame before the women of London and Bristol who have stood it for so long? And who would look after Daddy and make his meals and keep him well for work if I ran away?"[16]

Many of these flights to safety lasted for only a few days, as people sought temporary peace and quiet in rural districts. Special buses provided some transport. Soon most of these people were back in Barrow, if their homes remained habitable. Poorer families had to make do as best they could, patching up their dwellings with, say, canvas or tarpaulin and blocking up some glass-less windows; or they moved somewhere nearby, perhaps to live with relatives or friends, or to rent another property that afforded better shelter.[17] 'Our two-year-old house had no windows, no ceilings, and we could see the sky from the bedrooms', recalled a woman of her Barrow girlhood. 'It was devastating that we could no longer live there. We left the area for a year and lived in cramped conditions with a relative.'[18]

After a blitz it was normal for hundreds, if not thousands, of people to be on the move. Some became longer-term resident refugees in the countryside, and some of them took to commuting into the town. Nella's elderly Aunt Sarah lived in Spark Bridge, around a dozen miles north-east of Barrow, and Nella visited her on 19 April, a few days after the first raids (MOA). 'Every room for miles round, she tells me, is full of Barrow people who rushed out of town – "anywhere from sound of planes and guns" – and on the nearby farm they pleaded for a room to sleep in and would take meals *anywhere* and do *anything* to help on farm as well as pay a good price for room.' Nella did not try to conceal her own 'nerviness' but hoped for the strength not to give in. 'It must be dreadful to feel so frightened – and I hope I am never so nervy.' On 1 May she stopped by Barrow's WVS centre and spoke with one of the other women there (MOA). 'It seems so odd the way the bombs altered her from our capable secretary to a stranger who "will *not* sleep in so dangerous a place as Barrow again".[19] The prices people are paying for sleeping accommodation [outside Barrow] *amazes* me – not prices demanded but offered freely, and when people don't want or feel they cannot take "boarders" it's *doubled*.' Stories abounded of people searching, sometimes desperately, for private refuges.

A while later (18 May, MOA) Nella was back in Spark Bridge to visit her aunt and encountered more of these people, who had come to be known by the locals as 'jitter bugs'. Nella was struck by their panic. 'It's really astounding how people with cars rushed off and booked "safe" accommodation, paying *anything* in advance, and not giving a thought at all to whether their petrol would enable them to travel back and forward for a full week.' The mention of cars here and elsewhere clearly indicates that most of these people fleeing danger were, like the Lasts, at least lower-middle class. But even some workers were involved. 'Now', Nella added, 'there are tales of people having to walk two or three miles and catch a bus and travel up to 12 miles into Shipyard – to start on the 6 o'clock shift!' Schoolgirl Norah Bainbridge reported on 19 May that some of her fellow students had been evacuated, and that (here you detect a tone of annoyance) 'much inconvenience is caused to Dalton and Ulverston girls by the buses being filled by *Barrow* shipyard workers'. (Workmen's trains were, in fact, longstanding, though they were probably more heavily used at this time of emergency.)[20]

Nella Last's sympathies for fearful folk were especially scant for those with money. 'Pampered women are learning what primitive sanitation and no shops mean and, where cottages have been bought, are finding that as much more as [the] high figure paid will be needed to make them comfortable – even weatherproof! Furniture has been rushed into barns and outhouses that Joe [a relative of Aunt Sarah] says "swarm with rats" and where, as he says, "upholstered furniture will make grand breeding places!"' (18 May, MOA.) Class-consciousness and class resentment were not hard to find. 'There is a more bitter feeling about our "new rich" springing up than I've yet known,' according to Nella the following month (19 June, *DONL*, p. 78). 'It's caused by them being able to go out each night either in their own cars or "clubbing together" in a friend's car. They go out and stay at an outlying farm and have bed and breakfast – home-cured ham or bacon and eggs – and bring in butter and fresh eggs and in some cases cream and homemade jam and chutney bought at "fancy prices" from farmers' wives.'

The editor of the *Barrow Guardian* later (19 July 1941, p. 2) wrote more sympathetically about these movements of people. He was speaking of Dalton-in-Furness, some three miles north of Barrow, which, after the raids, 'became the temporary home of a great many families'. He praised Dalton's 'hospitality'. 'We have heard of scores of cases where homeless and frightened people were given shelter and rest, and were, let it be said, not by any means taken advantage of.' He downplayed certain uncomplimentary stories that had apparently been circulating. 'We have heard of very few cases of exploitation, and we hesitate to believe the solitary story of one and six-pence being charged for the use of a chair for one night.' All this had happened – or was rumoured to have happened – weeks before. 'Since those days there has been a considerable thinning off of evacuees in Dalton. In many cases new confidence has been restored. In others, homes in Barrow have been repaired and made fit to occupy again.'

Many evacuations were not voluntary. Families that had lost their homes had no choice but to move elsewhere. Many children – probably at least a couple of thousand – were evacuated officially to safer places, most of them to Westmorland.[21] Kendal, in particular, received large numbers of these evacuees in May, though the exact number was not publicised. Hundreds of Barrow's children were sent to the north of Westmorland. Another 500 were expected there in early September and a similar number in the south-west of the county.[22] The WVS in Westmorland, which handled most of the logistics, reported on this work in their monthly report for that month.[23] Some 1,460 of

Barrow's elementary school children were received in Westmorland. Kendal was the detraining centre for the south of the county and on the 20 and 21 May several hundred children arrived (perhaps as many as 1,000) and were fed, marshalled, sometimes re-clothed, and undressed for medical inspection. The majority of the children needed to be de-loused or "cleaned up" in some other way. Three WVS members had already spent time in Barrow seeing to 'the clothing of the hordes of children'; some of the girls were said to be 'covered with bites'.[24] Securing suitable accommodation for the evacuees was becoming an ever-increasing challenge. 'The job of finding billets for the many bombed out families arriving from blitzed areas is becoming a real problem.' This was partly because during the previous three weeks some 700 unofficial evacuees had been billeted in Kendal, mostly Barrovians who had made private arrangements, plus a few from Liverpool. In mid-1941 Kendal and its region were packed with evacuees. It was later claimed that more children had been evacuated by their parents privately from Barrow than were evacuated officially.[25] Happily, by the end of the summer, with the almost complete cessation of blitzes, significant pressures for new billets were not to increase.

Tensions concerning these evacuations became public. The alleged 'filthy' condition of Barrow's evacuated children in September was condemned by the editor of Penrith's main newspaper, who drew attention to such matters as inadequate clothing and shoes, scabies, and lack of immunization against diphtheria, which posed a threat to the receiving communities. 'Healthy children in clean homes have no right to have their own health imperilled by these filthy contacts.'[26] These charges were rejected by a senior official in Barrow, who described the precautions his town had taken. He also suggested an element of small-mindedness on the part of the critics. 'Dealing with our own scheme, possibly we could have refused to send a child possessing one nit or a few spots. What did the refusal mean to the children? They were being evacuated from DANGER and DEATH to comparative SAFETY, and to refuse the child the right to be evacuated was tantamount to its being condemned to death for a few nits and a few spots.... Would to God that you in Westmorland are spared the type of visitation which was our lot on nine consecutive days in May last.... A few nits in the hair and a few cases of scabies would hardly be noticed against the dark background of those tragic days in May.'[27] Class resentment fuelled these differing outlooks: Barrow was a strongly working-class town, a decided contrast to the more genteel and conservative Penrith region.

⋆ ⋆ ⋆ ⋆

While Nella never entered Barrow's giant shipyard, she sometimes heard from knowledgeable sources about what had happened there. On Saturday,

10 May she was visited by Ruth, her occasional home help, who told her of the raid on the shipyard on the night of 8/9 May (*NLW*, pp 142-43). Men 'were trapped for a while in deep shelter. She said Gerald – her sweetheart – had "not spoken all day" and then his mother had evaced him [i.e., evacuated] to "talk and get it out of his system".' (Gerald's mother was at that time apparently living outside Barrow.) Here was a suggestion of at least short-term post-traumatic stress, which dozens if not hundreds of others must have experienced.

The story conveyed elements both of terror and comedy. 'Ruth said that the men took cover as usual and as usual played cards by torch light and sat and talked – mostly doubtful jokes and stories and in the hard-boiled way of Yard workers cursed and blasphemed. After one frightful crash when a large crane came down the foreman went to see the damage and came back and said "I hope to God there is not another. It looks as if we are trapped now." As he spoke there was a worse *crrrump* and then a deadly silence. Gerald said torches dropped from nerveless fingers on to floor and by their light he saw the "sound" of knees as men instinctively dropped on their knees on playing cards or newspapers. He saw clenched or clasped hands and a glimpse of grey hollowed cheeks and then a calm steady voice rose "Father, into thy hands we commend our spirits" and then the Lord's Prayer started and Gerald recognized the voice as belonging to about the dirtiest mouthed and hardest swearing man in the shop – a footballer.' The men were indeed in peril. 'Above their heads the layer of concrete cracked and shifted with the weight of piling machinery flung on a heap by blast – and then a wide crack appeared on side of shelter side and light showed through. They managed to scramble out and all were saved – as by a miracle for the floor of the shop caved in on to their shelter shortly after.'

No doubt many other stories were told in Barrow of similar close calls. And some of them were probably true.

The telling of this story – and other stories by Nella – gives a sense of the mixed feelings that would have been involved in many people's experiences of the Barrow blitz. Fear must have been almost universal, though handled in different ways. Some succumbed, others stood firm. Some people thought only of themselves, or lost their nerve; at least a few engaged in looting.[28] Such unsavoury conduct was also reported from blitzed Manchester.[29] But other behaviour was also observed – appeals for, and the timely granting of, help, steadiness under pressure, minimal panic, and eventually a welcome sense of relief. Solidarities were often expressed, as citizens responded to the need to help others. A significant proportion of able-bodied Barrovians were engaged in these constructive tasks, before, during, and after the attacks.[30] There were powerful incentives to work together for the common good. 'Barrow is so small and we are "all in it together",' Nella remarked on 10 May. (These incentives did not, of course, work with everyone.) Women confined to home could also feel involved: Nella's elderly aunt in Spark Bridge made a pillow and a patchwork cot quilt, 'all by hand and so beautifully pieced and matched,' for the "poor people who had been bombed" (26 April). She seemed to be energised by the local emergency (10 May). Later Nella wrote of how, in her view, people – even those with modest talents – 'liked a worthwhile job and not to feel "futile"' (16 May, *DONL*, pp. 55-56). On 22 May at the reopened WVS centre she heard of women who had lost their homes being 'offered beds and sanctuary, or storage for a few salvaged treasures' by more fortunate women. Later that day she reflected on the WVS's collaborative efforts. 'It was so *good*, so *vital*, the way we all pulled together and worked and laughed together.' (*DONL*, pp. 59-62.)

Nella and her WVS colleagues were clearly of service to others when they went out in their mobile canteen, the 'Jolly Roger', to serve on post-blitz work sites (16 May, *DONL*, pp. 55-56). 'We went from one group of demolition workers to another and to bomb damage groups and grave diggers with our welcome hot tea and sandwiches. So many have been brought into town from districts outside town – Cumberland and Westmorland mostly and many "over age" miners and things are a bit at sixes and sevens yet. Others come into town by bus each day and returning to sleep have no hot drinks but bring food – and it's so bitterly cold.' Canteens were always valued, since outdoor workers rarely had any other means of refreshment. 'The men were glad of their tea when the Jolly Roger showed up', according to Nella on 21 May. 'I'd a fireman again to drive me – another "good help" like last one.'

⋆ ⋆ ⋆ ⋆

For some Barrovians, life would never return to normal. The ruptures were too severe. Nella Last reported on 22 May that 3,800 homes in Barrow were damaged; no doubt some were still being lived in, others abandoned. An official estimate suggested that about half the residences in the town received slight damage, in addition to those that were beyond repair.[31] Homelessness remained widespread for months. It was a lengthy struggle for the town to get back on its feet. 'There are still 7,000 people "homeless" in Barrow', Nella reported on 6 October 1941 (*DONL*, p 93), 'although everyone connected with repairs have worked marvellously and roofs and doors have gone on houses and plasterers work all the hours God sends'. Alerts, after May, were few and far between. Of course, precautions were still in order. 'Our last night of smoke screen till next full moon', Nella wrote on 12 June (MOA).

Ordinary pleasures and routines were in due course restored. On Sunday, 29 June (MOA) Nella and Will spent the afternoon in Bowness. There were cheerful crowds and a holiday mood. 'Few Servicemen were about and it was impossible to think of war or threat of invasion.' She then paused to reflect on the contrasting reactions of people in Barrow to the bombing of several weeks before. On the one hand were 'those who have tried to sell or let their houses and gone to live in tiny country cottages – *anywhere* to get away from Barrow.' These, she felt, were 'jittery' people. On the other hand were 'people who want estimates and are planning to make their houses "the same as before blitz".' But as she remarked, this probably wouldn't happen, for materials and labour were scarce, if not entirely unavailable, for such discretionary private repairs and renovations. She concluded by remarking that 'It's as if one lot of people think Barrow is a plague spot to be got out of and kept out of and the other think that we have had all in the way of bombs that we are going to do.' The latter were correct – but at that time no observer, however well-informed, possessed prophetic powers. The sense of danger in Barrow did recede, albeit gradually, but for many relief was accompanied by painful, even agonizing, memories.

Notes and References

1 J. Ray, *The Night Blitz 1940-1941* (London, 1996; paperback 2000), Chap. 9. The leading authority on raids nationwide is J. Gardiner, *The Blitz: The British Under Attack* (London, 2010). Barrow gets only a passing mention, with no details at all, in R. Overy's impressive *The Bombing War: Europe 1939-1945* (Penguin, 2014).

2 B. Trescatheric and D.J. Hughes, *Barrow at War* (Chorley, Lancashire, 1979), 10, and P. and R. Malcolmson, eds., *The Diaries of Nella Last: Writing in War and Peace* (London, 2012), 46-7.

3 Barrow Archives, 'Diary of Margaret Nora Bainbridge', BDX 555. (Later references in the text are to the same source.) She was born 22 December 1924 and lived at 37 Derby Street. Nora's facts were correct (The National Archive, HO 198/245). There was also an official awareness of the consequences of a German invasion, which was seen as entirely possible: R. Freethy, *Cumbria at War 1939-1945* (Newbury, Berkshire, 2009), 14-18.

4 Pre-war official estimates of the likely consequences of aerial attacks had usually overestimated the number of fatalities and underestimated the extent of the property damage. Bombing raids in Barrow as almost everywhere else proved to be more effective at destroying property than killing people – at least in the numbers once feared.

5 'Our public baths have gone', Nella wrote on 16 April (MOA). 'Such a pity, for all the soldiers stationed in Barrow and surrounding districts went [there] and there was always long lines of soldiers coming and going – and even lined up outside.'

6 *Barrow Guardian*, 21 October 1944, 5.

7 'The worst night we experienced', recalled one woman of the blitz, 'I can remember my mother lying on top of us on the shelter bed whilst bombs fell all around us. When the all clear sounded we discovered lumps of clay the size of footballs in the driveway but worse was to come when we entered the house' and saw, when it was light, 'the devastation inside'. (Cumbria Federation of Women's Institutes, *Cumbria Within Living Memory* [Newbury, 1994], 179.)

8 Houses numbered 39, 41 and 43 on Derby Street had been classified as 'Damaged and unfit for habitation'. Her house was no. 37. During this night's raid a housewife living in Bolton-le-Sands, Lancashire, on the east of Morecambe Bay, said that 'the house was shaking. Jack got up to watch the bombs and gunfire – he saw a number of incendiaries falling' (MOA, Diarist no. 5239, 5 May 1941).

9 These neighbourhoods housed mostly working-class families, many of whose members were employed by nearby Vickers-Armstrongs. The bombing of Barrow is remembered in an admirable 2016 short film by Matthew Dodd, *The Barrow Blitz: 75 Years On*.
10 The following night, 9/10 May 'started off so terribly', in Nella's words, 'that if it had gone on there would have been little of Barrow' (*NLW*, 142). Then there was a lull and 'the raiders were chased out to sea'. Thus concluded the 1941 blitz on Barrow.
11 B. Trescatheric, *A Shipyard Town: The Story of Barrow in the 20th Century* (Barrow-in-Furness, 2007), 42. His *The Barrow Blitz* (Barrow-in-Furness, 2009), 11-22, includes numerous photographs of some of the damaged properties.
12 TNA, HO 198/245.
13 B. Trescatheric and D.J. Hughes, *Barrow at War* (1979), 4. A later publication by one of these authors states that some 95 civilians were killed (Trescatheric, *A Shipyard Town*, 42). It also corrects an error in the earlier publication, which claimed (p. 4) that 10,700 houses received some form of damage.
14 Barrow Archives, Civilian War Deaths, BA/H/11/2/2.
15 Such 'trekking' overnight was common after heavy raids, though officially disapproved of: Overy, *Bombing War*, 143-44.
16 'Many people from the "better" houses have gone and left them as they stand', she remarked on 7 May, 'such an invitation to looters from the poorer end of the town who may have lost all'.
17 J. Thistlethwaite, *Cumbria, The War Years: Lake District Life during the 1940s* (Kendal, 1997), 10 and 52-53; and Freethy, *Cumbria at War 1939-1945*, 91-92.
18 Cumbria Federation of Women's Institutes, *Cumbria Within Living Memory*, 179.
19 A few days before (MOA, 26 April) Nella revealed that this woman hadn't even been in Barrow during the bombing, for she was away on an extended Easter holiday. 'She has resigned altogether from WVS, as also has her sister, who has gone to stay in the country further out. Mrs. Machin is going right away to Ruthin in North Wales where she "will feel safe from both bombs and invasion".' Nella was about to tease her, pointing out that Ireland might be invaded first and used as a base for invasion, and 'you are going nearer when you go to Ruthin', but she stopped herself from saying more 'when I saw how really terrified she was'.
20 Freethy, *Cumbria at War*, 65 and 71.
21 According to two local authorities, some 1,760 children were received from Barrow (J.F. Dow and M. A. Brown, *A Survey of Evacuation in Westmorland* [Kendal: Westmorland County Council, May 1943], 9). Another estimate put the number of Barrow's officially evacuated elementary students to Westmorland in June 1941 at 1,419 (*Westmorland Gazette*, 30 January 1943, 8).
22 *Westmorland Gazette*, 30 August 1941, 5, and *Cumberland and Westmorland Herald*, 30 August 1941, 1. The latter stated that 'there are already some 1,600 children [evacuated to the north of Westmorland] apart from those who have come outside the official evacuation organisation'. It is probable that this figure applied not just to those from Barrow but to all child evacuees, some of them from the North East. Thus far voluntary billeting had proven adequate and most of the billets, it was said, were 'in working class homes, but for the next batch compulsion will have to be resorted to for about half the evacuees'. It turned out that in September some 800 children from Barrow were officially evacuated to Penrith and the north of Westmorland, and compulsion was not used to billet them. (*Cumberland and Westmorland Herald*, 18 October 1941, 1 and 4 October 1941, 5.)
23 Kendal Archives, WDSO 92/1-2, WVS Narrative Reports for May 1941 for both Kendal and Westmorland. There was no press coverage of May's evacuation when it occurred, since any such reports would have revealed facts about the Barrow raids that might aid the enemy and were thus censored. The official plans called for approximately 2,000 of

Barrow's children to be evacuated over two days, 20 and 21 May, half for the South Westmorland Rural District Council, half for the North Westmorland RDC (Kendal Archives, WC/C9, Evacuation Bags, file 1/1).

24 Others also recalled some of the Barrow children as ill-clad: Thistlethwaite, *The War Years*, 112. As Dow and Brown pointed out, 'Many of the children had been sleeping in shelters and it was no wonder that they were in a dirty condition' (*A Survey of Evacuation*, 9).

25 *Cumberland and Westmorland Herald*, 18 October 1941, 1. One estimate puts the number of children officially evacuated in May at 1,500, the number privately evacuated at 2,250 (Trescatheric, *Barrow Blitz*, 28). By the late summer of 1942 only 20% of Barrow's children evacuated to Westmorland remained there (Westmorland WVS NR, August 1942).

26 *Cumberland and Westmorland Herald*, 4 October 1941, 5.

27 *Cumberland and Westmorland Herald*, 18 October 1941, 1; Trescatheric, *Barrow Blitz*, 31; *Barrow Guardian*, 18 October 1941, 6.

28 According to the *Barrow Guardian*, 3 May 1941, 2, 'quite a lot of thieving was done from damaged properties. The difficulty is that it is not easy to detect the culprits because they can hide their activities under the cloak of apparent helpfulness.'

29 G. Phythian, *Blitz Britain: Manchester and Salford* (Stroud, Gloucestershire 2015), Chap. 7.

30 More than 500 men were engaged in post-raid cleaning-up, salvage, and repairing property (Trescatheric, *Barrow Blitz*, 18).

31 *Barrow Guardian*, 21 October 1944, 5.

Fig. 1.Evacuees arriving at Wigton station, September 1939 *(Carlisle Library)*

Fig. 2. Underbarrow school, September 1939. Many of the children, some of them evacuees, are carrying gas masks. *(Kendal Library)*

Fig. 3. Soldiers at Kendal station *(Kendal Library)*

Fig. 4. Bomb damage to the Trevelyan Hotel, off Abbey Road in Barrow, April 1941 *(North-West Evening Mail)*

Chapter 4
Work

'The face of Westmorland has changed. The brant hill-sides are now an intricate patchwork of green grass and brown earth.' *Cumberland and Westmorland Herald*, 27 March 1943, p. 3.)

'Tonight of all things I've been harvesting. Mr. Preston has been cutting oats in the big field and Marian Clark was helping. She helps Mr P. as her war work as she has her father to look after at home. I thought it might be a good idea and asked her and as it appeared that they were shorthanded I donned an overall (and of course gloves) and helped to gather it into sheaves. I enjoyed it and we didn't stop till 10 p.m.'[1]

By the end of the second year of the war, virtually every able-bodied adult male in Cumbria was in paid employment, if not serving in the forces. This military call-up guaranteed a scarcity of labour on the home front. Consequently wage rates generally rose; some workers in jobs deemed essential were prevented from leaving them; factories sprung up or were reconfigured to produce munitions; farmers were directed to alter their modes of production; and women took on jobs that in the 1930s had been done almost exclusively by men. Most people worked longer hours than they had before, especially given such duties as fire-watching, which was mandatory from 1941. Many – women in particular – did some tasks that they had never previously done. These changes are well documented nationally. In this chapter we show some of the particulars of Cumbria's wartime workplaces and how changes came about.[2]

* * * *

Farming was central to Cumbria, and a major change to its agriculture was that much more land was mandated to be put into arable production in order to reduce the pre-war reliance on imports. These directives came from the War Agricultural Executive Committees (WAECs) of Cumberland and Westmorland. Thousands of acres of grazing land – this was a region where pastoral farming was often king – were newly ploughed up for crops and some unutilised land was reclaimed. As war got underway, Cumberland was required to find an extra 35,000 acres for crops, Westmorland 10,000 acres. Since more food could be produced from crops than livestock, while also reducing imports, some farmers, assuming they had suitable land, were required to plough up a certain number of grassland acres and sow them with oats, wheat or barley, or other crops suitable to a northern climate, including turnips which could be used as fodder.[3] There was a significant decline in the acreage of permanent grassland (around 50% nationally).[4] Government support was available to those farmers who had to shift some of their production to arable. Much was achieved: it was said that in Cumberland the acreage under potatoes in 1941 was nearly double that of 1940.[5]

Comprehensive surveys of all the farms in both counties in 1938-39 allowed the WAECs to determine in detail where changes were possible. As one report said of the new directives, 'Every farm had to be considered on its merits. There were some cases where 25 per cent had been asked for [in ploughed land], others where not one per cent had been requested'.[6] Even small farms – the norm in many parts of the North West – were required to cultivate more intensively, and wheat was sometimes planted on land where it had little chance of success. Appeals were possible and the merits of individual cases were to be given due consideration. However, farmers' choices, whatever the flexibility exercised, were suddenly greatly restricted. As one report concerning Westmorland stated bluntly, 'if the land is capable of growing a cereal crop it should not be sown down to rape and seeds in 1940'.[7] The quotas for 1942 required a substantial increase in the acreage devoted to potatoes.[8] A few farmers were prosecuted for ignoring cultivation orders. The Ministry of Food controlled livestock sales,[9] and official encouragement was actively given to farmers to make more silage for fodder and demonstrations were given showing how this could be done.[10] All these policies were expressions of a basic fact of wartime farming: much of it was under the direct control of the government, not of market forces.[11]

Various documents testify to this directive culture and the micro-management that it often involved. In July 1943 the agent for the Leconsfield Estate Company was authorised 'to stop up and plough the footpath (or bridlepath) crossing the field OS No. 288 in the parish of Cockermouth' – and restore these rights of way after the war. The previous year a notice was distributed in the Cockermouth district that set out new production targets. The acreage of lea was to be increased by 50% over 1942 and 3,000 additional acres were to be tilled. 'Will you please consider Autumn sown wheat on any suitable land which you have available.... Wheat may be successful on certain land out of lea, and part of your lea acreage will be accepted as lea wheat or potatoes.' Farmers with dairy stock were expected to provide their own feed. Potato subsidies were routinely applied for and granted to many farmers.[12] Co-operation was officially encouraged. A farmer in Caldbeck, Cumberland received a letter from the county's WAEC, dated 7 March 1941, which noted that because of inclement weather 'there is a large amount to be done in the short time available', and it was optimistic – or perhaps just hopeful – that farmers with tractors (He was one of them.) 'would be willing to do a little to help their neighbours if necessary'. The letter asked him directly, though tactfully, 'to assist in a small way by ploughing for any of your neighbours, should they supply to me [the machinery manager] to have their ploughing done'.[13] (It is not known how successful this appeal was or how many farmers were written to.)

When war came, farmers showed differing degrees of readiness. Some lowland farmers had taken advantage of the interwar years to improve methods and increase mechanization, leaving them well prepared for both increased wartime demands and labour shortages. Larger farms usually prospered during the war, commonly with the help of new machinery such as tractors. By contrast, hill farms, which were less capitalised, often struggled, including in years when upland areas suitable only for sheep were pushed to adopt some other form of husbandry. Recent research has revealed the striking variability in Westmorland farmers' prosperity. As one authority has put it, 'War was good for cattle in Westmorland. Despite a doubling of land under arable crops and a severe shortage of imported feedstuffs the numbers of cattle increased by about 10,000 between 1939 and 1945'.[14] Dairy cattle were highly valued; milk products were deemed to be essential to wartime nutrition. Farming realities meant that central government was often making shifts in policy to suit the particularities of landscape ecology, weather patterns, crop productivity, and the like. No one size could fit all. Extensive cropping probably resulted in soil exhaustion in some districts by 1945.

A second major set of agrarian changes resulted from the scarcity of farm labour in Cumbria, as men were called up to the forces or volunteered. If essential farm work were to get done, labour would have to come from unconventional sources. The main sources were, first, women, notably the Women's Land Army (WLA); second, Italian prisoners of war (POWs); and third, mainly at peak seasons in the farming calendar, volunteers or students – that is, cheap English labour. The problem of labour on farms was recognised early. In September 1939 provisions were even being made to allow soldiers to volunteer for a few days of harvesting when it could be shown that a farmer was in desperate need of workers (The soldiers were to be paid no less than the usual minimum rates.).[15] Harvesting was time dependent, and since nobody wanted crops to rot in the field, the needed labour was sought from various untraditional sources.

The Women's Land Army played a prominent role in wartime Cumbria. Recruitment began in 1939[16] and remained active up to 1943, though at first the WLA numbers grew rather slowly. The opening in mid-1941 of Westmorland's first Land Army hostel, for twenty young women, was an opportunity to publicise the merits of employing these 'girls', many of whom were said to be 'already busily engaged in thinning turnips'. 'As the summer advances, haymaking, harvesting, turnip pulling, potato lifting and other important jobs will keep them very busy.'[17] At the end of 1942, 770 land girls were employed in Cumberland and Westmorland; by 1943 this number had grown to 1,100, and, whatever initial reservations there had been, by then their value to farmers was generally acknowledged.[18] As the *Cumberland and Westmorland Herald* for 20 November 1943 (p. 1) remarked, there was a 'revised outlook to the employment of Land Girls. At first members of the Women's Land Army were looked upon with amusement; now there are many farmers very glad that they took advantage of their services before Mr. Bevin [Minister of Labour] stopped recruiting for the WLA.' (The priority by then was to employ more women on munitions work.) The following year, at the time of the Whitsuntide hirings, with scarce male farm workers sometimes claiming and getting fabulous wages, up to £5 a week plus board and lodging, one consequence, according to this Penrith-based paper, was 'a far wider appreciation of the services of the Women's Land Army, some of whom have now been settled in their present situations for a long period and against whom prejudice has ceased'.[19]

The diverse experiences of land girls are reasonably well documented. Most did not come from farming backgrounds; most had opted for the WLA as their outlet for national service (in preference, say, to one of the auxiliary military services or, in particular, munitions work) for various personal reasons. Once recruited they received about a month of basic training and then were posted to work in some country district, usually living in either a WLA hostel – there were at least eight in Cumbria by 1943[20] – or billeted in a farmer's house. A woman later observed about Lazonby that wartime 'brought a culture shock in the form of about 40 land girls who were billeted in a specially built hostel near the auction market'. One of the girls, a 16-year old, had lied about her age.[21] The work was often physically demanding and sometimes done in weather that, in their previous lives, would have kept these young women indoors. The jobs assigned included milking cows, other dairy-related activities such as delivering milk, driving tractors, pulling root crops, weeding, vegetable gardening, and various aspects of harvesting (Fig. 6b).[22]

Mobility was a key feature of the work of some land girls, especially when they were tasked with threshing. The demands for labour fluctuated throughout the seasons and from farm to farm. One woman recalled being put in charge of a threshing machine and its gang of four. 'The gang travelled from farm to farm spending about three days at each. A mechanic came along with us to maintain the thresher.'[23] Farmers sometimes phoned a hostel when they needed help, and, if feasible, a land girl might cycle to the farm.[24] Another former land girl recalled that she had worked on numerous farms in the Longtown area. 'After you'd done your jobs on one farm, they wanted somebody at another one and you were moved from there.' Occasionally, she added, the Land Army would 'split the girls up and send them to different hostels. I used to think that was a silly thing to do because you'd all made friends. Still, I didn't feel too unhappy when I was moved to Silloth. Our hostel there, Causeway Head, had been a vicarage and had no electricity so we had oil lamps.' There was compensation in the form of a large RAF base, lots of invitations to social events, and a local dance hall.[25]

Foreigners, mainly Italian prisoners of war, whose work is often mentioned in the press from 1941, were a second novel source of farm labour. A special agricultural hostel was built for them in Longtown, accommodating some nineteen men, and others were under construction elsewhere in the county.[26] Initially there was some complaining about the POWs' efforts in Cumberland, but less cause for dissatisfaction by the second half of the war: 'as farmers well know,' according to the *Cumberland and Westmorland Herald* for 13 March 1943 (p. 1), 'most of them appear only too glad to work on the land, and some, indeed, have a very high standard of proficiency'. A few months later it was reported that these POWs, for the first time, would be permitted to 'live in' for up to three months for harvest work. 'Up to now this permission has been granted only where the "living in" arrangement has been on what might be described as a permanent basis. There are many prisoners so employed in certain parts of the county and they are giving general satisfaction.'[27] In mid-1944 many farmers were said to 'now speak appreciatively of the work of Italians' and feared they might be assigned to work elsewhere.[28] Some Italians worked in gangs, many on reclaimed land. The harvest in Cumberland in 1943 was expected to depend heavily on Italian labour, and the area served was to be more extensive than the previous year, 'as satellite camps have been opened'.[29] Numerous oral recollections mention Italians doing farm work locally.[30]

Sometimes POW labour was supplemented by the work of formerly interned 'enemy aliens', foreign refugees, or conscientious objectors, particularly when they had some knowledge of farm work.[31] In later 1941 it was still felt necessary to emphasize that the foreigners housed in a new land workers' hostel at Lazonby 'are really political refugees who have escaped from the Nazi domination'.[32] In Cumberland some 600 foreigners were available for farm work in 1943.[33]

The final significant new source of farm labour was a miscellaneous group of 'volunteers' – though most were given room and board when required (which they might have to pay for), and some adults were paid modest stipends. In 1940 schoolboys were volunteering to work on Westmorland farms during their summer holidays – or perhaps adults in authority were volunteering their labour[34] – and teachers were being asked to donate part of their summer vacation to helping with the harvest.[35] In following years schoolboy holiday-harvesters were often mentioned, some from evacuated grammar schools, others from local schools; they worked for not more than six or seven weeks, usually less.[36] A report in July 1944 indicated that boys from Carlisle Grammar School 'will again this year have a shortened summer vacation, two weeks being reserved for assisting the farmers in potato picking during October. A similar arrangement is being made in many of the rural schools of the county.'[37] In 1943 plans were underway for the girls' school at Casterton to attend a 'holiday camp' for potato picking in the Windermere area; Carlisle schoolchildren worked hard at lifting potatoes in 1944.[38]

Farm work also drew in adults and late adolescents. Some teenage girls and young women from cities had offered to do short-term farm work in the summer of 1941 and were working out of Penrith; some young women in Carlisle in 1943 were planning to spend parts of their weekends helping with potato planting in the spring and with the summer harvest, as they had done the previous year.[39] The Cumberland Guild of Agricultural Workers drew most of its young volunteers from 'local factories, shops and youth organisations'. (Lakeland Laundries was one.)[40] By the last couple of years of the war ordinary citizens were being invited to devote some or all of their summer holidays to helping with the harvest; in 1944 special camps were being constructed to accommodate them.[41] The plans that summer of Cumberland's WAEC were quite elaborate, with provisions for camp dormitories, sanitation and bathing facilities, evening entertainment, vouchers for rail travel, and free train transport for volunteers' bicycles. The YMCA was to be in charge of the camps. Some 700 men were wanted (to bolster the 300 students already promised) to work for at least a week between mid-July and the end of September. Depending on the season, they were to harvest hay, corn or root crops.[42]

The results of all these special measures were said to be admirable.[43] Compared with pre-war figures, it was claimed in 1943 that in Cumberland the acreage of potatoes had increased threefold, barley fivefold, and wheat seventy-fivefold. These were all crops for direct human consumption. The oats acreage had also increased, helping to replace imported feedstuffs. In Westmorland the area for tillage crops was some 30 per cent higher than in 1870, the year with the previous highest figure, and over three times higher than in 1939. Dairy farming was thriving and much more of the feed for these cattle was being produced locally. By the end of the war Cumberland's farmers were producing more food than ever.[44]

* * * *

Cumbria as a whole, with the significant exception of the shipbuilding town of Barrow, was generally thought of as a relatively secure haven in a dangerous world. It gave young airmen a fairly safe place to learn their skills. Its recharged agriculture helped to sustain an island nation at war. And its secluded beauty offered mental sustenance and emotional renewal. Vacationers and hikers continued to visit, though in smaller numbers. Of course, its citizens shared with the rest of the nation the trials of rationing, the blackout, erratic transportation, and worries about the health and well-being of friends and relatives in the forces. But almost everyone saw the far North West as well removed from the front lines.

This was not, though, the whole picture, for over time military sites and munitions works became features of the Cumbrian landscape. In part this was a consequence of the government's commitment to the dispersal of factories and other war-related facilities. There are passing references that testify to these projects. On 2 February 1942 a young man living just outside Maryport wrote in his diary that 'Labourers working at aerodrome near Carlisle were taken in usual bus this morning. Found the snow was too deep for work so the bus turned round and came back.'[45] This was only one of numerous airfields then under construction. An explosives factory was sited at Drigg on the Cumberland coast.[46] People concerned with billeting or child care sometimes mentioned munitions workers. In September 1941 the WVS reported that billeting was 'becoming even more difficult as Kendal has now to find billets for industrial workers at the Standard Company's munitions works about to start up' (Kendal WVS, NR September 1941).

Some of these expanding industries were hiring women, which led to social side effects. There were already in 1941 pressures to set up day nurseries 'to enable married evacuees with small children to take up munition work locally' (Westmorland WVS, NR October 1941). There are several references in the press in the middle years of the war to war workers needing billets in Penrith. In February 1943 the WVS claimed that the biggest problem concerning billeting 'is the growing number of local housewives who are now taking up whole or part-time war work and have really no time left to look after lodgers' (Westmorland WVS, NR February 1943). Full-time housewives could be expected to do only so much. The single largest industrial employer in Cumbria was Vickers-Armstrongs in Barrow; it had the capacity to employ almost everyone available locally and others from farther afield. Westmorland's WVS was finding in 1943 that 'some Barrow women who had taken their children home months ago are now trying to re-billet them here as they themselves want to take whole-time, well-paid jobs in the dockyard' (Westmorland WVS, NR April 1943). After the depressed 1930s, Barrow and its shipyard were booming. The 'Yard', as locals knew it, employed at the peak of its wartime production over 17,000 people, many of the men in reserved occupations.[47] The wages and behaviour of munitions workers were often a sore point for others. One letter-writer from Keswick complained in late 1941 that the parents of some evacuated children 'are free to make their pile in large or small degree at various forms of war work with no cares and no responsibilities'.[48]

The construction of airfields was a major source of employment, and many civilian jobs were linked to their maintenance. At least 100 men were employed to level the site for an airfield at Hutton-in-the-Forest; 755 civilians were working at Silloth's airfield by early 1941; close to 750 civilians had jobs at Kirkbride at the end of the war.[49] The contractors that built the runways and associated facilities created an abundance of jobs, mainly in Cumberland, and made one firm with roots in Carlisle, John Laing & Son Limited, very rich.[50] Then there were all the ripple effects of these bases. As one authority has written, 'Individual local people bought lorries and went to work transporting various items, including wood, sand and gravel, to help in the construction of the airfields. Although most airfields were constructed in an average of ten months, the Air Ministry paid well and many people reaped the rewards.' These beneficiaries included those in the drink trade, who were happy to enjoy the custom of many thousands of airmen.[51] Cumbria's airfields were used principally for at least one of three purposes: training, maintenance, or storage.

Other wartime industries were found in various Cumbrian locations. K Shoes in Kendal had government contracts to produce, among other things, kit bags, RAF flying boots, and shoes for the ATS and WAAF.[52] Castle Mills factory, also in Kendal, which had manufactured rugs and carpets, converted during the war to produce aircraft engines and parts and was operated by the Standard Motor Company of Coventry.[53] There was a shell-forging factory in Workington.[54] The steel works there probably absorbed around a quarter of the coal dug by West Cumberland's almost 5,500 miners.[55] H. Edgard and Sons in Whitehaven, with around 400 employees, was manufacturing battle dress for the army.[56] Silk mills in Hensingham near Whitehaven produced parachutes; and later in the war a firm manufacturing thermometers moved to Cleator Moor as a result of the V-1 attacks on the South East.[57] After 1940 aircraft parts were being produced at three sites in Sedbergh, employing 274 workers in 1941 and posing a challenge for the billeting authorities.[58] In Pica, a rather poor village south of Workington, almost all of the working population was said in late 1943 to be 'engaged in war industry' (pre-war its unemployment rate was around 30 percent).[59]

A number of other industries moved to Cumbria. After the bombing of Coventry in November 1940, in the words of a historian of Ulverston, 'Armstrong Siddley took over the now disused Paper Mill buildings on the canal, and used the site for repairing and refitting aero engines, while Fred Broome's "Ulvex" factory on Morecambe Road was used by Ashley Accessories, originally based in Liverpool, to manufacture electrical components for the military'.[60] In early 1941 Wagon Repairs Ltd. of Birmingham moved its entire office staff to Appleby, including some families, which meant finding housing for another 120 people in the town.[61] Oxley, an electronics firm that had relocated to Ulverston from London, produced night-vision equipment for aircraft at a works in Priory Park.[62] In Ings, Westmorland, near Windermere, a factory producing precision tools for munitions works grew from almost nothing after its arrival from Kent to engage around 50 staff, mainly women.[63]

In Carlisle, war-related production was carried out at Carr's Biscuit Works (special biscuits for the forces) and at Teasdale and Company (confectionery). Other companies manufactured various kinds of ordnance – storage boxes by J.W. Hetherington, makers of packing cases; containers for supplies, plus some 600 million cans for the armed forces, by the Metal Box Company.[64] Morton Sundour Fabrics in Carlisle, which normally produced furnishing fabrics, converted its looms to the production of covers for aircraft engines and cockpits, dinghy packs, parachutes, camouflage and anti-splinter material, pinnace covers, blankets, kit-bags, bitumised blackout cloth and other special fabrics, one of which, a lifting jack for crashed bombers, was thought to be especially ingenious. 'Placed under the wings of the machine ... air was pumped into each of the jacks till the aircraft was lifted clear for removal. Average time for the job – seven minutes.'[65]

Some munition works were very substantial. High Duty Alloys Limited, constructed at Distington from 1940 by John Laing & Son, eventually employed close to 3,000 men and women.[66] The Royal Ordnance factory at Sellafield was one of the largest. It was started by John Laing and Son in February 1942 and completed in May 1943, at a cost of £3 million. The complex comprised 257 buildings. The construction project employed some 3,400 to 3,500 workmen at its peak, which made for problems of transportation and local accommodation. Special rail and bus facilities covered a large area beyond the worksite, and, in addition to local billets, workers were housed in seven hostels and in hotels at Millom, Silecroft, and Stanley Gill. At roughly the same time the company was also constructing a large power station at Carlisle, valued at approximately £850,000.[67] Engineering and manufacturing works and airfields were vastly more prominent in Cumbria in the early 1940s than they had been in the 1930s.

* * * *

One of the most striking and unexpected locations for military production was Windermere, long regarded by many as the jewel of the Lake District. In 1940 it was about to become the site of the manufacture of the huge Sunderland flying boat – albeit accompanied by lots of local controversy. The government was casting around for places to build amphibious military aircraft which would be neither obvious nor easily accessible to the Luftwaffe. To military planners, Windermere was an obvious choice. It was relatively remote from large centres of population, away from the coast, and boasted a deep twelve-mile-long lake upon which seaplanes could take off and land. The lake also had a history of experimentation with early seaplanes going back to the first decades of the twentieth century.* Seaplanes, the Sunderland flying boats, were being manufactured by Short Brothers Ltd. in Rochester, Kent as well as in Belfast (with another company, Blackburn, doing similar work in Dumbarton, Strathclyde), but these factories were becoming too vulnerable to enemy attack. In November 1940 the Ministry of Aircraft Production (MAP), under the leadership of its bombastic minister, Lord Beaverbrook, endorsed the development of a production site at Windermere. Under wartime powers this initiative was well within the government's prerogative.

The Sunderland was a much different beast from the nimble and beloved Spitfire. It was a huge aircraft, weighing 58,000 lbs., which could be configured on two levels. It was heavily armoured with three gun turrets and an additional gun in the cockpit on later models. Its primary wartime mission was the protection of transatlantic convoys of food, supplies and troops. It was unusual in having a lot of space for the crew. A Sunderland 'had rest bunks on board, a galley and a wardroom where meals were made and served and even a toilet. Towards the rear there was even a small workbench for repairs to be carried out while an aircraft was at its mooring. All this had to be installed along with the military equipment, the bomb racks which winched the depth charges out under the wings, the gun turrets and radar aerials' (King, p.42).

Many local people were initially opposed to the notion that such a behemoth should be built in their beautiful and tranquil land. Especially appalled by the proposal were the Friends of the Lake District, a powerful environmental protection group dating back to the nineteenth century, whose secretary, Rev. H.H. Symonds, wrote in their report for 1940, that the proposed factory was 'an abomination ... which profanes the [natural] sanctuary and makes desolate a famous and frequented part of it'.[68] Another early objection came from the Westmorland County Council, which took the view that Windermere had already done its bit by accepting so many refugees from bomb-threatened areas. In an undated letter to the Ministry of Aircraft Production, Isobel McGregor-Rose argued that to turn the area into a military site was 'the height of folly. Soon, at this rate of spoliation, there will be no safe spot left not to mention beauty spots' (quoted King, p. 17). The thick file of objections held by the National Archives [AVIA, 15/3622] as well as the deputations to, and lobbying, of the minister's parliamentary secretary,

* Unless otherwise indicated, this chapter draws upon Allan King's fine and amply illustrated book, *Wings on Windermere: The history of the Lake District's forgotten flying boat factory* (Sandomierz, 2008). Also of value is Chorlton, *Cumbria Airfields*, 228-236.

Col. J.J. Llewellin, by Conservative private members, the National Trust, and Friends of the Lake District may have left Whitehall officials wondering if these Cumbrians really understood their country's peril. Officialdom made efforts at accommodation. Another site, an old seaplanes works at Lytham St Anne's, was researched as a possible alternative and quickly discarded as it was on an unsuitable and dangerous mudflat. Time was of the essence. One of Shorts' factories had already been bombed and expansion of the Belfast works was untenable due to the dangers of transporting parts across the Irish Sea.

The Windermere project was soon quickly moving forward. Objectors were partly mollified by an assurance that the factory was to be a temporary facility that would be removed from the site after the war as soon as practicable (a promise that was eventually met). In addition, the minister, Lord Beaverbrook, agreed to a stipulation that 'only the absolute minimum amount of flying be undertaken from the lake'.[69] In fact, all the aircraft produced at Windermere were flown directly to a maintenance unit in Dumfries where the test flights of new Sunderlands took place. This was a significant concession. The factory and hangar themselves were camouflaged by rows of trees, designed both to baffle the Germans and maintain the natural beauty of the Lake District. It was reported that many who worked at Windermere actually described it as a 'garden factory', surrounded by beautiful trees and rhododendron bushes, and readily accessible to the beauty and recreational possibilities of the surrounding landscape. Not everyone put a premium on rural tranquility. Some experienced workmen who had been transferred to this remote worksite missed the shops, pubs, and diversions of city life, as did some adult evacuees from bombed areas.

Another local perspective on this major development was revealed in the WVS's Westmorland report to headquarters in November 1940. 'We have had to help to find billets for 400 industrial workers in Windermere,' the county organiser wrote, 'a very unpopular influx, and the Lake District is upset at the prospect of having a huge aircraft factory starting up in an area that up to now has been considered the safest in England and therefore filled with schools, invalids and the aged.' This safety, many felt, had now been compromised. 'It will soon become a vulnerable area (flares have already been dropped on the Lake) and it does rather strike one as an instance of one Government Department encouraging the cramming of a "safe" area and then another Department making it decidedly unsafe.' Non-Cumbrians and later generations have found it easier to accept that in such a situation 'military/security' considerations were bound to be given priority.

Construction was undertaken with some urgency to build the factory and the airplane hangar even though controversy over building a prefab village to accommodate workmen rumbled along in the background. By July 1941 the detail shop, where small parts were manufactured and partial aircraft pieces assembled, had been erected. Training and manufacture began, the canteen was soon in operation, and work began in earnest even though the hangar was not finished until March 1942, ready to receive the first flying boat hulls that had been put together in the detail shop. The hangar was a massive undertaking that dwarfed all other construction in the area. It was 300 by 250 feet, 70 feet high, and capped by a huge single-span cantilevered roof which carried four 10-ton cranes for lifting aircraft parts, all erected on an 8-9 foot concrete base.

At its peak in 1942 Shorts in Windermere employed over 1,500 people. A core of foremen, senior staff, and skilled workers came from Shorts in Rochester, along with local boat builders who were thought likely to make good aircraft builders; but fully 47 per cent of the staff were so-called 'diluted labour', that is, a combination of women and teenage boys too young to be conscripted. As with war factories elsewhere, all this meant significant social change in Windermere. Substantial wages were funnelled into the pockets of teenagers of both sexes and older women. Lucrative opportunities were created in an overwhelmingly rural region; new skills were learned; and the young and fit were able to benefit from the challenges of piece work (albeit subject to rigorous inspection by both government aeronautical inspectors and Short Brothers' own staff). Since the factory was begun in a rush, it became adept at what would later be called 'just-in-time' working, with unskilled trainees being given segmented small tasks with patterns and tools to guide their first attempts at aircraft production; then they moved on to other processes geared to ensuring that various stages of the complex process yielded what was wanted when it was wanted.

With so many new employees armed more with enthusiasm than skill, on-the-job training was to be a hallmark of the factory's system. At first many workers' output was consigned to the recycle or waste bin, but gradually, as experience was gained, the factory was able to produce aircraft to the RAF's standards and timeline. In the beginning many jobs were done by hand until the Lend-Lease agreement with the US made possible the importation of sophisticated milling machines and other technically-advanced equipment – equipment transported by convoys protected from German U-boat attacks by an earlier generation of Sunderland flying boats. On 10 September 1942 the whole workforce was encouraged to down tools and watch the launch of their first aircraft into the bay at Lake Windermere.

Working at Shorts in Windermere yielded a range of experience for locally engaged staff. They learned new skills but endured working conditions that were not always pleasant. Workers, it was reported, did not wear ear plugs against the noise of rivet guns; hard hats were rare; and the chemical baths used in parts of the production process could be toxic. Later in the war, when the factory was tasked with repairing damaged aircraft, special efforts were taken to prevent staff – often young women – from entering the aircraft until the blood of dead airmen had been sluiced away. Another kind of education came with the later arrival of union-savvy employees, who moved from car plants in the West Midlands and brought with them a thorough knowledge of industrial working practices, union cards, and demands for a proper bonus scheme and double-time rates, measures that were pretty much unheard of in rural Windermere. Then there were the 'perks' – the unofficial bonuses. Scraps of aluminium and other industrial materials were turned by workmen to such other uses as making cigarette lighters, bookends, letter knives, candlesticks, toasting forks, and even models of fighter aircraft, all evidence of a high level of skill as well as a taste for minor graft. The most blatant use of company property involved a panel beater who managed to make a sidecar for his motorcycle that was panelled with aircraft aluminium and even fitted with little perspex windscreens (King, p. 35).

On the whole it seems from the recollections of former workers that the factory was a friendly and happy place to work, and not without its humorous side. Allan King's book includes a copy of a playful inter-factory communication from Miss Renée Birchall to Miss Vera George, dated 27 December 1944, announcing the arrival of a Sunderland from Pembroke with its crew. The latter was to consist of '8 smashing-looking airmen, ages about 19 to 22 respectively, no older'. They were to stay in Windermere for about a fortnight, 'by which time we shall have no further use for them, and they will be allowed to return if undamaged'. While the crew was to include Canadians and Englishmen, the majority would be Australians. 'This arrangement', the memo declared, 'is made solely for the benefit of Miss George, who seems to have a preference for Australians'. Finally, each member of the crew was expected to be 'the exact double in every detail to one of the following' – then offering the names of such film stars as Errol Flynn, Tyrone Power, John Wayne, and Alan Ladd – all of whom would be required 'to stay long enough to be at the dance at Bowness on Thursday next' (King, p. 56).

In fact, members of the RAF were a common sight in wartime Windermere and the factory was often used as a training base for aircrews, who not only attended dances but also played football against German prisoners held at Grizedale Hall or the guards at Ambleside. Recalling the latter, a former worker reported that the RAF had a decided advantage because their left winger had been a professional footballer who had played for Cardiff and Wales before being called up (King, p. 60). The factory at Windermere also maintained a Shorts tradition by having its own sports clubs. Annual sports days were held at the Phoenix Centre in Windermere when Shorts teams played against each other and some from across Cumbria.

Another major social impact of the Windermere plant was the building of Calgarth, a village created specifically to house factory workers. As was the case with the factory, the village attracted considerable opposition throughout the planning process despite the fact that the Ministry of Works, responsible for the design of site, consulted with the Friends of the Lake District. The Friends were again able to extract a promise to dismantle the village after the war. However, in January 1942 the wording of the commitment was revised to reflect anticipated post-war housing shortages. It read that the houses would be removed 'as soon as the military situation made it safe to do so at the end of the war and as soon as the Ministry of Health is satisfied that the housing needs of others parts of the country no longer make advisable the retention of this temporary housing accommodation in the Lake District' (quoted King, p. 57).

This temporary housing was simple but built of brick rather than timber, apparently due to a shortage of wood, and perhaps better able to stand up to Lake District winters. Erected quickly and meant to be short-lived, the buildings were poorly insulated and often suffered from damp. However, unlike many Lakeland farmhouses, they boasted indoor plumbing and baths. Eventually over 500 people lived there and did their best to make their quarters homelike. While its structures were fairly basic, Calgarth was much more than a workmen's temporary housing project. In its nearly twenty-year existence, the village, with its 200 bungalows for married quarters and hostels for 300 single people, evolved into a dynamic community with a school, corner shops run by local merchants, its own policeman, and even a village hall. The latter was to host a variety of homegrown entertainments and social events as well as visiting performers from ENSA (Entertainments National Service Association), whose job was to go to armament factories as well as troop sites. Homegrown groups, such as one called the 'Six Pin-up Girls', would come to be so well regarded that they might even tour regional airfields and hospitals. The sports pitch was well used and helped to integrate the newcomers into the broader community; the venue was especially popular with visiting teams who found its changing rooms much superior to many in the district. The factory sports club, for the modest sum of a penny a week, organised a wide variety of athletic and other recreations, including swimming, rowing, table tennis, darts, bowls, and card games. In the winter there was even ice skating on a nearby tarn and 'some brave attempts at ice hockey' (King, p. 60). Activities like these were open to all employees, whether living or billeted in the area or in the village. This inclusiveness helped to thaw the initially frosty relations between outsiders and local people and blunted the loneliness of workers posted far from home and often without their families.

Here, then, was a major facility – and community – that was built from scratch and dedicated to military purposes. It probably could not have been constructed satisfactorily anywhere else in Britain. And because it has been studied so closely in *Wings on Windermere*, its remarkable history can be recounted in detail.

* * * *

Many everyday services were affected by the war. Domestic servants did not vanish entirely but their numbers dramatically declined, particularly from late 1941 when most young unmarried women became liable for national service. The lack of domestic help is frequently mentioned in WVS documents from the second half of the war, and it is certain that many middle- and upper-middle-class housewives worked much harder than they ever had before. Some left-wing observers had little sympathy for their plight – at least initially. 'Our local rag still full of adverts for large domestic staffs', wrote a young woman on 11 October 1941 from outside Ulverston. 'The laziness of the people in these big houses makes me boil.'[70] In fact, such laziness was about to become unsustainable. This diarist was more open to the needs of farmers' wives: 'inside help for farms [is] just impossible. Some branch of the Land Army should take it over, as it is a serious hindrance.' Since the employers of land girls were prohibited from assigning them domestic tasks, farmers' wives, it was said (probably correctly), had unreasonably heavy burdens to bear. This problem was raised at a meeting of the Carlisle branch of the National Farmers Union in February 1944. 'The farmers' wives were the hardest worked members of the farming community. If they did not get help in the house they were going to lose a lot of heart and suffer in health, and in consequence the war effort would suffer.' Critics attacked the prohibition placed on the WLA being asked to help with domestic tasks, some of which might involve feeding farm labourers.[71] Beyond private households, other traditional women's jobs became harder to fill. On 8 October 1941 a solicitor's clerk in Maryport wrote in his diary that 'Office cleaner has gone to the Isle of Mull to be near sailor husband. So, unable to endure lighting fires etc. on coming in, Irene, the typist, and myself came earlier to straighten the place up. Very hard to get a new cleaner.'[72] Paid cooks for larger canteens and British Restaurants became increasingly difficult to find from 1941, a problem that cropped up repeatedly for WVS organisers.

The work of women was suddenly in great demand – just as it had been in the Great War, and even in the French Revolutionary and Napoleonic Wars almost 150 years before. From mid-1941, and sometimes even earlier, there were pressing appeals to women to offer their services for the national good. Women's labour was sought in all sorts of capacities, some full-time and paid, others part-time and paid; some in uniformed service;[73] others in civilian employment, such as the civil service; some for jobs traditionally held by women, such as nursing, others for jobs that had normally been held by men. Women recruited for the Timber Corps (Fig. 7) were clearly doing jobs that women had rarely if ever done before. There were quite a few of them in Cumbria. One published photograph showed members at Grasmere sawing up larch logs for pit props in coal mines; another was titled 'Whitehaven Girl Forest Worker'.[74] The mere fact that such images were published was testimony to both the novelty and official approval of strenuous women's wartime work. (There was also acknowledgement that, with men absent and building workers committed to high-priority jobs, women might have to become their own home handymen – fixing plumbing faults, for example.)[75] In early 1945 more than 12,000 women were employed in West Cumberland industries, compared to fewer than 500 a decade before.[76]

Other heavy work no longer excluded women. Women welders and machinists at Barrow's shipyard were certainly a novelty. Women porters were being employed at the goods yard at Whitehaven's station as early as March 1941, and a laudatory story, accompanied by a photograph of the six women, made a splash in the local press. In this report, and others, patriarchal attitudes were, if not completely abandoned (that would be too much to expect), at least much diluted. 'I saw the women trucking all kinds of goods from one platform to another – and they didn't stop to gossip on the way.' The reporter asked them about their previous occupations. 'Some had been doing seasonal work in seaside resorts; others had been at home. Now all of them are doing work of real national importance – and doing it exceptionally well. This latter fact is also the verdict of the foreman, the goods agent, and others in the railway service.'[77] This was typical talk. The endorsement of women in the work force – there were some sceptics – became all the rage in the middle years of the war, at around the same time as pro-Russian sentiments were suddenly being widely championed, including by many who had never before professed such views. Having backs to the wall was a powerful antidote to conventional wisdom.

* * * *

Just as the character of labour and daily routines was changing, so too was the Cumbrian social landscape in other respects. Cumbria had long received visitors, but they had been predominantly tourists, drawn especially to the Lake District. While war undercut much of the tourist trade, it brought into the county large numbers of other outsiders, a few from choice, most from necessity. The following chapter presents a portrait of these newcomers and their experiences in unfamiliar territory.

Notes and References

1 Letter of 7 August 1944 (in private hands) from a woman living in Bowness to her husband in the army. For full details, see below, Chap. 7, 118-19.

2 Unpaid and volunteer work is discussed mainly in Chapter 6.

3 Kendal Archives, Kendal Oral History Group, interview no. RO152.
4 *Fighting with Figures: A Statistical Digest of the Second World War* (London, 1995), 67.
5 *Carlisle Journal*, 23 September 1941, 1.
6 *Cumberland and Westmorland Herald*, 9 December 1939, 5.
7 *Westmorland Gazette*, 30 December 1939, 4.
8 *Cumberland and Westmorland Herald*, 9 August 1941, 1.
9 *Cumberland and Westmorland Herald*, 30 December 1939, 1 and 20 January 1940, 1.
10 *Cumberland and Westmorland Herald*, 17 August 1940, 1, 21 June 1941, 7, and 28 June 1941, 2.
11 This paragraph is based principally on F. Thompson-Schwab, 'The Farmer's War, III: Cumberland', *Country Life*, 9 March 1940, 260-61, and numerous newspaper reports from 1939-41.
12 These documents are in the Whitehaven Archives, SUDC/1/3/119.
13 Carlisle Archives, DX 2232.
14 H. Crowe, 'The Profitability of Upland Agriculture in Westmorland, 1910-1947' (Ph.D. thesis, University of Sussex, 2009). We are very grateful to Dr. Crowe for allowing us to consult chapter 6 of her informative and thoughtful thesis, upon which this paragraph is based.
15 *Cumberland and Westmorland Herald*, 9 September 1939, 10.
16 An early appeal for women to join the WLA is in the *Cumberland News*, 15 April 1939, 8.
17 *Westmorland Gazette*, 21 June 1941, 9.
18 *Whitehaven News*, 4 February 1943, 4, and *Cumberland and Westmorland Herald*, 11 September 1943, 3 (almost a quarter of these members of the WLA were at work in Westmorland: *Cumberland and Westmorland Herald*, 27 March 1943, 3). The numbers cited represented less than two per cent of the national membership in the WLA, a reflection in part of the still modest scale of arable farming in the two counties and the absence of very large farms.
19 *Cumberland and Westmorland Herald*, 3 June 1944, 7.
20 An incomplete list, citing seven locations, was supplied in a letter to the editor of the *Westmorland Gazette*, 3 April 1943, 4.
21 *Cumbria within Living Memory*, 204.
22 There are numerous pertinent testimonies in M. Bates, *Snagging Turnips and Scaling Muck: The Women's Land Army in Westmorland*, edited by A. Bonney (Kendal, 2001). Other locations of WLA hostels included Longtown, Aspatria, Cockermouth, Gosforth, Penrith, and Milnthorpe (*Westmorland Gazette*, 3 April 1943, 4).
23 *Cumbria within Living Memory*, 206.
24 Bates, *Snagging Turnips*, 85.
25 J. Thistlethwaite, *Cumbria – The War Years: Lake District Life in the 1940s* (Kendal, 1997), 12-13 and 14.
26 *Carlisle Journal*, 10 October 1941,1. This report took pains to emphasize how well the Italians were being treated.
27 *Cumberland and Westmorland Herald*, 12 June 1943, 1; also *Farmers Weekly*, 20 February 1942, 126n, on Cumberland.
28 *Cumberland and Westmorland Herald*, 3 June 1944, 7.
29 *Cumberland and Westmorland Herald*, 7 August 1943, 1.
30 *A Parish Remembers: The War Years 1939-1945, Dalston Parish* (Dalston Parish Council, 1995), 44; Bates, *Snagging Turnips*, 99; Kendal Library, Kendal Oral History Group, Interview no. 0240, 10-11; and Thistlethwaite, *Cumbria*, 43, 80-81, 88, 113, 146, 158-59, and 169 (Three of these reminiscences were uncomplimentary about the efforts of the Italians.).
31 *Cumberland and Westmorland Herald*, 11 October 1941, 1.

32 Ibid.
33 *Cumberland and Westmorland Herald*, 27 March 1943, 3.
34 In July 1940 some 100 senior boys of the Newcastle Royal Grammar School, which had been evacuated to Penrith, were hard at work helping local farmers, with another 150 boys expected to be available in the near future. It is likely that the boys' efforts were a consequence of a request from the district's War Agricultural Executive Committee to the school's authorities. Whatever the boys' opinions, their elders wanted them to be seen as cooperative. 'Keen and hard-working, they are thoroughly enjoying – and, no doubt, benefiting by – the healthy outdoor life, in addition to doing very good work.' (*Cumberland and Westmorland Herald*, 6 July 1940, 1.)
35 *Cumberland and Westmorland Herald*, 8 June 1940, 4 and 6.
36 *Carlisle Journal*, 30 March 1943, 3.
37 *Carlisle Journal*, 11 July 1944, 1.
38 *Westmorland Gazette*, 29 May 1943, 5; *Carlisle Journal*, 17 October 1944, 1.
39 *Cumberland and Westmorland Herald*, 2 August 1941, p. 1; *Carlisle Journal*, 5 February 1943, 1.
40 *Carlisle Journal*, 15 February 1944, 3.
41 *Carlisle Journal*, 11 July 1944, 1. Some provision had also been made for holiday harvesters in Cumberland in the summer of 1943, and several hundred working people in Carlisle were expected to offer their services on weekends for potato picking, which happened later in the calendar year (*Cumberland and Westmorland Herald*, 7 August 1943, 1).
42 *Cumberland and Westmorland Herald*, 10 June 1944, 1.
43 This paragraph draws on a detailed article, 'Two Counties' Farmers at War', in the *Cumberland and Westmorland Herald*, 27 March 1943, 3.
44 *Carlisle Journal*, 4 May 1945, 1.
45 MOA, Diarist no. 5226.
46 J. Hyams, *Bomb Girls: Britain's Secret Army: The Munitions Women of World War II* (London, 2013), 10.
47 J.D. Scott, *Vickers: A History* (London, 1962), 292. He portrays this 'gigantic organization', largely supplying the navy, as having a 'prodigious programme of ships of all kinds, of gun mountings, control towers and ammunition hoists; of turbines, gearing and boilers', along with mines and depth charges and associated foundries. Submarines were the shipyard's specialty.
48 *Cumberland and Westmorland Herald*, 22 November 1941, 4.
49 M. Chorlton, *Cumbria Airfields in the Second World War* (Newbury, Berkshire, 2006), respectively 94, 209, and 157. One estimate is that 1,800 workers in West Cumberland were engaged in aircraft maintenance (J. Wilson, *West Cumberland at War* [privately printed, 1999], 34).
50 *Team Work: The Story of John Laing and Son Limited, Building and Civil Engineering Contractors* [*c*.1950], 43-45 gives details on the company's wartime construction of aerodromes around the country. A man born in 1935 recalled that 'my earliest memories are of the building and subsequent use of Silloth aerodrome. Contractors' trucks and steel erectors seemed to be everywhere.' (M. Scott-Parker, *Silloth* [Carlisle, 2nd edn., 1999],70.)
51 Chorlton, *Cumbria Airfields*, 242.
52 Ibid.
53 Kendal Library, file no. 940.5.
54 Whitehaven Archives, YBSC/2/2/1/4 provides a technical account of the production process.
55 B. Supple, *The History of the British Coal Industry, vol. 4, 1913-1944: The Political Economy of Decline* (Oxford, 1987), 21; *West Cumberland Times*, 14 October 1944, 7; O. Wood,

West Cumberland Coal 1600-1982/3 (Cumberland and Westmorland Antiquarian and Archaeological Society, 1988), 223. Coal mining was exceptional in being a war-related industry that contracted: Cumberland mines employed almost 20 per cent fewer workers in 1942 than in 1939 and per capital productivity declined throughout the war (Ibid.).

56 *Whitehaven News*, 17 April 1941, 3.

57 *West Cumberland Industrial Exhibition* (Workington, 1948), 35 and 55.

58 K.B. Lockhart, 'Wartime Sedbergh, 1941', *Sedbergh Historian*, VI, no. 6 (Summer 2015), 39 and 45-46.

59 *Whitehaven News*, 9 December 1943, 3.

60 H. Shacklady, *Ulverston: An English Market Town through History* (Sedbergh, 2016), 186.

61 Canon Matthews and J. F. Whitehead, *History of Appleby* (revised edn., 1950),57-58.

62 Freethy, *Cumbria at War*, 50.

63 J. Scott, ed., *A Lakeland Valley Through Time: A History of Staveley, Kentmere and Ings* (Kendal: Staveley and District Historical Society, 1995), p. 113; also Kendal Library, Kendal Oral History Group, Interview no. 208, pp. 3-4.

64 *The Official Guide: Come to Carlisle* [1946], 84 and 86.

65 *Sundour at War* (Carlisle: Morton Sundour Fabrics Ltd., 1946), unpaginated. This booklet is held in the Imperial War Museum, A/C 07/136. The company made most of its steel anti-torpedo nets at a factory in Scotland. Further details on wartime products are in J. Morton, *Three Generations in a Family Textile Firm* (London, 1971), 430-31.

66 *Serving a Nation at War: A review of the building and civil engineering works of John Laing & Son Ltd., London and Carlisle* [1946], 44, and Wilson, *West Cumberland at War*, 35-36.

67 Wilson, *West Cumberland at War*, 89-90; *Serving a Nation at War* [1946], 45; and *Team Work* [*c.* 1950], 24 and 32.

68 Chorlton, p. 229. The controversy and conflicting views are discussed in J. Cousins, *Friends of the Lake District: The Early Years* (Lancaster University: Centre for North-West Regional Studies, 2009),108-12.

69 Chorlton, 232.

70 MOA, Diarist no. 5290.

71 *Cumberland and Westmorland Herald*, 4 March 1944, 2. Farmers' dissatisfaction with this restriction was aired at a meeting in Carlisle with the WLA in September 1943 (*Cumberland and Westmorland Herald*, 11 September 1943, 3).

72 MOA, Diarist no. 5226.

73 'Life is Grand in the ATS: Carlisle Girls "Thoroughly Recommend It"', is the headline to a very long and gushing article published in the *Carlisle Journal*, 4 April 1941, 3, encouraging recruitment to the army's women's auxiliary. This write-up was typical of its time, in Cumbria and elsewhere.

74 *Westmorland Gazette*, 16 January 1943, 8; *Whitehaven News*, 4 May 1944, 4.

75 Advice to women concerning household repairs was published in the *Barrow Guardian*, 16 August 1941, 7.

76 *West Cumberland Times*, 10 January 1945, 2. Nationally there were almost 50% more women in waged employment in 1943 than there had been in 1938, excluding the forces and auxiliary services (*Fighting with Figures*, 38).

77 *Whitehaven News*, 13 March 1941.

Chapter 5
Offcomers and Transients

'Grasmere contains an odd assortment of people now – one half looking with disapproval at the other half.' (MOA, Diarist no. 5239, 22 February 1941.)

'It was quite difficult to make a firm attachment during the war really, because you were never in one place for long.' (Reminiscence of Mary Fedden in Mavis Nicholson, *What Did You Do in the War, Mummy? Women in World War II* [Bridgend, 2010; first published 1995], p. 69.)

War inevitably undermined the stability of millions of households and families. There were numerous possible causes of this instability: bomb damage to your home; being evacuated or having a child evacuated; having a billetee in your house; having a son or husband away on military service or an unmarried daughter working away from home; reduced family income, mainly as a result of the lost wages of a husband (usually the breadwinner) who had been called up; and an increased work load for most mothers, sometimes to the detriment of their health. Running a household in wartime became more taxing, physically and emotionally; the single parent in charge was almost always a woman. People in their millions were being dispersed around the country, often to places they didn't want to be. Changes in address became much more frequent, partly as a result of changing employment opportunities or the dictates of national service – the GPO registered some 39 million changes of address during the war.[1] Young women entering the Land Army or Timber Corps almost always moved away from home, most of them from cities; new munitions works were located mainly in the Midlands and western regions of the country, and lots of workers had to move to these locations. Newcomers were especially noticeable in smaller towns and rural areas – or if they were foreigners. Some regions were full of foreigners, many of them refugees, others were uniformed nationals of one of Britain's many allies, plus numerous prisoners of war.

* * * *

Wartime Cumbria was home to many more non-Britons than before. There were Czech refugees in Maryport, at Edmond Castle in Hayton, at a former school in Caldbeck – most of the men there were employed by the

Forestry Commission – Belgians in Ambleside and elsewhere. Poles were scattered around the county, including at Barrow-in-Furness and various air bases.[2] In March 1944 five young Polish artists, all serving in the army, held an exhibition of their work at Tullie House in Carlisle.[3] In the autumn of 1941 young men of Czech and Austrian nationality were living in a hostel at Lazonby and supplying labour to farmers in the Penrith area.[4] Some 150 Belgian refugees who were settled in or near Penrith (they had a school there) gathered together on 19 July 1941 to celebrate their national day.[5] Undoubtedly this list could be readily extended.

Austrian and Czech refugees were among the earliest groups of newcomers, many of whom had endured harrowing journeys to escape oppression as the Nazi noose tightened in 1938-39. In September 1939 Catherine Elizabeth Marshall was housing eleven Czech refugees, nine men and two women, at her spacious home, Hawes End, Keswick, along with five evacuated children from Newcastle. The latter she described as 'such dirty little scamps' they were children the billeting officer had had difficulty placing since they had already been kicked out of other billets. For her adult billetees she had nothing but praise.[6] 'I could not have a nicer house full', she wrote on 12 September, 'they are most helpful in every way'. They performed housekeeping, kitchen work, and cooking on alternate days with her cook; did ARP work; cleared brush; and did lots of garden and yard work. In the evenings they entertained themselves with chess – they were all great chess players, Marshall noted, not too surprising since one man had been a professor of mathematics in Prague – draughts, or listening to the wireless. They were an independent and amiable lot, no doubt grateful and relieved to find themselves in a large house on a lake after the horrors they had endured. Their hostess even acquired several used bikes for the refugees' use and intended to get all of them out into employment as soon as practicable.

Catherine Marshall was an exceptional hostess. She was a leader in coordinating refugee admission and placement, appointed by the Home Office as advisor to the Czech Refugee Trust. Letters held at the Carlisle Archive Centre testify to her activism and advocacy on behalf of refugees, wherever they were headed. She was able, she noted in a letter of 28 March 1939, to have some refugees accepted by the Croydon Airport immigration authorities, including one man so distraught at the thought that he might be sent back that he was considering suicide. The refugee committee she worked with had connections with aid organisations that helped people who had made the arduous trek across the mountains on foot or skis to Poland and continued on to the UK. Once on British soil they were vetted to ensure that there were no Nazis among them and, if given security clearance, were issued temporary visas

In June 1940 Patterdale Hall, Ullswater, an unoccupied building, was rapidly converted into a hostel for Czechoslovakian refugees, an initiative that benefitted from a great deal of support from local people. The mansion had been 'rented by the Czech Trust Fund, under the control of the Home Office, to accommodate about 60 men, women and children' – political refugees opposed to Nazism in their own country – 'who have had to be removed from a restricted area'. The men were to be employed doing work for the Forestry Commission while the women would run the hostel.[7] Local women, such as Mrs. Eric Crewdson, also a member of Westmorland's WVS, developed considerable experience in working with these refugees and continued to do so over several years.[8]

The refugees, many of them escapees from concentration camps that had already imprisoned half a million people before war was declared, were only too glad to express their gratitude in whatever way they could. They did so as individuals and as a group. One German woman doctor, speaking at a Kendal YWCA/YMCA gathering celebrating 'the annual week of prayer and fellowship' in November 1939, said she had worked in her profession in Berlin but 'all she wished to do now was to give her services to Westmorland County Hospital in Kendal, as a token of gratitude for the kindness she had received in Britain'.[9] Needless to say her offer – delivered in both English and German – was well received. Others spoke of their revulsion at Nazi brutality and their joy at now living in a country of freedom and self-government, some hoping that they would someday be able to enjoy these blessings in their home countries. In August 1940, the more than twenty refugees living at the Friar Row Forestry Hostel in Caldbeck gave a performance widely attended by local people entitled 'Seven Years of Escapes'. The programme consisted of German and Czech folk songs, 'typical of happiness before Hitler's regime'; songs composed in concentration camps giving voice to anguish over missing relatives; and displays of Austrian and Czech folk dancing by performers in national dress. The concert ended with renditions of the refugees' national anthems, to which the audience replied with 'God Save the King'.[10] In November 1940 more than 300 residents of Patterdale were treated to a similar concert in aid of the local branch of the British Red Cross. On this occasion the performance was enhanced by a film on Prague, the Czech capital, and a sensitive reading of 'Impressions of a Czech poet about the English Lake District'.[11]

Having a common enemy was a major inducement for mutual encouragement and support. At Windermere in August 1941 a concert on behalf of the National Library for the Blind (Manchester) – which had lost many Braille manuscripts under enemy bombardment – benefitted from the performances of several talented Austrian and Czech refugees. A violinist and pianist living in Ambleside contributed their skills, as did a Viennese violinist from Bowness, a Czech soprano, and other refugee instrumentalists, some living in Windermere. Eleven pounds were raised for the cause and perhaps some hearts and minds won too.[12] These newcomers were mostly welcomed. Their skills were appreciated. Their endorsement of British values was applauded, and their generally fine education and eager adaptability were often acknowledged. Young male refugees were appreciated for helping to source timber for aircraft at a critical time when their British counterparts were being called up. The *Cumberland and Westmorland Gazette* for 31 August 1940 (p.1) featured the picture of a seven-year old Czech boy at Hawes End peeling potatoes along with a Newcastle Grammar School lad as part of weekend kitchen duty. No doubt the photo was staged, but it does suggest the desire to see these migrants as integrated into local life. The paper wanted its readers to know that 'The Czech boy speaks English fluently'.

⋆ ⋆ ⋆ ⋆

Another group of refugees that made a solid impression on their adopted communities were the schools which, with children, teachers, and head teachers, moved as a body to Cumbria and sometimes stayed for several years. One of the largest migrations was that of the 600 boys of the Newcastle Royal Grammar School, which shared facilities in Penrith with the Queen Elizabeth Grammar School. The Newcastle boys, along with their masters, were fed, housed, and educated in the town for five years. Many students were billeted with families while others occupied large houses acquired by the school for dormitories as well as class rooms. They were the bearers of income and youthful vigour, as well as their distinctive blue uniforms. They were also thought – by the editor of the local newspaper at least – 'to bring much intellectual prestige to Cumberland in general and to the Lake District in particular'.[13] The editor went on to praise the headmaster, Mr E. R. Thomas, as 'an educationist of some distinction' and predicted that the mingling of local scholars with boys possessing 'what amounts to a public school outlook cannot but have its influence for good'. Whether readers shared these elitist enthusiasms we cannot know. But we do know that Mr. Thomas acted quickly to get some of his students involved in the harvest as part of their summer vacation. The boys were seen to be 'making a very substantial contribution to food production by helping local farmers over a wide area'.[14] This inspired gesture seems to have been popular with the boys themselves, who continued to help with the harvest in later years. Such seasonal work made a contribution to the war effort and probably helped boys to make friendships that otherwise would not have developed and to identify with their new communities. (Further details concerning the experiences of these and other evacuated students are presented in the appendix.)

Numerous other schools evacuated to Cumbria. The Newcastle High School for Girls was said to 'form by far the larger part of the evacuee children at Keswick' early in the war, though it seems later to have moved to Kendal, where Newcastle's Heaton Secondary School for Girls had also been evacuated.[15] The South Shields Grammar School was evacuated to Kirkby Lonsdale.[16] The Leas School from Hoylake, Cheshire, took over the Glenridding Hotel, Ullswater, in a private arrangement between the school and the owner, with the latter continuing to provide catering and hotel management services.[17] The Lycée Français de Londres relocated to and near Rampsbeck.[18] The Roedean School for girls, as we have seen, moved to Keswick from Brighton in 1940. Dame Allan's Boys' School from Newcastle evacuated to Wigton. Huyton College evacuated some 170 girls from Liverpool to Blackwell, Bowness and Rydal Hall near Ambleside; the East Sussex Moira Girls' School occupied Windermere's Ferry Hotel; and Mowden Hall School, a preparatory school, moved from Darlington to Fallbarrow Hall, Windermere, while a Methodist boarding school from Harrogate found safe haven in the Hydro Hotel.[19] So the young, whose families were (mostly) comfortably-off, or their sponsors were, found safe quarters away from the bombs – although occasionally, as with the Methodist school, they were later displaced by those with more clout, such as the RAF.

One notable evacuation, that of the Royal College of Art (RCA) to Ambleside, along with at least 200 students and staff, brought both culture and a perhaps somewhat uncomfortable bohemian tinge to the Lake District – even though it had long been used to artists. Many artists' work needed lots of space and considerable ingenuity, as with pottery kilns, sculpture studios, and the like. Mural design, for example, required locations across the town, including the town hall. With due respect for wartime restraints, the college's convocation day in 1941 was conducted with little fanfare except for the presence of 'notables in the artistic world' from London, who gravely viewed the work of 'the sculptor, the artist in colours, glass, metals'. Never before, it was thought, 'had such an important event taken place in such quietude and one for which one would hope that in the future Royal College of Art some painter will depict for the walls of the Convocation Hall in the little town of Ambleside, with students dressed in shorts, slacks, open-neck shirts, and all the outfit of the hiker coming up to the dais to receive their diplomas'.[20]

Art was a source of some controversy in the war years. War artists recorded the horrors of battle and the valour of the combatants and several came from the Royal College of Art. But was it acceptable to continue the training of those whose life's work might be (in some eyes) jewelled baubles for the rich? On the other hand, could the nation risk losing a generation of artistic skills? Flexibility was clearly called for. The RCA, reflecting either sensitivity to national opinion or political good sense, revamped its curriculum to permit students liable for call-up to complete their programmes in two years rather than three. It also reduced the minimum age for admission from 19 to 18 to allow students to study for a year before reaching the age for call-up for national service.*

Looked at from another angle, would worldly London aesthetes be happy in a remote rural area? We can never really know the answers. But Edward Bawden, John and Paul Nash, and Burnett Freedman, among others who honed their skills in the Lake District, became war artists and Gordon Ransom left an enduring contribution to local culture in the Ambleside parish church. There Ransom created and installed a mural called 'Rushbearing' using his fellow students and several villagers as models (Duxbury, pp. 252-3). He had learned that this rush-bearing ceremony was part of local custom. The *Westmorland Gazette*, knowing that the many new residents were not well informed, explained to its readers on 12 July 1941 that the rushbearing festival 'originates from the days when our places of worship had not tiled floors but earthen aisles' and the rushes were renewed annually and accompanied by a celebration'.[21] Another artist, Fred Brill, who had a more modernist bent, drew and painted home guard members, although again some of his models were fellow art students (Duxbury, p. 239).

A few local eyebrows were probably raised concerning the cloth, yarns, and dyes that art scholars used. These were rationed goods and not everyone would have known that the Board of Trade signoffs, including a commitment not to resell materials on the open market, was needed to acquire them (Duxbury, p. 40). Reservations may have been raised by the students themselves, drawn from many backgrounds, cultures, and ethnicities and often dressed in self-consciously 'artistic' or bohemian fashion. 'The trouble about going round with foreign students with beards', wrote a young intellectual woman on 16 September 1941, who had been spending time in and near Ambleside, 'is that everyone kept on mistaking us for inmates of the Art School evacuated to the place'.[22] Later the students were joined by a few disabled and invalided ex-servicemen with an artistic vocation, who returned to the school in Ambleside (Duxbury, p. 182). By early 1941 the college organised Saturday night hops while the RCA theatre group put on plays intended for locals – favouring traditional costume dramas to avoid potentially controversial modernist material. These performances strengthened the skills of students interested in theatre arts, such as stage and costume design; they were also thought to increase the standing of the college with local authorities and promote good relations with the permanent residents (Duxbury, p. 166). Long-haired and often oddly-dressed, these visitors did their best to fit into Ambleside society

* J. Duxbury and C. Perry, eds., Leslie Duxbury, *Bohemians in Exile: The Royal College of Art in Ambleside, 1939-1945* (Cheltenham, 2008), 4. Leslie Duxbury's work was unfinished and later brought out by the two editors. Details concerning the college in this and the following two paragraphs are drawn from Duxbury's book unless otherwise indicated.

and probably made life a bit livelier during these often dreary years.

* * * *

'A few soldiers billeted on this village [Bardsea, near Ulverston] have nearly all found fiancées among the village girls', according to a MO diarist in her early twenties on 25 July 1941.[23] ('Can't help wondering how many of the marriages will be happy', she added.) Another MO diarist was walking in the Grizedale area on 29 March 1942 and saw 'a little group of WAAFs and two or three ATS, each party, like myself, apparently seeking relief from life in a crowd'.[24] On 1 December 1940 Nella Last was told by a cousin that 'there's over 1,000 soldiers at Ulverston and the food and treatment is so bad that as soon as they get pay on a Saturday they clear off for the weekend'. (MOA) The forces, wherever they were stationed, usually came from elsewhere. In Cumbria they were often posted for training, staying a few weeks or a few months; or perhaps they were manning some remote defensive battery. Most of them probably made an impact on their localities, though perhaps not for long, in contrast to other regions, such as Lincolnshire, where almost 25 per cent of the county's wartime population was in uniform, mainly because of its dozens of air bases,[25] Cumbria had no such massive and sustained presence of servicemen. The largest number cited (to our knowledge) comes from the spring of 1940, when an estimate put the number of soldiers in the Carlisle area at 1,500.[26] This was no doubt exceptional.

Still, the forces were certainly present in Cumbria, scattered around the county, and usually in small units. There are numerous references to mobile canteens serving men in uniform at isolated posts (for security reasons these were not identified).[27] As we have seen, the airmen, including exotic young foreigners, who came to Windermere to collect new seaplanes were exceedingly popular with young local women – particularly if they stayed for a dance. Some young men, unhappily, stayed forever. There are 18 military graves in Haverigg (St. Luke's) churchyard near Millom, 10 of them of Australians or Canadians. Of the 56 airmen buried in Silloth's cemetery, 31 were from Commonwealth countries, one from New Zealand and the rest from Canada or Australia (details from the Commonwealth War Graves Commission). These facts reflect the multi-national character of airpower in wartime Britain. Air bases, many for training, were notoriously dangerous places. 'Many aeroplanes and their crews perished on our fells,' recalled a woman of wartime Lorton in Cumbria.[28] Young men commonly lost their lives before getting a chance to fight the enemy.

Much of the evidence about the military who spent time in this rural area is fragmentary, caught only in snatches of memory or testimony. When the Cumbria Federation of Women's Institutes gathered their wartime memories, there were numerous references to the military presence in the region but without much specificity. 'The RAF was stationed at Silloth', wrote one woman, and 'some of the men were billeted at Mawbray'.[29] The Derwentwater Hotel was taken over by the army.[30] Later in the war soldiers of the Royal Tank Corps came to Melmerby Hall and a woman recalled that her young brother observed the exercises carried out nearby and was once thrilled to sit inside a tank. The soldiers, she suggested, were perhaps equally enchanted by local dances, whist drives and other social events.[31] A woman who lived as a girl on a farm near Howtown on the banks of Ullswater remembers growing carrots, turnips and potatoes for servicemen stationed locally.[32] The WVS in Kendal routinely dealt with soldiers, many of them in transit (Fig. 3) and eager for canteen refreshments. Tens of thousands were probably served by this canteen, almost daily, between 1940 and 1945.

There are many passing references to servicemen stationed in Cumbria, usually without further details – for example, at or near Penrith, Windermere, Appleby, Lowther (The army took over the castle and much of the adjoining grounds of the Earl of Lonsdale.), Kendal, Milnthorpe, Grasmere, Ambleside, Longtown, and Brampton. In Kirkby Lonsdale a battalion of the Royal Engineers was quartered in Lunefield House and encampments by the river.[33] These facts are reminders that many men in Britain's forces would have spent perhaps a few weeks or a few months in Cumbria before being moved somewhere else. It was not uncommon to undergo basic training in one location, and engage in specialized learning somewhere else, before being posted to what might be the first of many deployments. Troops in Whitehaven were numerous enough in February 1941 that their attachment to a Salvation Army canteen was written up in the local press.[34] Uniformed men, both British and allied, make frequent appearances in Nella Last's Barrow diary. On 14 January 1941 (MOA) 'a lot of soldiers are being billeted round about', and on one occasion her laundry was late to be delivered because Lakeland Laundries, a big commercial firm, was overwhelmed with demands from the many troops in the region; on 29 January 1941 [MOA] she noted an industrial protest by the laundry's 'girls', prompted by their long working hours – 'they wash hundreds of soldiers' clothes entire'. The presence of the military in a locality is recorded in all sorts of ways. In February 1942 a young solicitor's clerk living just outside Maryport heard a story that, even if not entirely true, testified to the stationing of troops in Cumberland, which everyone must have known about. He was told of a former town hall clerk, aged 24, now aide to an officer: 'His sole job is to arrange dances, engage bands and see that lorry drivers bring in ATS and WAAFs from the outlying districts for the night of the dance'.[35]

Americans were seen as the most glamorous of the soldiers posted (if only briefly) to Cumbria. One woman recalled in the 1990s that some Americans arrived shortly before Christmas 1944 (She seems to have lived in or near

Ulverston.). 'We were asked to be hospitable to them and invite them into our homes. Dan, who came to our house, was only a young man, having had his 18th birthday on the ship coming over to England. He had never seen a coal fire before and enjoyed sitting beside ours. He had only been used to electric bars at home.' She remembered well his fascination with gas lighting.[36] The WVS canteen on New Road in Kendal was serving 'large convoys of USA troops passing through the town' as early as September 1942 (WVS NR) and was said to have been 'filled with American soldiers' on Boxing Day 1942 (WVS, NR December 1942). They 'demand large quantities of coffee' (Kendal WVS, NR January 1943). At one time, probably in or just before 1943, some black American troops were billeted in Carlisle.[37]

But Americans were not present in Cumbria in significant numbers until the last year of the war in Europe – and they were never as prominent as, say, in East Anglia, with its many air bases,[38] or in areas near the south coast in 1943-44. In August 1944 the Penrith Troops Entertainment Committee 'ventured into a somewhat new sphere by providing entertainment for American soldiers [some 50 of them] temporarily in the district'.[39] The editor of Barrow's *North-Western Evening Mail* chose to publish on 26 August 1944 (p. 5) a photograph of an attractive member of the US Women's Army Corps from Auburn, New York. She was probably a recent arrival in the city, as were the two US army majors who spoke to the Barrow Rotary Club later that year.[40] US servicemen were sufficiently numerous in Barrow by later 1944 (but not before) that their presence warranted a visit from an American YMCA canteen, which delivered refreshments to fellow citizens. One of its crew of women wrote several letters home that winter detailing her time in Barrow.[41] Nella and Will Last and their neighbours befriended a pair of US soldiers in Barrow, who were paying social visits as the European war was ending, and the following month Americans were still being served at Barrow's WVS canteen.[42] When Mrs Last asked a teenage girl, aged around seventeen, how she planned to spend VE Day, the girl replied: 'Oh, I don't know. I hope this rumour the Americans are coming back into the camp when the Marines go is true. I bet *they* liven things up that day.'[43]

⋆ ⋆ ⋆ ⋆

The history of one Cumbrian estate testifies to the shifting realities of life in wartime, as new demands suddenly sprang up and traditional practices abruptly dissolved. Hutton-in-the-Forest was inherited by William Vane (later the first Lord Inglewood) in 1931. His careful efforts to manage the estate were starting to bear fruit when war was declared and Vane was among the first to be called up.[44] In keeping with wartime patterns of female management, William Vane gave his younger sister, Margaret, power of attorney over the estate in his absence. Many and varied were the challenges she had to face. Immediately after war was declared, two mothers and their children were evacuated to Hutton from Newcastle. One mother found the country too quiet and quickly returned to the city, but scuttled back again when she found the bombing too frightening. Upon her return, the Hutton housekeeper declared that the evacuees were too much for her to cope with, given her fragile health, and the women and children were eventually moved to several farms in the Skelton district – for how long is unknown.

Meanwhile, there were many eyes on the possibilities afforded by this large estate. Several people used Hutton to store furniture after being bombed out of London. Others considered the estate as a possible residence for Czech refugees who would work on Forestry Commission land. Still others contemplated an admiralty training school, or a girls' school, even a BBC facility. (In 1942 the BBC took over two farms on the estate to build the Skelton transmission station, deemed to be one of the largest and most up-to-date short-wave stations; it sent 65 per cent of its transmissions to Europe and the remainder worldwide.) While these discussions were going on, Margaret Vane and her staff pondered how the building's panelling and tapestries could be preserved and priceless furnishing stored when the inevitable requisition took place. The family retained a five-room flat on the estate, which was also used by relatives and friends 'who always took their own rations with them'. Perhaps some of their visitors were among the self-evacuated seeking safety in the countryside.

In due course the RAF decided they needed the house, and in short order Margaret Vane arranged for the chimneys to be swept and servants' bedrooms colour-washed to accommodate their new occupants (usually officers and guards). Men slept in huts in the grounds. Others were billeted locally and their wives, perhaps, came to stay with them for a short time. The hall and the pele tower were used as offices. The RAF also wanted to install electricity in the house (the estate agreed to pay a portion of the costs). William Vane joked to his mother in a letter that she could expect to have electricity in her bedroom when the war ended, but until this was accomplished oil lamps were used and the RAF bought a second-hand engine and generator. In fact, the RAF did not stay long, concluding that communications were too difficult that far from Carlisle. They were soon replaced by the army (which got the generator). This army contingent was a tank company stationed at Lowther which used Hutton for overflow, with the largest uniformed contingent on the estate being around 150. Hutton helped with provisioning, for the troops bought their fruit and vegetables from the gardens; the rose garden became an onion bed and the herbaceous borders grew vegetables. Visitors expressed amazement at so many people living in and around the house. They could hear singing and whistling, but it was not considered too loud. The house was now much warmer and Margaret Vane contended that the troops had not spoilt the peace of Hutton.

A soldier's perspective on this region was offered by E.P. Malpress, who in 1943 was posted to the Royal Army Corps at Lowther Park, just south of Penrith. 'Horrified at what I saw,' he wrote. It was 'a largely tented camp situated in a sea of mud and water, soaked by pouring windblown rain'. After arriving he was sent to the regimental orderly room and instructed 'to swear an oath of secrecy'.[45] His following days were dominated by rain, mud, and cold. One somewhat mitigating feature was a 'huge NAAFI marquee in which was a huge brick fireplace', while nearby Penrith, 'which one could visit in the evenings and weekends, contributed various canteens and a warm cinema'. His misery continued despite a large workforce devoted to building huts designed to give some relief from the dreadful living conditions. As luck and army machinations would have it, just as the huts were completed the regiment was transferred to Northumberland, and noisily trundled their cumbersome tanks along the main street of Penrith.

Malpress and his colleagues were among the many temporary residents of Cumbria, and it appears that they left behind little but tank tracks. In Hutton-in-the Forest, by contrast, there were still much activity and many workers. It remained an agricultural estate that now employed land girls and local farm workers, who by then would have included more women and youngsters working as regular farmhands. The Air Ministry had further plans for the estate's farmland and woodlots. In 1940 it had requisitioned land on the estate for hiding and storing aircraft. But to store aircraft they needed to get them there. The first site they chose, part of the Home Farm, turned out after several weeks of work to be totally unsuited to an airstrip. William Vane had warned that the land was too sloping for an airstrip. However, despite his expertise and status as a serving soldier, the military authorities took no notice and tried to make the difficult site work. Having failed, it took a couple of years to restore the land to productive farming but it appears no permanent damage was done. A second attempt, a second site, and expert advice did bring success – and many more people. At one time it was estimated that about 100 men were employed in building the airstrip using tons of quarry rubble to level the land, which was then covered with soil and seeded. In addition, a track of about forty acres was driven through the middle of the woods for taxiing the aircraft to camouflage cover. There was standing room for about one hundred planes in the woods, including some of the first Hurricane fighters. Of course, all this activity meant lots of incomers, all making their mark on Hutton, its environs, and nearby Penrith.

Margaret Vane kept a watchful eye on all this activity, circling the estate regularly on her bicycle. She kept in touch with her absent brother, and deputised for him at local agricultural events such as a ploughing match held in 1942 in aid of the Lord Mayor's Air Raid Distress Fund. For his part, as a soldier fighting abroad, William Vane was able to send his family welcome parcels of figs, almonds, raisins and beautiful fabrics from his posting in the Middle East. At war's end he returned safely home and was elected MP for Westmorland in 1945. The next year, shortly after the army de-requisitioned his property, he gave a party to celebrate the end of the war and his sister's successful management of Hutton-in-the-Forest.

* * * *

Some outsiders in Cumbria were very much birds of passage. The most transient were members of the forces who were passing through the North West en route to somewhere else. They appear in local sources mainly because they commonly travelled in large numbers and, needing refreshment in the course of their journeys, canteens were set up and largely functioned to serve just them. An early indication of this routine movement of men was reported in late 1939. 'The Carlisle Citizens' League have opened their canteen on the island platform of the Carlisle Citadel Station, and their restaurant and rest room, with 14 beds and comfortable furnishings, at the old Beaconsfield rooms at the Viaduct. Everything there is for the comfort of troops who may be halted at Carlisle on their way North or South, and volunteer staffs are working day and night to attend to them.'[46] In March 1942 Westmorland's WVS was given the big job of assembling 'all available mobile canteens to feed the very large number of troops on the move' (NR March 1942). Serving these men in transit through Kendal lasted for much of the war.

In later years the managers and servers in these canteens were commonly members of the WVS – the cooks were usually paid – and many of the monthly reports testify to the demands of serving these soldiers. In September 1942 the 'large numbers of USA troops' passing through Westmorland were severely straining the food resources of Kendal's WVS canteen. In 1943 Kendal's busy canteen was open daily and often at night too and served tens of thousands of men in uniform. 'We have a great reputation with the Forces up and down the country as our work is chiefly for transport services, and is much appreciated.'[47] Serving servicemen in transit was central to the work of Kendal's WVS. 'The canteen has a reputation for good cheap food and comfort of which it is very proud, and is known, as they say, from Land's End to John O'Groats.'[48] In the summer of 1944 American soldiers passing through Penrith by train were said to have been throwing chocolates from windows, as had also happened in the Carlisle area; and three schoolboys in search of these treats found themselves in court for trespass.[49]

Other migrants came to Cumbria, mostly for work, sometimes from choice, more often because of decisions others had made. A number (probably a small number) of military wives moved temporarily to Cumbria to be near their husbands: there were enough of these wives in Kendal in April 1941 that the WVS was helping to start a club for them (Kendal WVS, NR April 1941). Other newcomers included many munitions workers, most of them men. Most members of the Women's Land Army working in the county were outsiders, some of them perhaps struggling to adjust, at least at first. 'Yesterday we required a Land Girl for the garden,' wrote a young woman on 12 August 1941 from the Windermere hotel where she was temporarily employed. 'She's 23, from Liverpool, and has never left home before, and still shy and homesick.'[50] Her outsider status was not unusual: in early 1941 an invitation appeared in the press for women in Cumberland and Westmorland to sign up for the WLA, noting that half of the land girls then 'working in the district have come from other counties'.[51] Later, in March 1943, a letter in the press appealed for books and newspapers for members of the WLA, observing that their 'greatest hardship is the sense of isolation and being cut off from the amenities which most of them enjoyed in the towns from which they came'.[52] Sometimes, as in Lazonby, where the women were posted in a hostel in the village, these outsiders arranged their own entertainment, holding dances and film shows and 'inviting soldiers from nearby army camps as well as the locals'. This informant added that their presence caused some resentment among local girls, 'and with some cause as quite a few of them later married local boys and settled down here'.[53]

There were outsiders that Cumbrians saw not at all or only as farm labourers – the enemy prisoners of war. The Cumbrian sites of Italian POW camps included Milnthorpe, Calthwaite, Dalston, and Plumpton near Penrith. Throughout the war there would be a great many POW camps throughout Britain, some 600 by 1945. Some German officers were held in the Shap Wells Hotel. The No. 1 POW Camp was Grizedale New Hall, a 40-room mansion near the village of Satterthwaite in a picturesque part of the Lake District. Grizedale had been used as a hikers' hostel until 1939, when it was requisitioned from the Forestry Commission and used to house German officers, in particular submarine officers captured by the British navy in the early months of the war as well as Luftwaffe pilots. It became known locally as 'U-Boat Hotel'. While surrounded by barbed wire and lit by searchlights, the local press thought it a bit posh and advised its readers that 'the German officers have the benefit of a library in which there is a full-sized ping-pong table; they feed in a large oak paneled hall' (though it was admitted that the fare was not 'Ritzy'), played football, enjoyed sing-songs around a grand piano and soon were to be supplied German books.[54] Wooden huts were later built in the grounds and at its peak Grizedale held over 300 prisoners.[55]

Other prisoners – officers and men were usually confined separately – led much simpler lives. They were also much more often seen by Cumbrians because they were often sent out to work on nearby farms. Once interviewed by British government officials, those men not deemed to be an imminent threat to security or dedicated Nazis were assigned to prison camps where their labour could aid the British home front. First Italians and then (late in the war) Germans worked on farms in Cumbria, either in direct agricultural labour or on ancillary tasks such as drainage work. Officials inspected their work, partly to prevent sabotage.[56]

* * * *

Child evacuees have already been frequently mentioned and appear again in Chapters 7 and 8. Their experiences were extraordinarily varied. To speak of evacuees as a group and to generalize about what they felt and what happened to them is impossible. Some billets worked out well, others did not. Circumstances sometimes militated against success: for example, while the parents of an evacuated child remained responsible for his or her clothing and footwear, a few were so impoverished that they could not (or would not) fulfill their obligations, leaving people in the reception area to foot the bill. These ill-clad children could not have found it easy to feel good about their lives. Then there is the length of a stay away from home to consider. Some evacuations lasted for months if not years, others for only a few weeks.**

Reminiscences highlight this diversity. Two women evacuated to Kirkby Lonsdale remembered their happy experiences as children there.[57] By contrast, a woman from Newcastle had a bad memory that stood out for her. She was one of a group of evacuees taken to a Cumbrian church hall 'where local families were waiting to take them in'. All the other children were chosen except her. 'An adult took her around the village in the dark and knocked on doors until someone would take her. Sixty years later she still remembers how upsetting this was.'[58] In the 1990s another woman recalled that at the beginning of the war 'we were told we would have to have some evacuees, and four children and their mother arrived. They were from the North East. My mother sat them all down at the table with the family and the children ate until they were sick. The mother explained that they had never before been told they could eat as much as they wanted. At night when my mother suggested going to bed, they said they usually just turned the table upside down and slept in that. This family', she added, 'only stayed with us a few months but later on a young boy of seven from Newcastle came to us and he is still a friend today, over 50 years on'.[59] A woman who was living in a big house in Carlisle remembered taking in three evacuees from Newcastle, two girls and a boy. The girls were sisters, and although their foster-mother doubted that 'this was the sort of place they really wanted to be in, they

** The reminiscences in B. Wilkinson, ed., *A Safe Haven: Evacuees in Keswick 1939-1945* (Carlisle, 2010) are mostly happy. Perhaps this is to be expected of people who, in their senior years, agreed to the publication of their recollections of childhood and preferred to dwell on the positive.

made the best of it in a very graceful way.' The boy, who arrived a little later, 'would only speak to my daughter Gail, who was then three. ...Otherwise he never said a word. Then I met his mother, and I realised why. She was an overbearing woman who spoke for him the whole time. He was about nine, and she had obviously done it from birth.' (This is one of a multitude of cases where we have the testimony of only one person.) She added that 'He settled awfully well.... The girls moved out when they were fourteen or fifteen and reached school-leaving age, but Jack was with me right up until we left Carlisle [in later 1943].'[60]

These are just a few of the remembered and recorded Cumbrian evacuations. Thousands of others, had they been recorded, would no doubt have included very different facts and feelings and judgements of praise or blame. Some children adapted well to their new homes away from home, others did not. No doubt being torn from home and family – for those who felt torn – was for some children a traumatic experience, even if their assigned caregivers were kind and conscientious, as many were. The intensity of a child's feelings might depend in part on whether he or she was housed with a sibling – almost always this was desirable. For other children, with parents who were (perhaps) negligent or distracted and unreliably affectionate, their lives as evacuees may have been felt to be improvements on their previous lives. The records produced by the Kendal Oral History Group, held in the Kendal library, include dozens of references to evacuees and several reminiscences of actual evacuees. They testify to the great range of experience and outlook.

To be evacuated, especially for a long time, must have been transformative for many children. On 12 May 1945, with Europe now officially at peace, Nella Last (*DONL*, 214) met some London evacuees on a bus to Millom – she had participated in taking them there the previous autumn. The changes in their lives were not (to her) distressing. 'It was their speech which really amused me – "summat", "lile", "yon", "gitten" for "something", "little", "over there" and "got" and the soft Cumberland dialect mixed with the quicker London way of speaking.'[61] Mrs Last said that 'One thing they all liked – being able to run and play on moor and field and "no one saying anything" and "it being so nice when you fell down, to smell the grass and heather". They had seemingly all had good homes and spoke as if their friends had been happy and of one little boy and girl who were staying altogether as they had lost both parents and grandparents in London raid.' The conditions of an evacuee's life were, on occasion, sufficiently happy and prolonged that in the end he or she was actually not eager to 'return home', for their new Cumbrian homes were what they had come to identify with. Nella Last wrote at length about this on 11 July 1945 (*DONL*, pp 218-19), citing one case in particular, that of John, aged 12-13, who felt unwanted by his own family and 'begged' to be allowed to stay with his Cumberland foster-parents and their son, an only child of about the same age, who had come to like him and had no qualms about receiving John as a permanent member of the household. Several months earlier the county organiser in Westmorland had written of the departure for home on 27 November 1944 of almost all of the official evacuees from Tyneside (Westmorland WVS, NR November 1944). 'There were many cases of tears on both sides, children not wanting to go home and hostesses who had looked after them for five years hating to part with them. Quite a few children are remaining on by mutual consent.'

As for those who received evacuees, there were stories – perhaps embroidered, perhaps just rumours – of evacuated children whose parents were (allegedly) getting big wages in some munitions factory while the billetors of their children were being paid paltry sums for child care. There were also individual complaints of dirty, unruly, and ill-mannered children, some of whom, it was thought by the complainants, were accustomed if not inured to squalid conditions. By contrast, there were untold instances of evacuees who behaved admirably. One of these was 12-year-old schoolboy, John Finley, from Newcastle, who was billeted with Mr and Mrs Robinson at Myrtle Cottage in Bowness. His industriousness in collecting waste paper in the Windermere district was so impressive that his accomplishments were written up in the *Westmorland Gazette*, 5 July 1941 (p. 7), accompanied by his photograph.

Two adult women's recollections are reminders of how cautious historians must be in portraying and assessing the diverse experiences of evacuees. One girl was evacuated at age seven from Barrow (after its blitz), for ten months, first to Great Asby, five miles from Appleby, and later to Long Marton, three miles the other side of Appleby. She recalled not her own discontent but her father's: 'he said I was completely independent of the family when I came back. I made my own mind up about everything that I did and never consulted anybody'. She said she gained lots of confidence living there.[62] Another woman had mixed memories. Also a Barrovian, she was evacuated at the age of nine to Eskdale, 'which I loved', to people known to her mother. 'There was a rather bad thing that happened there which I don't like talking about – I was sexually assaulted ... by the man of the house.... But I loved the school, I loved the country, [and] the people.' She also recalled the solidarities of walking cheerfully to school with the other children.[63] Such recollections show that it is the individuality of evacuees' experiences that needs highlighting.[64]

Then there were the children who were placed in institutions, not family homes. Brathay Hall, Ambleside housed a nursery for some 34 children, aged two to five, who had been orphaned; a published photograph showed them and their care-givers out for a walk on Boxing Day 1942.[65] On 2 February 1942 a young man, on his walk from near Maryport to Cockermouth, 'Saw

Tallentine Hall where some Waifs and Strays have been evacuated'.[66] A home for babies from bombed areas had been opened in Arnside in early 1941 by the Waifs and Strays Society in cooperation with the WVS. Around thirty children were living there later that year, their parents elsewhere (though major raids were then largely non-existent).[67] From late 1940 a former workhouse on an open moor near Shap station in Westmorland was used to house evacuated 'mentally defective' children, around 45 girls, from southern districts, mainly London. The place was said to be quite isolated.[68] It is hard to imagine that many of the children in these institutional settings emerged unscarred from their wartime confinements.

All these outsiders made for a much more diverse population than Cumbria had known before the war. Some had talents that enriched local life. It was said that the refugee Czechs working in the Maryport area were active supporters of the arts and bearers of refreshing new outlooks.[69] Czech refugees occasionally organized concerts and shows – two examples among many were a performance in May 1941 of music and folk dancing in Caldbeck's parish hall and an exhibition in March 1943 in Carlisle of their drawings and photographs.[70] Many newcomers also brought with them special needs which, when combined with the wartime circumstances and needs of Cumbria's permanent residents, prompted and sustained a whole range of activities devoted to welfare, recreation, and morale. These are the subjects of the following chapter.

Notes and References

1 D. Campbell-Smith, *Masters of the Post: The Authorized History of the Royal Mail* [London, 2011], 327.
2 MOA, Diarist no. 5226, 18 February 1942; *Cumberland and Westmorland Herald*, 11 October 1941, 1 and 10 August 1940, 3; Ambleside Oral Archive, www.aohg.org.k, transcript K1.
3 *Carlisle Journal*, 10 March 1944, 3.
4 *Cumberland and Westmorland Herald*, 11 October 1941, 1.
5 *Cumberland and Westmorland Herald*, 26 July 1941, 1.
6 Carlisle Archives, File D/Mar/2/51. Subsequent references are drawn from this file unless otherwise noted.
7 *Cumberland and Westmorland Herald*, 29 June 1940, 1. ATS personnel were later billeted at Patterdale Hall: Cumbria Federation of Women's Institutes, *Cumbria within Living Memory* (Newbury, Berkshire, 1994), 183.
8 Ibid, 1 and Westmorland WVS, NR February 1941.
9 *Westmorland Gazette*, 25 November 1939, 7.
10 *Cumberland and Westmorland Herald*, 10 Aug 1940, 3.
11 *Cumberland and Westmorland Herald*, 23 November 1940, 3.
12 *Westmorland Gazette*, 16 August 1941, 5.
13 *Cumberland and Westmorland Herald*, 13 July 1940, 2.
14 Ibid; this page also features a photograph of Newcastle's Grammar School boys helping with the potato harvest.

15 *Cumberland News*, 23 March 1940, 4; *Westmorland Gazette*, 26 April 1941,5; Kendal WVS NR, July 1943.
16 Kendal Library, Kendal Oral History Group, Interview no. 148, 1.
17 *Cumberland and Westmorland Herald*, 29 June 1940, 1 and *Cumbria within Living Memory*, 184.
18 *Cumberland and Westmorland Herald*, 10 July 1943, 2.
19 *Cumberland and Westmorland Gazette*, 21 December 1940, 1; L. Campbell, *Village by the Water: A History of Bowness-on-Windermere* (Kendal: self-published, 2015), p. 289; E. M. Rees, *A History of Huyton College* (Liverpool: Huyton College, 1985), pp. 67-73.
20 *Westmorland Gazette*, 16 August 1941, 7.
21 *Westmorland Gazette*, 12 July 1941, 5
22 MOA, Diarist no. 5290.
23 Ibid.
24 P. and R. Malcolmson, eds., *A Londoner in Lancashire 1941-1943: The Diary of Annie Beatrice Holness* (Record Society of Lancashire and Cheshire, 2016), 79-80.
25 P. Otter, *Lincolnshire Airfields in the Second World War* (Newbury, Berkshire, 1996), 273. Our estimate takes into account the army's presence in the county as well as various air forces. A survey of some of the sites in the Lake District taken for military purposes is in John Cousins, *Friends of the Lake District: The Early Years* (Lancaster University: Centre for North-West Regional Studies, 2009), 113.
26 *Cumberland News*, 6 April 1940, 7 (also 8).
27 *Westmorland Gazette*, 16 August 1941, 7. On canteens for the troops, see also Chapter 6.
28 *Cumbria within Living Memory*, op. cit., 180.
29 *Cumbria within Living Memory*, 181.
30 B. Wilkinson, ed., *A Safe Haven: Evacuees in Keswick 1939-1945* (Carlisle, 2010), 20.
31 *Carlisle within Living Memory*, op. cit., p. 185.
32 J. Summers, *Jambusters: The Story of the Women's Institute in the Second World War* (London, 2013), 156.
33 A. Pearson, D. Kyle, A. Phillips and M. Gresson, *The Annals of Kirkby Lonsdale and Lunesdale Today* (London and Kirkby Lonsdale, 1996), 342.
34 *Whitehaven News*, 27 February 1941, 3
35 MOA, Diarist no. 5226, 5 February 1942.
36 *Cumbria Within Living Memory*, op. cit., 189; also R. Freethy, *Cumbria at War 1939-1945* (Newbury, Berkshire, 2009), 85-86.
37 M. Nicholson, *What Did You Do in the War, Mummy? Women in World War II* (Bridgend, 2010; first published 1995), 42.
38 The very mixed and mainly negative English opinions of Americans in East Anglia are documented in two books edited by R. Malcolmson and P. Searby, *Wartime Norfolk: The Diary of Rachel Dhonau 1941-1942* (Norfolk Record Society, 2004), 245-46, and *Wartime in West Suffolk: The Diary of Winifred Challis, 1942-1943* (Suffolk Records Society, 2012), see 'Americans' in Index.
39 *Cumberland and Westmorland Gazette*, 12 August 1944, 1.
40 *Barrow Guardian*, 2 December 1944, p. 5 and 16 December 1944, 4.
41 J. H. Madison, ed., *Slinging Doughnuts for the Boys: An American Woman in World War II* (Bloomington and Indianapolis, 2007), 107-37.
42 Information courtesy Margaret (Atkinson) Procter, daughter of the Lasts' next door neighbours; *Nella Last's War* (2006), 280; and *Diaries of Nella Last* (2012), 210-12.
43 MOA, DR no. 1061, May 1945.
44 R. Blake, *Hutton-in-the-Forest: The War Years 1939-1945* (Skelton Agricultural Society, 1996), 2. The discussion in this and the following five paragraphs is based on this pamphlet, unless otherwise indicated.

45 IWM, Document 12895, Private papers of E.P. Malpress, unpaginated.
46 *Cumberland News*, 2 December 1939, 5.
47 From the report to Westmorland's annual WVS meeting, held 13 October 1943 (Kendal Archives, WDSO 92/1-2).
48 Kendal Archives, WDSO 92/1-2, Westmorland WVS Annual Report, 1 November 1944, by Mrs Hornyold-Strickland.
49 *Cumberland and Westmorland Herald*, 22 July 1944, 1.
50 MOA, Diarist no. 5290. 'I had no idea that such a type would volunteer for the Land Army,' the diarist added. 'She used to work in a florist's shop and doesn't look remotely tough.' A volunteer from Manchester threw all four feet, ten inches of herself into the demands of farm work (*Cumbria within Living Memory*, op. cit., 205-06).
51 *Westmorland Gazette*, 11 January 1941, 8.
52 *Whitehaven News*, 25 March 1943, 2.
53 *Cumbria within Living Memory*, op. cit., p. 204.
54 *Whitehaven News*, 12 October 1939, 2. In the early stages of the war the 'intention was to ship POWs to Canada both to save the effort of feeding and guarding them plus to remove any possibility of an uprising in support of the expected German invasion'. http.// www.bbm.org.uk/Grizedale Hall.htm. In fact many thousands of prisoners were sent to Canada, some of them to be lodged in Fort Henry, a nineteenth-century fort in Kingston, Ontario, originally built to protect British North America from the Americans.
55 S. Tiplady and K. Baverstock, *The Parish of Satterthwaite: A Social History* (Satterthwaite, Cumbria, 2014), 284.
56 G. Edwards, *Moota-Camp 103: The Story of a Cumbrian Prisoner of War Camp* (Cockermouth, 2005), 26.
57 *Annals of Kirkby Lonsdale and Lunesdale Today* (1996), 344-45.
58 A. Clark, *Wartime Memories: Stories of the Second World War in the North East* (Newcastle-upon-Tyne, 2012),23.
59 *Cumbria Within Living Memory* (1994), p. 199.
60 Reminiscences of Pauline Crabbe, in *What Did You Do in the War, Mummy?* op. cit., 39.
61 In the summer of 1941 a 31-year old Londoner enjoyed with a friend a ten days' holiday on a farm at Crossale, near Lake Ennerdale, and noted that a domestic servant 'clattered about in Cumbrian clogs' and their host 'teased us with Cumbrian dialect'. (MOA, Diarist no. 5401, 12 August 1941.)
62 Regional Heritage Centre, University of Lancaster, Elizabeth Roberts Archive, Mrs. W5B, 9-10.
63 Ibid., Mrs. J1B, 15 and 86.
64 Other evidence concerning the diversity of evacuees' experiences is found in R. Freethy, *Cumbria at War 1939-1945* 92-94, and, for a county to the south, M. Graham, *Oxfordshire at War* (Stroud, Gloucestershire, 1994), chap. 3.
65 *Westmorland Gazette*, 2 January 1943, 5.
66 MOA, Diarist no. 5226.
67 *Westmorland Gazette*, 25 January 1941, 7 and 4 October 1941, 8.
68 TNA, ED 32/669, a report of 7 June 1941. Similarly, a Girls' Friendly Society hostel at Shap was described as 'a most isolated spot where an excellent matron copes with a large number of children in primitive conditions' (Westmorland WRV NR, December 1942).
69 MOA, DR no. 2845, March 1943.
70 *Cumberland and Westmorland Herald*, 31 May 1941,7; *Carlisle Journal*, 19 March 1943, 1.

Chapter 6
Well-being

'In wartime there were many opportunities for unselfishness, and they [members of the Women's Institute] should make the best use of these opportunities.' (*Cumberland and Westmorland Herald*, 3 May 1941, p. 4, speech of the president of Westmorland's Women's Institute, 26 April 1941.)

'A people at war – and that means, as a rule, a people that is working harder and under more trying conditions than usual – cannot get on without rest and amusement.' (George Orwell, January 1942, in his *Essays*, ed. J. Carey [London, 2002], p. 393.)

Welfare in peacetime fell well short of many people's needs. Welfare in wartime posed even greater challenges. Some needs were rooted in entirely new realities (e.g. losses from bombing), others were not new but larger in scale (e.g. family break-ups). Some needs were felt mainly by men in the forces, others by civilians who had been evacuated or were over-worked, as many women were. Children's basic needs were fairly obvious and generally agreed upon, adults' needs were less easy to agree on – who among them should have priority? – and more diverse. Since social welfare was one of the pillars of public morale, the state had a strong interest in ensuring that people felt supported in the trials and tribulations that war forced upon them. 'We are all in this together': this was what people thought or at least were encouraged to think. It would have been politically dangerous for the authorities to let citizens feel adrift and uncared for, or unnecessarily deprived of everyday pleasures and opportunities for relaxation. Ideally nobody's needs should have been ignored; ideals of service for others expanded, some of which were accepted as a state responsibility. A major consequence of the war was a pronounced shift towards a version of a welfare state.*

* At a time when the Government was trying to attract women into munitions work, the *Cumberland and Westmorland Herald*, 27 September 1941 (p. 5), ran an article headed 'Flowers in Factories, What is Being Done for Women Workers'. The author stressed the factory arrangements (no specific place was mentioned) that were designed to enhance women's happiness and how much better these were than in the previous war: a degree of freedom to choose the job she would do; the provision of medical staff 'ready to deal with minor cuts or injury' and a rest room 'with a homely woman in charge, a comfortable divan, and fresh flowers on the window sill'; and a canteen where concerts and other entertainments took place

Much social welfare in wartime Britain, however, was delivered not by the state directly but by volunteers and charities. The war was a major stimulus to their activities. While there were many volunteer organisations, the single most visible and widely-found provider was the Women's Voluntary Services, launched by the Government in 1938 in anticipation of war and headed by the Dowager Marchioness of Reading (Lady Reading). The WVS was a vital civilian service organisation in Cumbria, though some, perhaps many, of its activities were carried out in coordination with other bodies, such as the Women's Institute and the Red Cross, and occasionally the YMCA. We have already seen something of the WVS's work with regard to helping with evacuation. This was always one of its major tasks, along with preparing to deal with air raids (first aid, furnishing rest centres, and the like), which in the late 1930s was seen as its primary mission – a central pillar, it might be said, of civil defence. This priority was soon moderated and, with time, the WVS's agenda enlarged to encompass a great variety of matters concerning social well-being.

Providing support for the forces was always one of the WVS's priorities, as it was, too, for the YMCA, and various local bodies committed to boosting the morale of servicemen and women. In the middle years of the war most members of the army were in Britain, not abroad, and often living dreary and monotonous lives. Troops on the move were refreshed in canteens. Troops stationed somewhere could also benefit from the activities of the WVS – perhaps a lending library, mending services, or a mobile canteen. In 1941 Kendal's WVS was looking into finding sleeping accommodation for army transport drivers (NR, January 1941). Local communities took pride in sponsoring a canteen to serve the forces, especially in 1940-41. In the summer of 1940 three Women's Institutes in Westmorland (Temple Sowerby, Bolton and Dufton) took the lead in providing a mobile canteen to be run by the YMCA and manned by the WVS, and much was made of their success (the names of donors were commonly inscribed on such a canteen).[1] Accommodation of some sort for the troops – a canteen, reading room, 'hut', or hostel – was central to a lot of the work of the YMCA, as a report of 1943 emphasised.[2] In 1941 YMCA mobile canteens were very active with the forces in the North West: serving refreshments, providing comforts, including cigarettes, lending gramophones, and supplying books and magazines, free writing paper and envelopes, shaving materials, games, and the like to men at isolated posts. 'Only those who work on the mobile canteens', it was said,

---

and where 'there is space for dancing, to music from a gramophone, and for table tennis and other games'. This (essentially) promotional piece ended with words that encapsulated the then conventional thinking. 'You do not need to be a psychologist to realise that people who enjoy working do a much better job. We have to make more guns, more tanks, more planes – and welfare is part of the answer to Hitler.'

'knew how much the men welcomed the daily visits from the canteens, and what tremendous disappointment was caused when, as sometimes happened, though very rarely, they failed to get to a post [perhaps because of bad weather]. ...In some instances they were the men's only regular contact with the outside world.'[3]

Local people found other ways of helping out men in service, be they near or far. Comfort funds were particularly common. In 1943 the work party of the Watermillock Women's Conservative Association was making woollen comforts for the RAF and the Missions for Seamen in Blyth; Dacre was sending three parcels of comforts a year to each of the 59 men and women from the parish who were serving in the forces.[4] The Greystoke Comforts Fund arranged a series of events on 14 October 1943, including a bring-and-buy sale – 'produce, groceries, new and second-hand goods met with a ready sale' – followed by a supper and dance.[5] Some of the £32 raised was probably used to buy wool for knitters. The proceeds of whist drives in Kirkby Stephen and Langwathy in early October 1941 were to provide comforts for local men and women in the forces; in July 1943 the Keswick Women's Work Guild's flag day raised £85 in aid of the local Forces Comfort Fund.[6] Several fund-raising efforts for comforts (one a pantomime) were held in and near Whitehaven in early 1942.[7] Occasionally servicemen publicised their needs. The *Whitehaven News* for 5 February 1942 (p. 3) reported that 'West Cumberland soldiers in a Royal Artillery battery in an isolated part of Yorkshire request cards and games for diversion in off-duty hours'; the men also acknowledged gifts recently received, including books and a pair of boxing gloves. People in uniform might be 'comforted' in other ways. The WVS in Barrow bought a piano in September 1940 to entertain members of the forces.[8] In March 1943 the newly-formed Appleby Troops Welfare and Entertainment Committee held a concert in the public hall, which was 'free to members of the Forces stationed in the area'.[9] Penrith had its Troops Entertainment Committee (as did Appleby) that was charged with bringing cheerfulness to members of the forces, and from June 1943 a social evening, featuring singing, was held every Sunday in Wordsworth Hall, attached to the Methodist church, for the benefit of servicemen posted locally and their civilian friends.[10]

* * * *

Perhaps the most widespread welfare activity of women was knitting, along with mending. Knitting comforts for members of the forces (and sometimes Russians) – sweaters, socks, scarves, gloves, mitts, helmets – comes up again and again. A key merit of knitting was, first, that it could be done almost anywhere, notably in a woman's own home. She did not have to go elsewhere to do it, so physical isolation or lack of mobility was not a deterrent. Second, shyness and lack of social confidence were not impediments to knitting. Third, women who were not physically robust, or elderly, or tied down domestically, could, as knitters, still be of service to the nation and give help to strangers. There was a statement in the WVS monthly report from Cockermouth for September 1943 that can stand for dozens of other testimonies: 'Bothel have acquired mending wool to repair socks for the guards of the Italian Prisoner of War Camp on Moota.... Loweswater, Lorton, Gilerux, and Bothel are knitting frocks and jumpers etc. for the Russian children.'[11] 'A fine bale of woollen remnants has reached us from a Yorkshire firm', reported Westmorland's WVS June 1942, 'for the Windermere working party to make up into children's garments for us when they are not doing Hospital Supply work.' A photograph of a meeting of Carlisle's WVS knitting party in March 1944 showed some twenty members, and there were undoubtedly more not present on that occasion.[12] The productivity of knitting parties was often noticed in the press.

Basic needs were widespread, and many could be alleviated by women. The Comforts Fund in Wigton was well established by mid-1940, and the knitters there had already produced hundreds of woollen items for men in the forces.[13] The working party of Alston's Red Cross took pride in its accomplishments in June 1943: 96 garments were sent away that month, 64 to the army depot, 13 to the RAF, and 19 to the Carlisle Red Cross. A total of some 5,882 garments had been made in Alston thus far.[14] One appeal for women to work on comforts was titled 'The Knitting Needle Brigade' – an appropriate military metaphor.[15] Individual feats of knitting productivity were occasionally announced, and, while hardly typical, they would not have been publicised had not many other women been similarly occupied and presumably attentive to reports of these impressive accomplishments. Women in small villages were routinely knitting hundreds of pairs of socks for the troops annually.

Clothes were a major challenge for almost all citizens, except for the rich, with their already large wardrobes. New clothes were rationed from 1941 and often hard to get; old ones might or might not be available to a family, and if they were, someone would have had to possess the skills necessary to turn them into suitably reusable garments. 'Make Do & Mend' campaigns encouraged these efforts, which gave tens of thousands of women a common mission, for themselves, their loved ones, and perhaps strangers, such as homeless people. Wartime put a premium on getting as much value as possible from material goods and prolonging their shelf lives – and women were vital to carrying this out.

One way of dealing with scarce clothing was to exchange outgrown or unneeded clothes with others. The garment that one woman might want was, perhaps, owned by another woman who didn't need it and was perhaps prepared to give it up; she in turn might hope that an item of clothing she wanted, perhaps for a growing child, could be spared from someone else's wardrobe. To encourage and facilitate exchanges of clothing was common sense and was put into practice in some towns during the last couple of years of the war. It was said by the WVS that in early 1944 in Cockermouth 'There seems to be a sort of unofficial exchange system going on in the Secondary School,' – teenage girls were probably the principal exchangers – 'and of course amongst relatives, friends, and neighbours, and it apparently works quite well'.[16] From late 1943 the WVS was active in setting up such exchanges, mainly for children; in Westmorland, in acknowledgement of the rural and scattered nature of much of the population, an exchange was being run from a mobile van.[17] Boots and shoes were also candidates for organised exchanges: one was set up in late 1943 in Penrith.[18]

Another major activity was fruit preservation (Fig. 6a), a particular concern of the Women's Institute, which was widely present in Cumbria. 'The country has always fed the town', according to a report from Cumberland on 19 September 1939, 'and now is our opportunity of showing what it can do'.[19] With the severe rationing of commercially-produced jam, there was a clear incentive for women to produce their own, mainly through the WI, and this was actively encouraged by the Ministry of Food, which allowed the WI to purchase substantial quantities of sugar. It is probable that by the third year of war almost every Cumbrian parish with a WI (and some without) had a centre for jam-making – there were 115 institutes in Cumberland in 1942.[20] Of the 55 jam centres in the autumn of 1942, 48 were run by the WI.[21] These centres, some in village halls, kept village women very busy at certain times of the year. By early 1943 American sealing machines were making canning easier.[23] Ideally, no fruit was allowed to go to waste – such prudence was long practised by careful village housewives. The jam produced was sold, by retailers and at WI stalls, mainly, perhaps, to women who were not in a position to make their own – perhaps they lacked enough sugar, which was rationed. Fruit preservation, along with the increased cultivation of vegetable gardens, clearly contributed to meeting basic needs. It was also an ideal outlet for country women's practical skills.[23]

There were other ways of contributing to domestically-supplied food or medicines. One was through collecting nettles for tea; another was collecting rosehips, an important source of vitamin C – the hips were made into syrup. Members of the WVS, including those in Westmorland, were routinely involved in both activities, which in some places also involved the efforts of children. (Collecting of almost any kind was perhaps the main way of mobilising children for worthy wartime causes.) The WVS also managed herb-drying centres. In Penrith in mid-1943 (NR June 1943) such a centre had been recently opened in a room over the ovens of a local bakery and the town's WVS organiser gave a detailed account that month of what had been done so far and what she hoped to accomplish. 'My area covers 37 villages in Cumberland and 21 in Westmorland, Penrith being roughly in the centre so there should be a good response from all these. We have been well supplied with foxglove leaves [to make digitalis] to be dried. In fact last week we had so many we couldn't cope with them at the bakery and have temporarily borrowed the lecture hall at the local ATC [Air Training Corps] headquarters, which is completely filled with leaves.' She concluded by noting that 'The drying centre is open every evening for two hours. The staff of three schools are responsible for an evening each and the remaining evenings are undertaken by other organisations, whose members are mostly also members of WVS.' This sort of overlapping of work between women's groups was fairly typical. In September 1943 special mention was made of a herb-drying centre, run by the WI and WVS together, in a hamlet near Cockermouth; though small, it had just sent 108 lbs. of dried foxglove leaves to a processor in Derby. Volunteers in Windermere contributed to the nation's food supply by setting over 600 traps for perch, which were canned for sale.[24] Belonging to a pig club was another way to combine self-interest and the public good – a portion of a keeper's slaughtered pig had to be made available to others.

Food was of course central to the functioning of British Restaurants, another wartime innovation, which functioned mainly in larger towns. These restaurants were intended to provide hot, nourishing, full-course midday meals, at price of a shilling or less. The meals were good value for money; they also minimised wastage. British Restaurants – initially known as communal feeding centres: this collectivist slant was disliked in some Conservative circles – were especially attractive for people without kitchen facilities, for evacuees, for schoolchildren whose mothers had (usually) war-related, employment, and for others away from their homes for the day. A man visiting Carlisle's new British Restaurant in October 1941 'found that a mother whose husband was in the Army, and who was herself in business, could take her young child there and get a comfortable meal'.[25] Ration cards were not needed – a crucial virtue for almost all consumers – service was cafeteria style (then a novelty almost everywhere), paid staff were few, and the servers were volunteers, mainly members of the WVS.

Kendal's 'Riverside Restaurant', in a former men's club, opened in June 1941 to much fanfare and applause. This substantial building seems also to have included a quiet room for reading and writing and bathing facilities (with evacuees especially in mind).[26] It was soon serving meals to around 500 people each day.[27] The British Restaurant in Staveley, which was launched two months later, made use of a former Methodist chapel and could accommodate 100 to 150 persons. Its midday meal was priced at 11½d.[28] Dalton's British Restaurant, in the old market hall, opened in November 1941, and Cockermouth's at Waterloo House in late March 1943.[29]

Most Cumbrian towns had a British Restaurant, Barrow and Workington among them, and even modest-sized Millom and Kells.[30] A British Restaurant – 'The Eden' – was opened in Carlisle in September 1941, in a large room in Christ Church School, and there too, as in most places, it was lavishly praised. It also offered a cash-and-carry service.[31] Carlisle's second British Restaurant, opened in early 1943 in South Henry Street, included a cooking depot 'where 3,000 meals can be cooked and, if needed, carried to other centres in insulated containers'.[32] 'The narrow old-fashioned street presents quite an animated appearance with the coming and going of diners taking advantage of the British Restaurant.... No one in our country need go hungry when such facilities are provided.'[33] In rural areas, where no restaurant could flourish, the war witnessed the development of the pie scheme, often initiated and managed in part by the WVS, which was designed to supply nourishing midday meals to scattered agricultural workers, often at work in the fields; this usually depended on the joint efforts of bakers, local authorities, and volunteer distributors.[34]

The monthly WVS reports from all over Cumberland and Westmorland testify to the diverse work that women – most of them middle-aged or older – undertook. Some members did camouflage knitting for the army (nasty work). Others made hospital supplies for both civilian and military requirements – slippers, socks, pyjamas, bandages, blankets, surgical supplies, and the like. The efforts of Barrow's Hospital Supply Depot, which was closely linked to the WVS, received extensive coverage in the press in mid-1942: it was said to have produced almost 50,000 useful articles during the previous three years.[35] WVS help might be given to the Food Office by distributing new ration books, which was especially valuable in places with a scattered population, or to local authorities by assisting with salvage collections. Blood donations were organised, some with the help of mobile vans. Staff were provided to school canteens, and much-prized Wellington boots (hundreds of pairs, perhaps close to 2,000 by mid-1944) were distributed to children in Westmorland, mainly in rural areas. By 1943 home help was being provided for people who were ill, especially in the countryside.

The uniformed services were not overlooked. Members of Cockermouth's WVS provided 'hospitality' to American and Dominion troops in May 1943. A contingent of the ATS also arrived in town that month, looking for help. 'We set to it, and did everything possible – begging many comforts, books, games etc., and even securing a piano for their recreation room. Their quarters are in the old [Poor Law] Institution, and look pretty grim. We helped make them curtains, and tried in every way to help, by giving advice on local affairs etc.' In early 1942 Westmorland's WVS found several billets for members of the ATS (Westmorland, NR February 1942). On 1 November 1944 Westmorland's county organiser commended the work of the Windermere

Hospitality Committee, which, since its beginning, had hosted 1,202 service personnel 'including 363 Australians, 293 Canadians, 85 New Zealanders, 61 USA, and a Belgian Congolese, Dutch, French, Bermudan, Newfoundlander and Pole'. She added that the WVS member in charge 'also dealt with many requests to find hotel accommodation for honeymoon couples'. We should remember, too, the vast amount of time that the WVS spent during 1942 and 1943 in training to respond to possible air raids – raids that never actually happened.

* * * *

The record of volunteering, fund-raising, and philanthropy could be extended almost indefinitely.[36] Flag days proliferated, perhaps counter-productively after a while, as people wearied of them. A flag day was responsible for some of the money raised (over £6,000) in 1942-43 for Cumberland's Red Cross and its POW fund – and much more had been done. 'School children, often acting entirely on their own, have raised quite substantial amounts by carol singing, sale of rose hips, concerts and performances, and donations have been received from bowling, tennis, cricket and football clubs, churches, private parties, sales of sheep and logs, from schools, choirs, Women's Institutes, WVS parties and British Legion.'[37] In August 1943 the Patterdale Girls' Club held a bring-and-buy sale and raised over £40 for the Red Cross and the St. John Prisoners of War fund.[38] War Weapons Weeks, Salute the Soldier Weeks, and the like – these were big, often annual events – were designed to encourage people to invest their savings in the war, and depended on the work of dozens if not hundreds of volunteers. Funds were sought for mobile canteens, especially in the second year of the war, when civil defence efforts were particularly active.[39] The boys of Kendal Senior School made coat hangers for the WVS's clothing depot; the wire was donated by the paper mills in Burneside (Westmorland WVS, NR October 1942 and August 1943). 'Smokes funds' for soldiers were actively promoted, including by newspapers; some cigarette funds were specifically for British POWs.

The dislocations of wartime broadened the range of perceived needs. In mid-1944 the Citizens Advice Bureau in Penrith reported on its activities since its opening three years earlier: the 1,600 enquiries it had dealt with, many from servicemen, concerned housing issues, clothing, rationing, communications with persons abroad, war damage, price complaints, income tax, which was then imposed on many more people than in peacetime, and more.[40] Rules and regulations had expanded and many people needed advice in grappling with them. Others, barely literate or actually illiterate, needed help with letter-writing, which some had not done at all in peacetime. More people in wartime were of no fixed address and wanted help finding temporary accommodation (key work for the WVS). Nurseries were needed to care for the very young children of women who had paid employment; the WVS was active in providing volunteer care-givers.[41] Occasionally volunteering was not related to material concerns. In the summer of 1943 Crosthwaite Church near Keswick was coping with a dearth of bell-ringers. Several families had been providing bell-ringers for two or three generations, but 'As more and more men were called to the Forces following the outbreak of war, the Crosthwaite bell-ringing tradition might have been broken had it not been for the fact that several women members of these old bell-ringing families volunteered to take the place of their men folk at the ropes.' Most of these women were the wives and daughters of peacetime ringers, and there were usually three or four of them in a team of eight. When there had been a ban on church bell-ringing (up to November 1942), they had practised by working on muffled bells.[42] The opportunities for volunteering were virtually endless.

It is worth noticing aspects of well-being where little was probably achieved. One was the age-old problem of restless adolescents. In Kendal in early 1944 efforts were underway to start a cafe 'in the evenings with facilities for young people to enjoy themselves, the object of course being to try to keep them off the streets, but without appearing in any way to "patronise" them'. The WVS and others were seeking, apparently with some success, the cooperation of cafe proprietors (Kendal WVS, NR February 1944). Carlisle, too, at this time was discussing the possible provision of non-alcoholic social centres for youth,[43] and a few months later a cooperative youth centre was formally opened outside the city, in Dalston Hall, to considerable fanfare.[44] A small sign of inter-generational cooperation was revealed the following month, when it was reported that Kendal's British Restaurant was soon to be re-decorated by students from the Ambleside Art School (WVS, NR March 1944). Concerns about wayward and under-occupied young people and providing them with 'healthy amusement'[45] probably increased as peace was on the horizon, by which time there were many more adolescents whose lives were relatively unsupervised by responsible adults than there had been a half dozen years before.

Inadequate bus transportation was another common headache. On 28 August 1941 a young woman travelled from her work in Windermere to Bardsea, near Ulverston, observing that 'any journey by bus here is unbearable. One has to queue up for half an hour to get a good seat, and everyone in the queue complains that people going short stages are often picked up while those going further are left behind'.[46] A fundamental principle governing wartime transportation was that trains would be mainly for long-distance travel, leaving buses for local services. 'Bus travel now is a nightmare', declared Nella Last on 12 August 1943 (MOA), thinking about her imminent journey from rural Spark Bridge to Barrow. Journeys by bus, a heightened wartime necessity for most people, were a real trial, and travellers' grumbles abounded – about waiting, crowdedness, no-shows, unsatisfactory schedules, and buses not stopping for passengers, commonly because they were already full.[47] Factory workers, most of them engaged on war-related projects, were given priority over other travellers. A special meeting in Carlisle at the beginning of October 1943 heard that the most frequent complaint was 'that people living in rural districts, who wished to travel to the nearest market town for shopping, were unable to board the buses because they were full when they left the starting point, and consequently did not stop to pick up passengers at intermediate points'. Sometimes, it was said, buses returned 'empty from war factories after taking the workers to work' and did not stop for people who wished to travel but had been unable to board earlier packed buses.[48] Some of these problems were virtually insurmountable. Wartime bus services were severely constrained by restricted supplies of fuel, rubber, spare parts, and other material necessities.[49] Some young men working at the Shorts factory in Windermere were said to make the most of the constraints on transportation by rushing for a seat on the first bus home, the better to offer a friendly male lap to a young female employee who would otherwise have to stand or wait for a later bus.[50]

By the second half of the war many of the taken-for-granted comforts of life, certainly for members of the middle class, were in short supply. Scarcities came to affect all sorts of matters: in early January 1943 the WVS was appealing for old buttons 'for the many garments made by the WVS work parties in Westmorland';[51] rubber teats for babies' bottles became very hard to find and this was causing some women considerable distress;[52] shoes were liable to be worn unmended since repairs might take weeks to do;[53] watches were not repaired (not quickly, at least); underwear wore out and could not be easily replaced (women often spoke of this); toys, if obtainable at all, were very expensive – the list of scarce 'necessities' could go on and on. People had no choice but to make do with worn-out goods. 'Darned some socks', wrote Nella Last in Barrow on 12 February 1943 (MOA), 'reflecting I'd have thought them a year past repair at one time!' Thousands of Cumbrian women must have had similar feelings.

Finally, we note a specific example of hardship – the diet of the iron ore miners of West Cumberland. In early 1944 a resident of Egremont wrote to the press concerning the failure to provide canteen facilities for these men. As a result, he said, their productivity was reduced and they were prone to illness. 'How on earth miners are expected to deliver the goods on a pitifully small meat allowance of 1s 2d per head, cheese, and a little jam passes my comprehension.' Other workers, with access to decent canteens, were not so heavily dependent on rations.[54] The following week a spirited letter was published from an 'iron ore miner's wife' in Moor Row. She was grateful for this understanding of the miners' special circumstances, and spoke of her own experiences. 'I can honestly say we are sick to death of our main diet – cheese. For five long years we have had an extra ration of cheese, but even a mouse likes a change of food. The meat and milk and bacon supply are the worst. How can a wife make a little porridge and small pudding for her man out of half-a-pint of milk a day for both herself and her husband? ...With only one half pound of meat extra a week I could do much better.' Hers – incontestably – was not an easy life, but it could, she said, be made a little easier. 'We women are up in the morning early to get our men out to work. We don't need physical jerks [she may have been thinking of the exercises promoted on the wireless] – we get plenty of them in queues and trying to look over and under the counters. What we need is a little extra for our men and to be able (at least once a week) to sit down to a rasher on a plate all for ourselves.'[55]

⋆ ⋆ ⋆ ⋆

'Two chambermaids are going to a dance at Patterdale and are spending 25 shillings on a taxi to get there. They consider it quite cheap and would have paid more. The dance ticket will cost about 1s or 1s 6d. Amazing to compare different ideas of a good time.' These words were written on 4 August 1941 by an intellectually-inclined woman in her early twenties, an aspiring writer, who was working that summer at a residential hotel in Windermere and presumably had direct information about these two fellow employees' recreational plans.[56] Her words are reminders that well-being was also related to relaxation, and that leisure activities featured prominently in wartime society, along with hardships and austerity.

Many of these activities were continuations of pre-war pleasures. The cinema remained a powerful attraction; virtually all Cumbria's newspapers routinely carried advertisements of the week's films, though the rural character of much of the North West, and restricted bus services, put limits on attendance. Still, almost all towns had cinemas, some of them large. In the early 1940s there were at least ten in and near Barrow, five in and near Carlisle, five in Workington, three in Whitehaven, three in Kendal, two in Penrith and Maryport, and one each in Appleby, Kirkby Stephen, Cockermouth, Aspatia, Wigton, Egremont, and Kells. (The nation as a whole had some 5,000 cinemas, and attendance rose by over 50 per cent during the war, with some 30 million tickets sold weekly by 1945.)[57] Some papers, such as the *Whitehaven News*, provided summaries of the films that were much like advertisements. Films were constantly changing – those who wanted to attend often could easily do so – and admission prices were low for the cheapest seats, around the price of a newspaper. Rural districts were inevitably less well served: this was why on several days in April 1943 a mobile cinema van visited sixteen places in the area around Penrith, though it was probably showing government information films, not entertainment.[58]

While live musical and dramatic performances were bound to be offered less regularly, they were still noteworthy. Amateur theatre, drawing on the talents of local players, was alive and well in wartime Cumbria, as the press routinely – and enthusiastically – noted. Dozens of modest-sized communities put on occasional dramas. References to concerts of various sorts – military, classical, religious – are also abundant. In October 1941 the Manchester Women's String Orchestra was on tour and due to perform in Carlisle, Windermere, Penrith, and Keswick: such travelling engagements became staples of wartime.[59] Many concerts were explicitly linked to wartime fund-raising. In October 1940 a Czech refugee concert at Caldbeck raised £15 for the Red Cross.[60] One account of several upcoming concerts, partly sponsored by the Pilgrim Trust, explicitly remarked on their value for sustaining morale and maintaining artistic standards.[61] The actress and writer Nancy Price not only worked on a Cumberland farm in 1941, but she also gave 'recitals to rural audiences in the little spare time at her disposal. These performances – sometimes given from a farm cart in a barn – have raised money for charities. ...People have travelled long distances over the hills to attend the recitals at Croft Farm, Buttermere.'[62] Other prominent performers in wartime Cumbria included several principals in the D'Oyly Carte Opera Company who were staying in Penrith.[63] Big-name ensembles made occasional appearances. An American woman temporarily in Barrow-in-Furness with the US Red Cross wrote on 21 January 1945 that 'This afternoon we heard John Barbirolli conduct the Hallé Orchestra, a great treat for Barrow and a greater treat for us . The concert was in one of the local cinemas, which was naturally without heat and everybody listened with coats on. It took me until intermission to warm up.'[64]

Dances were ubiquitous. The recollections of land girls in Cumbria repeatedly mention dances and dance halls, and the press was full of advertisements for forthcoming dances and reports on dances recently held. Indeed, hardly a week went by without at least one dance occurring within the catchment area of the *Westmorland Gazette* and the *Cumberland and Westmorland Herald*. The latter advertised 21 forthcoming dances in its issue of 12 April 1941 (p. 4), 20 on 8 January 1944 (p. 4), and around two dozen for the holidays at the end of 1944 (23 December 1944, p. 4). Some places held regular Saturday night dances, among them Penrith, where the dance was held in the drill hall; Moresby, where the miners were the prime sponsors; and Barrow, where the Strand Rink offered dancing on Friday evenings as well. The Empress Ballroom in Whitehaven commonly held several dances each week. Dances had many non-commercial sponsors – the Home Guard, local charities, social clubs, and sports groups, not to mention such (perhaps) unexpected organisations as the Gosforth, Seascale and District Nursing Association.[65] 'Dances are great events in the villages,' according to the *West Cumberland Times*, 21 October 1944 (p. 8), 'and all the villagers attended them.' Some were linked to whist drives. In the early summer of 1943 the WVS in Kirkby Lonsdale was 'organising fortnightly dances for the troops at the request of their Commanding Officer', and a warm welcome was no doubt issued to local women (Westmorland WVS, NR June 1943).

The 'imported' war-workers in Windermere – presumably associated with the local aircraft factory – gave a dance on 13 August 1941 that was attended by a recent university graduate who was working at a local hotel during the summer and who described the occasion. 'It was crowded', she reported, 'with dancers and onlookers, the latter standing rows deep. The atmosphere was so thick that one would have thought that beer and tobacco were being given free instead of being scarce. Dancing was painful, as there was never an empty square foot of space. The band was composed of factory workers, including an accordionist with an Italian name who was said to have broadcast a lot; if the loudspeaker had been better he might have sounded good. Certainly no sign of British "restraint". Everyone was very happy, on the surface at least, and when the M.C. said there would be an encore to one dance "if you promise to jitterbug", everyone went mad and stayed mad. The Northerners and the Southerners disapproved strongly of each other's mode of running a dance and actually dancing. The whole thing was like a rugby scrum and 20 or so people in long frocks were unlucky.'[66] This same dance probably struck other participants (non-writers) differently; and, as she suggested in distinguishing northern from southern customs, a dance in one place may have been in some respects quite unlike a dance in another .

Many dances were promoted in association with some special feature, designed to enhance their appeal. In May 1941 the dance on Thursday 8th in the village hall sponsored by the Eamont Ladies' Social Club was in aid of the YMCA Hut Fund and offered a 6d reduction in admission to members of the 'Forces in Uniform' ('Come in Crowds', the notice declared). The organisers of the dance at Burn Banks the following evening in the recreation hall, with music 'by Rosalind and her Boys', had taken account of transportation – 'Bus leaves Sandgate, Penrith, at 7.30 p.m. Fare 1s each'.[67] On 14 April 1942 there was a 'Free Salvage Dance' in the market hall at Egremont sponsored by the Thornhill War Efforts Council. 'Admission by 7lb. bundle paper, magazines, etc. (minimum quantity).... Prizes for Lady and Gent. Bringing the largest amount of paper, etc.'[68] In March 1943 the Keswick section of the Ribble-Cumberland Motor Services Social Club raised some £126 for the local branch of the Ladies' Guild of the British Sailors' Society by means of a 'military whist drive' and dance at the Royal Oak Hotel.[69] A dance at the

Unemployed Centre, Cleator Moor on 18 July 1944 was organised by the National Fire Service(NFS) – 'the MC was Fireman Bowman' – with the proceeds going to the NFS's Benevolent Fund.[70] The dance in 'the Institute' at Plumpton on 27 November 1941 was to benefit the Minesweeper and Local Comforts Fund; a dance at Beckermet in July 1944 was to help raise funds for the district's hospital; a concert and dance in Pica in aid of the Red Cross in February 1944 was promoted by local farmers and held in the Miners' Welfare Hall; the proceeds from a dance arranged by the Endmoor Girl Guides in July 1943 were for the Soldiers' Parcels Fund; and a lavishly promoted Monday evening dance in Workington in September 1944, featuring 'Joe Daniels and his Hot Shots' (all members of the RAF), attracted some 350 people to the town's drill hall for the benefit the Border Regiment Benevolent Fund.[71]

It is possible to go on and on in a similar vein.[72] Most people did not – and could not – travel far, at least for leisure. Everyday lives were confined mostly to community. Still, within these communities a lot was done to gather people together for accessible social pleasures. Local initiatives for recreation abounded, many of them from clubs and associations. These events were antidotes to the grind, dreariness, and tedium of wartime. Working hours were often long and conditions unpleasant, material necessities (food, drink, clothing) were limited, and confinement at home was prevalent, though eased, no doubt, by listening to the wireless and (for some) increased reading of books and receiving letters.[73] The large collection of letters between housewife Evelyn Harwood in Kendal and her husband, absent in the army, provides rich testimony to the vital importance of correspondence to help people cope with the strains of prolonged enforced separation.[74] And the stresses did drag on. By the last year or so of the war a lot of people were run down and very tired – these are recurrent complaints. But efforts were not lacking to ease their strain, lend helping hands, and lay on, at modest expense, recreational diversions. And whatever private and unrecorded weariness or frustrations may have existed, throughout the war the public discourses in Cumbria in the press and elsewhere were decidedly buoyant and focused mainly on positive news. Gloominess and discontent were not much reported. Indeed, reports of this nature would usually not have been permitted.

* * * *

'Well-being' is not easy to define. Dictionaries speak of 'the state of being comfortable, healthy, or happy', 'a good or satisfactory condition of existence', and 'the state of feeling healthy and happy'. Sometimes it is used more or less synonymously with 'welfare'. Welfare depends on the satisfaction of both needs and desires – and the boundary between them in wartime was blurred. While conditions of life were clearly pinched, if not worse, for many people, extensive and organised efforts were made to help people get by and deal with ill fortune and deprivation. Aid was commonly available; people were not left to cope on their own. Citizens did, to a considerable degree, support one another. And those who rendered support – many of them volunteers – clearly gained from their work a sense of purpose and of solidarity with others; Nella Last's diary provides much evidence in support of this proposition. Civilians enjoyed a feeling of connection with the ideals of national service that flourished in wartime (Fig. 5) – these ideals, of course, were sometimes tarnished, for example, through black market transactions and petty looting.** Service and pleasure were closely linked. One of the purposes of the monthly meetings of Westmorland's Women's Institutes was to 'introduce a little brightness into the lives of members',[75] and newspaper accounts of the multitude of WI meetings indicate that this goal was pursued assiduously throughout the war. Even dances and whist drives and bring-and-buy socials, with their diversity of sponsors, were part of these impulses of service.

'It's good to feel nowadays', wrote Nella Last on 15 July 1943 (MOA), 'that one's efforts are to "help" and "care for". I know I could not work as hard for any kind of "distinction".' Wartime allowed some people – perhaps, most strikingly, middle- and upper-middle-class women of all ages – to become rather different sorts of people. Their sense of self was enlarged. Work carried them into more public spaces. Leadership was often required. And this work was outward-looking and often broadly conceived. Working for *common purposes*, sometimes in the face of formidable difficulties, and usually achieving worthy goals, was central to many civilians' sense of satisfaction and well-being. This was one of the central psychological facts of living in wartime Britain.

Notes and References

1 *Cumberland and Westmorland Herald*, 24 August 1940, 3.
2 *Cumberland and Westmorland Herald*, 24 April 1943, 1.
3 *Westmorland Gazette*, 16 August 1941, 7.
4 *Cumberland and Westmorland Herald*, 9 January 1943 and 8 May 1943, 5.
5 *Cumberland and Westmorland Herald*, 16 October 1943, 5.

** There is an inherent bias in press accounts concerning wartime welfare, which almost always showcased citizens' eager support, financial or otherwise, for the war effort. Morale, clearly, should not be undermined in public. The unusually detailed reports by the *Whitehaven News* between December 1943 and April 1944 on social life in five villages in the area, based on personal visits, stressed their residents' values of public service and good citizenship, notably their generosity and cheerfulness in donating money and time to benefit others. (The villages were Pica, Gosforth, Distington, Ravenglass, and Calder Bridge.) Patriotic acts were always highlighted.

6 *Penrith Observer*, 30 September 1941, 2; *Cumberland and Westmorland Herald*, 24 July 1943, 1.
7 *Whitehaven News*, 15 January 1942, 3 and 12 February 1942, 3.
8 Barrow Archives, BDSO 27, WVS Minute Book, 16 September 1940.
9 *Cumberland and Westmorland Herald*, 27 March 1943, 2.
10 *Cumberland and Westmorland Herald*, 12 August 1944, 1; 22 January 1944, 1; 1 April 1944, 2; and 10 June 1944, 1.
11 RVS Archive and Heritage Collection, Devizes, Wiltshire, Cockermouth NR, September 1943.
12 *Carlisle Journal*, 31 March 1944, 1.
13 *Carlisle Journal*, 9 July 1940, 1.
14 *Cumberland and Westmorland Herald*, 10 July 1943, 2.
15 *Whitehaven News*, 28 August 1941, 3.
16 RVS Archive and Heritage Collection, Cockermouth, NR January 1944.
17 *Cumberland and Westmorland Herald*, 9 December 1944, 6; Westmorland WVS, NR October 1944.
18 Carlisle Archives, SUDP/1/3/3/N2 HOSP 18, Box 49.
19 Women's Library, LSE, 5FWI/A/3/073.
20 *Whitehaven News*, 23 April 1942. Planning for Cumberland's 'communal jam making' is reported in the *Cumberland and Westmorland Herald*, 14 June 1941, 3.
21 *Carlisle Journal*, 27 October 1942, 3. It was said that some 27,000 pounds of jam had been produced, apparently that year or during the previous twelve months.
22 *Carlisle Journal*, 2 February 1943, 3.
23 *Cumberland and Westmorland Herald*, 14 June 1941,3.
24 J.L. Campbell, *Village by the Water: A History of Bowness-on-Windermere* (Kendal, self-published, 2015), 290; and The National Archive, MAF 99/792.
25 *Carlisle Journal*, 10 October 1941, 1.
26 *Westmorland Gazette*, 10 May 1941, 7; 7 June 1941, 5; and 14 June 1941, 5.
27 Kendal Archives, WDSO 92/1-2, letter of 11 August 1941 to Miss Clarkson from Mary Hornyold-Strickland.
28 *Westmorland Gazette*, 30 August 1941, 5.
29 *Barrow Guardian*, 29 November 1941, 2; *West Cumberland Times*, 24 March 1943, 1 and 2.
30 *Whitehaven News*, 2 December 1943, 2 and 7 June 1945, 5.
31 *Carlisle Journal*, 19 September 1941, 1 and 5.
32 *Carlisle Journal*, 12 January 1943, 1. It was said that the city's 'Eden' Restaurant had served over half a million meals during its sixteen months of existence.
33 *Carlisle Journal*, 5 March 1943, 5.
34 *Whitehaven News*, 3 June 1943, 4; Kendal Archives, WDSO 92/1-2, County Organiser's Report of 1 November 1944, 3 and letter of 7 June 1945, 2.
35 *North-Western Evening Mail*, 3 July 1942, 3 and 13 August 1942, 4.
36 For one town, see G. Edwards, *The War Years: Life in Cockermouth and at Moota POW Camp* (Cockermouth, 2009), 63-70; also R. K. Bingham, *The Chronicles of Milnthorpe* (Milnthorpe, 1987), 397-98.
37 *Cumberland and Westmorland Herald*, 16 January 1943, 2.
38 *Cumberland and Westmorland Herald*, 28 August 1943, 5.
39 It was pointed out that there were nearly 1,000 civil defence workers in Whitehaven, 'so that one if not more mobile canteens will be needed under crisis conditions' (*Whitehaven News*, 13 February 1941, 2). At the same time money was being raised for a YMCA mobile canteen in the Lune Valley, and a speaker at the market hall in Orton 'outlined the good work done by the canteens' (*Cumberland and Westmorland Herald*, 22 February 1941, 4). Instances of such useful work were clearly evident after the bombings in Barrow a couple of months later.

40 *Cumberland and Westmorland Herald*, 1 July 1944, p. 7.
41 An appeal in Carlisle to get more married women into war-related production emphasized the availability of places in nurseries for their children (*Carlisle Journal*, 24 March 1944, 1). Such nurseries had rarely existed in Cumbria before the war.
42 *Cumberland and Westmorland Herald*, 28 August 1943, 5.
43 *Carlisle Journal*, 31 March 1944, 5.
44 *Carlisle Journal*, 26 September 1944, 3.
45 Kendal WVS, NR March 1945.
46 MOA, Diarist no. 5290.
47 The problems and diverse experiences of wartime bus journeys are richly documented in a diary kept by a women living in Morecambe, a few mile from Cumbria: P. and R. Malcolmson, eds., *A Londoner in Lancashire 1941-1943: The Diary of Annie Beatrice Holness* (Record Society of Lancashire and Cheshire, 2016). Cumbrian bus travel would have been much the same.
48 *Cumberland and Westmorland Herald*, 2 October 1943, 1. A letter-writer from Hensingham alleged that some workers' buses 'refuse to stop at recognised stops even when half empty and, when forced to do so by dismounting passengers, usually do so very many yards before or after the stop and, as happens daily at Hensingham Square, in the middle of a busy cross-road to the danger alike of those alighting and those hoping to embark.' (*Whitehaven News*, 20 July 1944, 5.) Her complaints seem to have been directed against both the buses' conductresses and drivers; she went out of her way to describe the travelling workers as 'without exception always considerate'. The silk mills at Hensingham made parachutes – about 120,000 during the war; most of the workers were women (Jeff Wilson, *West Cumberland at War* [privately printed, 1999], 88).
49 J. Howie, *The British Bus in the Second World War* (Stroud, 2013), 100-01. Further details on Cumbria's bus services are in J. Howie, *Ribble in World War Two*, published by the Ribble Enthusiasts' Club in 2010. We are grateful to Barnard Ashcroft for supplying us with a copy of this booklet. A long explanation of the company's struggles to provide satisfactory services in wartime was published in the *Carlisle Journal*, 28 November 1944, 1.
50 A. King, *Wings on Windermere: The History of the Lake District's forgotten flying boat factory* (Sodomierez, 2008), p. 58.
51 *Cumberland and Westmorland Herald*, 23 January 1943, 4.
52 Kendal WVS, NR August 1944. 'We have mothers (and grandmothers on behalf of their daughters) almost in tears asking for our help.'
53 Kendal WVS, NR October 1944. Commonly there were shortages of both leather and skilled workers.
54 *Whitehaven News*, 6 January 1944, 2.
55 *Whitehaven News*, 13 January 1944, 5.
56 MO Diary no. 5290. The diarist had just graduated from university.
57 J. Gardiner, *The Second World War on the Home Front: Life in Britain during the War* (London, 2015), 17 and J. Richards and D. Sheridan, eds., *Mass-Observation at the Movies* (London, 1987), 12.
58 *Cumberland and Westmorland Herald*, 24 April 1943, 1; also R. Freethy, *Cumbria at War 1939-1945* (Newbury, Berkshire, 2009), 105-06.
59 *Carlisle Journal*, 10 October 1941,5.
60 *Cumberland and Westmorland Herald*, 19 October 1940, 4.
61 *Cumberland and Westmorland Herald*, 4 October 1941, 3.
62 *Westmorland Gazette*, 12 July 1941, 5. An accompanying photograph showed the actress feeding calves at this farm.
63 *Cumberland and Westmorland Herald*, 12 August 1944, 1.

64 J. H. Madison, ed., *Slinging Doughnuts for the Boys: An American Woman in World War II* (Bloomington and Indianapolis, 2007), 133.
65 The latter, *Whitehaven News*, 9 April 1942, 1.
66 MOA, Diary no. 5290.
67 *Cumberland and Westmorland Herald*, 3 May 1941, 4.
68 *Whitehaven News*, 9 April 1942, 1.
69 *Cumberland and Westmorland Herald*, 6 March 1943, 5.
70 *West Cumberland Times*, 22 July 1944, 5.
71 *Cumberland and Westmorland Herald*, 22 November 1941, 4; *Whitehaven News*, 20 July 1944, 5; *Whitehaven News*; 24 February 1944, 5; *Westmorland Gazette*, 10 July 1943, 3; *Workington Star*, 29 September 1944, 7.
72 It is estimated that some four million people across the nation in 1942 attended commercial dance halls weekly (J. Nott, *Going to the Palais: A Social and Cultural History of Dancing and Dance Halls in Britain, 1918-1960* [Oxford, 2015], 52). Dances in Cumbria were held mostly in smaller venues.
73 'Only one post a day,' wrote MO's young Westmorland diarist (no. 5290) on 21 July 1941, who was then living in Bardsea, a village near Ulverston, 'and it has become so important since the war, as everyone is so scattered and the railway fares are so ruinous'. It was reported in later 1942 that the library in Tullie House, Carlisle was more popular than ever and that there was in increase in serious reading (*Carlisle Journal*, 4 December 1942, 1).
74 Imperial War Museum, Harwood Papers, Documents 16878.
75 Women's Library, LSE, 5FWI/A/3/073, Westmorland Reports, Kendal, 16 September 1939.

Chapter 7
Summer 1944

'Requests for help to get billets are reaching us from all quarters.' (Westmorland WVS, NR June 1944)

'One mother wept with gratitude to the billeting officials the next day. She never dreamt that anyone would want her and her four little girls, but she had had a wonderful welcome from a lonely spinster in Arnside that she would remember all her life.' (Westmorland WVS, NR August 1944.)

From mid-1941 the dynamics of war were transformed. First, Britain gained two powerful – or at least potentially powerful – allies: the Soviet Union in June and the United States in December 1941. The nation was suddenly full of pro-Russian publicity and propaganda, and public events abounded in support of Russia's resistance to the common enemy. From 1942 American troops and airmen were flooding into the country. By the end of that year it was looking as if victory was not just possible but probable, as the weight of allied force started to bear down heavily on the Axis powers. Second, the threats to homeland security receded. After serious raids on Hull in the summer of 1941, no major port or industrial city was subjected to intense aerial attack until 1944. With the exception of the symbolic Baedeker raids of 1942 on five historic cities – Exeter, Bath, Canterbury, Norwich and York – almost all other raids during these three years, aside from London's 'little blitz' in early 1944, were comparatively small in scale, albeit still lethal for some unlucky inhabitants in a few unlucky places.

One consequence of this comparatively raid-free reality was that many evacuees returned home. Cumbria became less congested with outsiders than it once was. It is estimated that between May 1941 and August 1943 Cockermouth's population fell from some 5,762 to 5,245. The number of people billeted there at the latter date was only about a quarter of the number billeted at the earlier one.[1] Westmorland had received a total of some 11,610 officially evacuated unaccompanied school children up to September 1941. By the end of 1942 the number remaining in the county was down to 1,714.[2] The number of schoolchildren privately evacuated to Westmorland declined by some 70 per cent between June 1941 and January 1943.[3] Half of Barrow's children evacuated to Westmorland had gone home by early 1942 and no more than twenty per cent of them were still in the county by the end of the summer (WVS NR, January and August 1942). Almost all had returned to Barrow by April 1944.[4] The Heaton Secondary School for Girls returned to Newcastle from Kendal in mid-1943.[5] In January 1943 the total number of evacuated children in Kendal (official and private), both at the elementary and secondary level, was approximately 500, much lower than it had been – in December 1941 the number of officially evacuated children alone was around 1,100 (WVS Westmorland, NR January 1943 and WVS Kendal, NR December 1941). The numbers of evacuees continued to decrease during the following two years.

Early 1944 saw a modest reversal. Renewed raids in the South East prompted an increase in the flow of evacuees to the North West. According to Kendal's WVS Narrative Report for February 1944, 'The last week or ten days have produced many enquiries from people in the London area with regard to billets (in a private capacity), and we have two or three families already housed'. These migrations continued in March: 'already a considerable stream of self-evacuated people are coming in and accommodation is getting harder and harder to find; this may complicate matters later on' (Westmorland WVS, NR March 1944). Pressures on accommodation were reported from Grange-over-Sands, where boarding houses were said to be full of private evacuees.[6]

June 1944 brought major though relatively short-lived changes. Almost all British eyes were on the Second Front, which had been launched with the D-Day invasion. This allied offensive had been long anticipated, and its progress and associated losses of life must have been matters for discussion, and sometimes anguish, in thousands of Cumbrian households. On the Home Front there was one major new threat: the launching by the Germans from 12 June of thousands of V-1 missiles – also known as doodlebugs, buzz bombs, flying bombs, and pilotless planes – against South-East England. (Their range did not allow them to strike more distant targets.) For more than two months the residents in one part of the country were terrorised by this new form of aerial attack. One consequence was the evacuation of as many as 900,000 people, mainly women and children, to safer districts, one of which, though far away, was Cumbria.

⋆ ⋆ ⋆ ⋆

This was the fourth (and final) major wave of wartime evacuees to arrive in the North West. It began in early July and continued for several weeks. Local authorities, members of the WVS, medical and social services, and billeting officials throughout Cumbria did their best to apply lessons learned from the experiences with earlier evacuations. On the whole rest centres were well stocked and staffed, trains and buses efficiently organised, and evacuees accompanied by helpful care-givers. Evacuees who arrived at a rest centre in Carlisle were attended to by the WVS. 'Clothes baskets were borrowed to make cots for the babies ... [and] clothes ropes were rigged up and pegged out for baby garments.' The next day most evacuees were billeted in nearby villages; in one Cumberland village an empty cottage was quickly fitted out by the WVS for two mothers with three children each.[7] The evacuations of mid-1944 were in many places better carried out than those early in the war.[8] There was, for example, a detailed plan for transporting and receiving evacuees from Dagenham, East Ham, West Ham, Wanstead, and Woodford to Keswick, Penrith, Cockermouth, and various rural districts in Cumberland.[9] For the most part the refugees, both official and private, met with sympathy and were warmly received, especially by local authorities and publicists. A photograph in the *Westmorland Gazette*, 16 September 1944, showed London evacuees happily picking blackberries. Such an image was in tune with the positive narratives featured in the news that summer. WVS reports, not written for publication, were also upbeat. 'Windermere have organised a weekly club [for evacuees]; Ambleside a meeting place where the women can wash and iron etc.; and Patterdale have done excellent work getting their major batch into Patterdale Hall, released by the military at very short notice. They were most grateful for the loan of USA quilts' (Westmorland, NR July 1944).

There were, though, sensitive issues, chief among them billeting. Penrith, said the editor of the *Penrith Observer*, had, 'unlike many other towns, done its full share in catering for evacuees since the war started'.[10] (Because of newcomers, Penrith's wartime population probably expanded at a greater rate than that of any other Cumbrian town.) In Carlisle there was concern about trying to accommodate more evacuees in a city 'already under acute housing pressure'; and with so many people employed outside the home, 'Housewives may be reluctant, even if accommodation is available, to leave their houses to the care of strangers during the daytime'.[11] At a council meeting in Keswick on 6 July the chairman of the Evacuation Committee advised that a message had been received asking that the area be prepared to receive evacuees 'at any time within the next few days'. His committee's strategy, in common with other jurisdictions in Cumbria, was to target billeting notices on householders who either had not previously taken evacuees or had only had them for a brief period of time. He hoped that when billeting notices were received, 'they would be taken in the right spirit' and no one would refuse to take in evacuees, while admitting that 'a lot of grumbling' was to be expected.[12]

And grumbling there was in some communities, large and small, along with a little compulsory billeting – or, more likely, the threat of it – and occasional prosecutions of recalcitrant householders.[13] A few instances of individual grievance or non-compliance were inevitable with evacuation on this scale. It was said that in Kendal 'some hostesses are trying the "freezing out" process [on evacuees], some evacuees demand to have everything done for them, adopting the "we are the guests of the Government so why should we wash up?" attitude (and expecting their husbands to be put up also by their hostesses), but they are the minority and on the whole most of them have settled far better than expected' (Kendal WVS, NR August 1944). Pregnant mothers were likely to be unwelcome as billettees.

The press and local officials went out of their way to counsel against social intolerance, and to remind readers that any inconvenience they might experience as hosts to evacuees was minor when compared with the dangers and difficulties endured by London mothers and children. Reports of the evacuees' arrival in Penrith, Keswick, Kirkby Stephen and in the north of rural Westmorland stressed the stoicism and 'exemplary courage' of their guests and the amiability of the children; 'not a single child was heard crying or whimpering', despite a very long and tiring day of travel.[14] An account of the arrival of evacuees in Keswick (117 mothers, 231 children) noted that some of the children 'were from the East End', but they 'had been kept neat and tidy and clean in spite of having to travel and rest under difficult conditions.[15] Kendal's WVS organiser appreciated the strains these London mothers were under. Most had arrived after long journeys. They had no idea where they were being sent (some hoped for Blackpool), and many, she said, 'had lost all their luggage, including the precious prams, and some are still without'; the WVS had tried to collect what prams, cots, playpens, and the like that they could and had started an afternoon social club for the women and their children (Kendal, NR August 1944).

These generally optimistic accounts sometimes glossed over the problems of accommodating slum refugees, a few of whom had, at best, rudimentary notions of hygiene, were prone to bed-wetting, and had little understanding of middle-class manners. Like the adolescent slum recruits to the army described by historian Alan Allport, some were probably unfamiliar with either a toothbrush or underwear and were functionally illiterate.[16] These issues were well known: as it was reported from Ennerdale, 'previous evacuees had not left behind them a favourable impression'. This view was shared in Maryport, where the chairman of the Maryport Urban District Council tried to counter reluctance to billet people by reminding readers that these women and children were the victims of Hitler's Nazism and should be received with 'open doors and open hearts'. He hoped that residents would have 'warm feelings for these unfortunate people'. Another councillor acknowledged the poor impression prior visitors had left but added that some of the new evacuees would have husbands and sons in Normandy or other battle fronts, whose minds would be eased by knowing that their women and children were safe.[17] Such complainants were probably in a minority. A later (1946) account of Westmorland said that the refugees 'were in the main reasonable and patient'; these authors were struck by 'their indomitable pluck and genuine gratitude for all we could do' and concluded that 'the fear of the Kendal householders of having people of a low standard in their homes was not justified'.[18]

This evacuation differed from previous ones in that many of the refugees were primarily in search of rest and a short-term respite from the strain of almost constant alerts. Most arrived as families, minus husbands and fathers. Mothers were not separated from their children. Most evacuees had their own homes to return to, though some might have needed repair. People secure in Cumbria should, it was declared, be prepared to put up with a little inconvenience to assist the less fortunate. Similar views were heard about the evacuees arriving in lightly-damaged Leeds.[19] These arguments convinced some people to accept refugees, especially as many reckoned that the war was near its end and the new guests would not likely be staying for long.[20] But other householders, especially some in crowded towns long accustomed to billetees, were more resistant. The thankless work of the billeting officers was sometimes difficult indeed. Why, wondered refugees and billetors, couldn't the evacuees stay in the well-organised and equipped rest centres? (These were actually designed to accommodate only short-term homelessness.) Wasn't such a temporary fix preferable to billeting?

⋆ ⋆ ⋆ ⋆

Cockermouth was one place where increasing difficulty had been encountered in finding billets for new arrivals. Here the problem was well documented by F.H. Mason, chairman of the town's Evacuation Committee, in a report to Cockermouth Council concerning the challenges and achievements in managing the billeting of 123 evacuees – almost 200 more were being sent into the rural district. All over the town there were cases of householders who had either never had evacuees or only had them for a brief period in 1939, and these people were evading their duty by not taking in the 1944 refugees. On the other hand, he reported, there were 'outstanding cases of hospitality', as in the case of one woman who had had an average of half a dozen children over the whole period of war.[21] Analyzing the problem, Mason gave several reasons for billeting resistance including continued food restrictions; the scarcity of household goods and appliances, owing to rationing and the lack of supplies; the growing number of housewives in full- or part-time employment; and the element of chance concerning the type of evacuee a householder might be requested (or required) to shelter. Evacuees could fit into a family very well, but could also prove a disaster. Recently, he noted, he had had to send back a particularly obstreperous family as they 'had offended people here by uncalled for remarks concerning the inhabitants of Cockermouth and the place itself, with the result that no householder would take them in nor would help them in any way'.[22]

Endorsing practical necessity and acknowledging the widespread view that the burden of receiving strangers had not been fairly shared, Cockermouth's UDC, having received word that the town would be receiving V1 refugees, publicised its willingness to make use of compulsory billeting in the local press. Soon thereafter the chief billeting officer issued advance notification to some householders that they would be required to provide accommodation. Immediately excuses began to roll in, the first within twenty minutes of delivery, often accompanied by doctors' notes. While some excuses were deemed reasonable, others were thought to be in blatant defiance of the council and the law. (Local authorities had already culled from their list of potential billetors the obviously infirm and elderly – about 70 years of age and older.) At 8 p.m., 6 July a train arrived with over 300 aboard. They were taken to rest centres, with the WVS 'assisting in their usual admirable way'. There they were fed and made comfortable.

New challenges arose. Unlike the earlier children's evacuations, in 1944 there were numerous mothers with large families. The heads of these 'outsize families' often forcefully voiced their desire *not* to be separated from their children. These families could not usually be accommodated in modest-sized private homes. There were also a few cases where a woman wanted to be housed with a friend or her sister, as well as their various children. Mothers often stressed that for them the importance of keeping the family together well outweighed material comfort. Indeed, families sometimes said that a proffered billet was 'too posh' and walked out (Kendal WVS, NR July 1944).* In practical terms all this meant that a council could be pushed to take over condemned buildings and attempt to upgrade them – a difficult and time-consuming enterprise – or try to find space in requisitioned buildings not fully occupied by their designated users. Government officials, not possessing a crystal ball, were understandably reluctant to vacate space that still might be needed to meet some other wartime emergency for which they were responsible.

Elsewhere local officials, working under pressure to house evacuees, had sometimes made rash promises to householders that if they took in people for the night, these people would be moved to other billets in the morning. These assurances, in the view of the chair of the Evacuation Committee, effectively sabotaged the enforcement of compulsory billeting powers – and not incidentally infuriated the diligent chairman of the Cockermouth Evacuation

* Dow and Brown (*Evacuation* [1946], 36) wrote of one woman who refused a 'posh' billet' and 'said, very sensibly, that she knew what her boys were like and she was afraid that they would damage a house which she described as "all polish".' A similar concern was reported in the *Carlisle Journal*, 5 September 1944, 1. Also, some mothers 'were afraid that they might not be able to do their children's washing as and when necessary; they had not enough clothes with them to use the laundries'. This is evidence of realistic class-consciousness.

Committee. If this were not enough, the chief billeting officer fell ill (a heart attack, from which he later died). Given his illness, his whole organisation collapsed with him, and precious hours were consumed in getting through the red tape needed to deputise the town clerk to take over. In the midst of this chaos, one Ministry of Health official, Miss Thompson, was able to requisition a hostel and leap over some bureaucratic hurdles to free up and transport beds, blankets, chairs, and the like in order to furnish space for four mothers and fifteen children. Meanwhile, Nurse Lawson, 'by the exercise of that peculiar charm she seems to possess over children', managed the smooth removal of the children and their mothers to their new temporary homes. Other cottages were requisitioned and, by midnight Saturday, with the help of people willing to donate their time doing tasks ranging from financial management to fitting gas rings, 'all was calm and relatively settled'. You can almost hear the collective sigh of relief.

There was one other detailed account of Cockermouth's reception of evacuees – by the WVS organiser – and it is largely compatible with what the evacuation official had written (though the dates given differ). She described the arrival on 14 July of 333 evacuees – all mothers and children – plus 17 escorts.[23] Two halls had been set aside as rest centres, appropriately equipped to receive visitors. The train was met by billeting officials from both Cockermouth and nearby rural areas, the WVS, and a trained nurse. The evacuees were bused to the rest centres and fed; most stayed there for the night and 70 others were sent to two hostels. 'It was really surprising how soon everyone settled down, and the WVS members on duty throughout the night at both centres were able to report "no incidents"'. Billeting commenced the next day; some evacuees had to remain in the rest centres a second night. 'There was great difficulty in fixing billets, particularly in the case of large families.... The Local Authority accordingly requisitioned a large empty house, which in addition to the hostel took in all the remaining families, and the Rest Centre was eventually closed at 4 p.m. on Saturday the 15th. The following week ten condemned houses were opened and furnished, and the large families have been installed there, to their satisfaction.' The report on the reception of evacuees in Penrith's Rural District (RVS Archive, Quarter ending September 1944) was similarly proud of work well done.

In Cockermouth – in common with the rest of Cumbria – the emergency of the summer of 1944 was short-lived. By the end of September, 139 of 193 officially organised evacuees had returned home leaving a total of 206 in Cockermouth, including private evacuees. The furniture and other domestic equipment so urgently sought a few weeks earlier were now returned to storage (with the exception of items taken by returning refugees that the council was trying to retrieve). The anxieties of the billeting officers undoubtedly subsided upon receipt of an official government circular that placed clear limits on any future organised evacuations, restricting them to women in the last month of pregnancy who were destined for maternity homes and possibly a few elderly, infirm, or ill citizens whose housing was grossly inadequate. So uneventful were the following months that Cockermouth's Evacuation Scheme Committee records no more minutes until March 1945, when there is a relatively brief entry expressing sympathy for the death of the original billeting officer and another noting a claim for compensation from a householder who had hosted twenty-three evacuees from September 1939 to December 1944. This householder estimated the cumulative damage to her property to be at least £75. The council forwarded the claim to the national government, recommending that some sort of ex gratia payment be made, and especially that the mattress rendered unusable by a young bedwetting guest either be replaced or paid for.

⋆ ⋆ ⋆ ⋆

During these months there was a lot of constructive social action. This included looking for hard-to-find teats for infants' bottles (Rubber was scarce.) and a service in Kendal in which keen young volunteers carried messages, inflated mattresses, scoured the town for baby food, helped the sick from trains, searched for lost luggage, collected morning milk, and (not so enjoyably) washed nappies.[24] At Westmorland County Hall in Kendal in November the mood at the county's WVS conference was self-congratulatory. Much work had been done and done well; many hundreds of mothers and children had been kept safe.[25] In Workington in early July there was an appeal for Morrison shelters, which (it was felt) were no longer needed in the far North West. 'There were a lot of these shelters in gardens [the Morrison was intended for indoor use] and one, in fact, was being used as a hen-run and scratching-shed, according to the Town Clerk. That was altogether wrong. The need for these shelters was urgent elsewhere,' and the local authorities were prepared to arrange for their collection.[26]

The summer in Barrow was a little different, for the town was both an evacuation location and a proposed reception centre. Roughly 130 of its children were thought to be still billeted outside Barrow, and some people felt they should be allowed to return to their homes before mothers were required to look after other people's children.[27] Barrow's planners had done their jobs well, giving some 700 evacuees a warm welcome at the town's station. The intention was to billet them in outlying areas, notably Ulverston, Dalton, Askam, and Millom, rather than in Barrow, despite many offers of urban accommodation – 'far more offers than children' – so compulsory powers did not have to be exercised.[28] Offers of billets in Dalton were also abundant.[29] Greeting the children – there were few mothers in this first evacuation – Barrow's mayor told one small lad that 'It won't be long before Hitler goes down and you will be on the road home again'.[30]

The evacuation was a success. The largest family group, made up of two sisters and two brothers, was kept together. The children were reported to be happy, bright and excited; some were thrilled to see the huge shipyard cranes and others were keen to get their first glimpse of the sea. Later, when the children were enjoying a snack, the mayor dropped by again and assured them, with understandable hyperbole, that they were 'the nicest, sweetest, prettiest lot of evacuees he had ever seen'.[31] (Perhaps Barrow, a strongly proletarian town, was relatively unphased by the prospect of billeting working-class children from elsewhere. Also, many of the evacuees were from suburban London, notably Hornsey, not the impoverished East End.) Other officials applauded the excellent arrangements while urging grandly, 'Let us open our doors to these women and children if they seek sanctuary among us, as we would welcome men back from battle. We have not had to share their suffering; let them feel that they share our sympathy'.[32] Official letters of appreciation from London underlined the successful reception of, and the programmes created for, these children. Praise for the WVS was especially evident – among other things it later set up a social centre in Barrow's Christ Church schoolroom for evacuated mothers and their children.[33] Similar 'clubs' were organised at Ambleside, Windermere, and Whitehaven.[34]

Evacuations to Barrow later that summer, involving mothers as well as children, strained local resources. Housing unaccompanied children was not usually a problem; housing families, especially large ones, was. An editorial in the *North-Western Evening Mail* for 8 August 1944 (p. 1) mentioned some of the impediments. 'Barrow has had to provide accommodation for workers coming from other districts [mainly to work in the shipyard] and the considerable destruction of dwelling houses in the borough has also been a great handicap.' Billets were at that time still needed for around 300 children and 100 mothers, though this was just a sort-term matter: all but four of the large families were accommodated two days later. The billeting challenges were 'aggravated by the demands of unofficial evacuees, much more numerous than the official evacuees'. [35] Compulsory powers – or threats to use them – were sometimes employed.

* * * *

Different particulars were observed in other places. In Keswick, a billeting appeal was made to householders to accommodate evacuees from London but the planners focused their efforts away from the densely populated town to the adjacent rural districts and thus did not need to exercise compulsory powers.[36] Things seemed to go fairly smoothly and once the newcomers were registered, fed, and assigned housing, a boating company entertained some of the V1 evacuees with a free motor-launch trip around the lake.[37] In Penrith public notice was taken of evacuated women of call-up age. Some of these young women, noted a reporter for the *Penrith Observer* on 18 July (p. 3), presented themselves at labour exchanges within 48 hours to re-register for work. This was praiseworthy. Others, mainly single women, seem 'to spend an aimless time in the cafes sipping morning coffee and afternoon tea. Smartly dressed and comfortably housed, their chief desire appears to keep clear of the official centres where they might have to give detailed information about their presence in the area.' As usual, locals were quick to scrutinise the conduct of newcomers, and, unsurprisingly, it was observed that while some 'refugees' took seriously their wartime duties to the nation, others did not.

The pressure to keep families together could have a positive outcome. 'The billeting officer could not have made a better choice,' said the editor of the *Penrith Observer* on 25 July (p. 2), 'for the families, it is stated, are having the time of their lives and are doing more to popularise such communal living than any words of ours could possibly do'. Since so many of these families had lived a crowded, cheek-by-jowl existence in the metropolis, it is not surprising that living among others with shared experiences, a broadly common culture, and speaking in familiar accents would be a comfort in disjointed times. Some women found rural life dull and quickly returned with their families to their battered but bustling cities. But generally, it was thought, 'the evacuees are only too glad of the peaceful relaxation offered by a small Cumberland town and adjoining fells and rejoice in undisturbed nights and the absence of Germany's latest winged monstrosity'.[38]

One source permits (this is unusual) an inside, personal, and detailed view of the arrival of evacuees in July 1944. Barbara Miller-Jones (b. 1911), who was living in Bowness at Green Lodge on Longtail Hill, the large home of her parents, had a five-year old daughter, Angela, and a husband in the army in the Middle East. Their very full wartime correspondence has been preserved by their younger daughter, Lisa Bell, of Garth Row near Kendal, who was born after the war. In a letter of 11 July 1944, Barbara, who was then volunteering, perhaps with the Girls' Training Corps, described to her husband, Rodney, the arrival of evacuees in Windermere, mostly women and children from Kent:

> The train was very late but they came at last and I could have *wept* when I saw them – they looked so tired and worried. I could just imagine how they felt with tired children and crying babies. We gave them tea and sandwiches and biscuits and then they all saw the doctor and went to the billeting officer. They were such nice people – not slumites at all – lovely little babies and children, all clean and well cared for. ...It was their *patience* which was so pathetic. Never one grumble did I hear, though they were all terrified of their billets, dreading their reception and feeling they were not wanted.

Barbara's father, Sydney Hughes, had already written to the local authorities saying that his wife was not then well enough to take in any evacuees, 'but is willing to have them when she is better' (10 July). So their daughter Barbara found herself in a quandary when she noticed one evacuee mother, who had 'a sweet little girl' about three and who was obviously soon to give birth.

> She sat there for ages, waiting to go to her billet, and everyone was refusing to have her, because of the responsibility, I suppose. She was so tired and the little girl was crying. I felt *terribly* sorry for them. After everyone else had gone and they still hadn't found her a billet, I couldn't *bear* it any longer and went to the billeting officer and asked if they had sent anyone to Green Lodge. When he said No, I said, 'Well, if you'll promise it's only for two nights, I'll have her now'. Knowing I would bring down the wrath of HH [her mother] on my head but counting on [housekeeper] Bobo's support, I arrived at Green Lodge in fear and trembling but feeling also that I simply had to do it if it was the last thing I did. Luckily Bobo was grand and Mum could have been worse. ...Thank heaven I had the guts to do it.

As things turned out, the evacuees, Mrs Tuffee and young Valerie, got on very well with their Cumbrian hosts and were not asked to move on. The two girls played happily together. Mr Tuffee, who worked in a factory, visited in early August – Barbara spoke of him and his wife as 'such decent nice people ... and so brave' (12 August). Mrs Tuffee went to a nursing home to have her baby and on 6 September returned to Green Lodge, now with two daughters. 'Mrs T. looks very well but has had a horrible time in a short-staffed nursing home – no doctor, no night nurse and worst of all no chloroform. Also a most callous matron. It makes me shudder, especially as Mrs T. is pretty tough and had her first baby in an air raid....' On 13 September 1944, over two months after the evacuation, Mr Tuffee arrived in Windermere/Bowness and the following day took his family home. 'It seems safe enough now and they were longing to be home, of course. We feel quite sad and lost without them. They were so nice. I hope they won't regret their return.'** (Doodlebugs were largely disappearing from the scene, though V2 rocket attacks were then just beginning. These, though often lethal, turned out to be much less frequent than the summer's V1 bombings.)

⋆ ⋆ ⋆ ⋆

Billeting was a delicate matter. Women officers, such as those in the WVS, probably had greater empathy for the burden of household work in general

---

** We are very grateful to Lisa Bell for allowing us to see and quote from her mother's letters. She is currently editing her parents' correspondence and may in due course publish it.

– certainly in properties lacking modern conveniences and then, after five years of war, often missing the help of strong arms and backs in the form of servants and labourers, many of whom were by now employed on national service. When billeting was resisted, we can sometimes see the perspectives of both sides. To illustrate, a child might need housing, but perhaps the ageing bachelor on whom he was to be billeted knew nothing about children, did not even make his own meals, and feared the impact of another mouth to feed on his middle-aged housekeeper, who, in a time of a high demand for labour, would have had no trouble finding a position with no child care to fuss about. One WVS helper in Workington told of 'easy billeting, ending with use of empty houses for two large families'. She noted the apple-pie order of certain houses. 'Even if one billeted people on these smug citizens (lower middle-class, or working-class got on a bit), they'd only be desperately unhappy and leave.'[39]

Overall it was thought that 'working-class homes proved the best billets'.[40] Domestic standards were broadly shared, along with compatible views about health, hygiene, and cookery. Propriety and genteel appearances were rather further down the list of working-class priorities – but so too was the capacity of labourers' households to absorb a mother and several children into an already crowded house. Despite frictions and rough edges, evacuees often settled happily into their new quarters. The one close study of this evacuation in Westmorland thought that 'there were many cases where the visitors were absorbed into the homes as friends and joined the family circle'.[41]

In 1944 it was easier to see evacuees as 'guests' since no one expected them to stay in Cumbria for long. Few thought the war would last much longer, with allied troops victorious in France. (In fact, victory took several months longer than most people expected.) In addition, the maturation of wartime emergency provisions was complete: people who ran rest centres were delighted to be able to do what they had trained for, and on the high street facilities like British Restaurants made life easier for both billetors and billetees. The former were relieved of some domestic tasks and the latter had places to go to meet others and do things. Some evacuees volunteered to do local war work. Among many there was a 'general feeling of "not wanting to be a nuisance"'.[42]

Most of the summer's evacuees were returning home, or settled in some other acceptable habitation, within a couple of months. By the end of the year, the story of evacuation was almost over. For five years, on and off, it had been a crucial link between 'distant' Cumbria and other parts of England. Cumbria had been put on the map, nationally speaking, in its own distinctive way; and Cumbrians had encountered city dwellers face to face in unprecedented numbers.

* * * *

As 1944's evacuation crisis was concluding, there was an alteration in everyday life that was universally welcomed – the ending of the blackout and its replacement by the 'dim-out'. This occurred in mid-September. The *Westmorland Gazette* reported on 23 September 1944 (p. 5) that in Kendal 'the improved street lighting had been much appreciated and commented upon, and in corroboration of this fact, the almost complete disappearance of hand torches has to be recorded' – residents of the town could walk home from work, school or shopping without them. 'The topicality of the popular song "When the lights go up again" had been rather spoilt by the fact that the lights are beginning to go up before the war has ended,' commented an editorial writer in the *Workington Star*, 15 September 1944 (p. 2), while noting the satisfaction of the town's citizens. 'A few nights ago people going home from the second houses of the cinema were delighted to see that the street light situated between the air raid shelter exits in Oxford Street was ablaze in almost pre-war splendour.' Strange to think, he reflected, that soon 'brightly illuminated streets will be an entirely new experience for most children'. Improved lighting of streets and houses brought 'an added cheerfulness to the public mood at night time' in Carlisle while its surrounding villages and suburbs were heartened by the warm glow from curtained windows.[43] People in Kendal were happy to be able to return home at night without needing torches.[44]

The 'dim-out' was a gradual thing, a bit like a chandelier slowly being turned up. Municipal engineers planned to fan out lighting slowly from city centres as supplies and labour became available. Modifying or repairing lamps not used for many years would be a challenge to maintenance crews while searching for the 'tremendous amount of glass' which would have to be replaced before many more lamps could be lit would require considerable ingenuity. In both Workington and Kendal some of the lighting delay was attributed to the 'excessive and willful damage done to lamps', and sometimes to their fittings, 'by the youth of the town'.[45] No doubt some of these same youths were now in uniform while their peers and their elders were more than usually drawn to the bright lights of urban centres. In residential areas the relaxation of full blackout (except for skylights) was greeted with glee. In Penrith 'in many homes the hated black-out blinds were discarded in celebration. The usual curtains, if only for the joy of scrapping the old black crepe, were drawn across the windows'.[46]

The 'dim-out' increased hope as well as cheerfulness. Post-war dreams were renewed. A writer in Workington looked forward to seeing the demolition of bomb shelters he had long regarded as a public danger in the blackout and yearned for the day 'when we shall be able to stroll round the town gazing into shop windows blazing with light and full of goods now unobtainable or in short supply'.[47] Many more must have rejoiced in the dramatic reduction in civil defence hours to twelve per month – in Penrith in October, ARP was disbanded altogether[48] – and the abolition of all daytime fireguard duties and the overnight ending of them in some parts of the country, which must have included most of Cumbria, as well as the widely predicted standing down of the Home Guard.[49] Chairman of the Keswick Urban District Council, Mr. C.G. Bone, hoped that this easing of restrictions was finally a 'sign of the beginning of the end' and that it might be his 'privilege to switch on all the lights at full power before the end of his year'.[50]

In early November Westmorland's WVS, that unpaid workhorse for social welfare, took time to review the 'magnificent work' in its 89 branches of activity, involving a seemingly tireless membership of 2,875. While the WVS conference lauded their efforts, many members thought it was time to end their work and devote attention to home and family. Their organiser, the Hon. Mrs Hornyold-Strickland, was like-minded and told her colleagues that she had been assured by Lady Reading that after the war and the need for their emergency services was at an end 'the WVS would fade out, and not deprive any woman of a paid job'.[51] As the year wore down farewells were made to more evacuees returning home such as the party seen off for Tyneside in early December at Oxenholme station by the mayor and mayoress of Kendal, Councillor and Mrs. W. F. Pennington. Nearly all the children, 79 in all, had a doll or other toy to take with them. They were accompanied by members of the WVS and joined in Carlisle with other children billeted in Cumberland; and then, well fed, were sent on to their final destination of South Shields.[52] And, yes, the Home Guard did stand down, honoured by special ceremonials in Kendal and no doubt all parts of Cumbria.[53] For many people it was now time to look forward – to the challenges of the post-war world.

Notes and References

1 Whitehaven Archives, SUDC/1/3/254.
2 J.F. Dow and M.A. Brown, *A Survey of Evacuation in Westmorland* (Kendal, 1943), 10.
3 Westmorland *Gazette*, 30 January 1943, 8.
4 *Penrith Observer*, 2 May 1944, 3.
5 *Westmorland Gazette*, 17 July 1943, 4.
6 J. Welshman, *Churchill's Children: The Evacuee Experience in Wartime Britain* (Oxford, 2010), 280.
7 *Carlisle Journal*, 21 July 1944, 1.
8 Kendal Archives, WC/C9, Bag 1, file 1/1. Almost 900 mothers and children were embraced by the plans.
9 Whitehaven Archives, SUDC/1/3/158.
10 *Penrith Observer*, 18 July 1944, 2.
11 *Carlisle Journal*, 11 July 1944, 1.
12 *West Cumberland Times*, 8 July 1944, 8.
13 At a special meeting of the Ennerdale Rural District Council, its billeting officer was authorised to use his compulsory powers. These powers had long existed but it seems that the RDC thought that an open endorsement of them might induce greater public cooperation. (*West Cumberland Times*, 12 July 1944, 2.)

14 *Cumberland and Westmorland Herald,* 15 July 1944, 1. Initially Penrith received 274 official evacuees plus many evacuated privately (*Cumberland and Westmorland Herald,* 29 July 1944, 1); Workington received 346, the north of Westmorland at least 150, and Carlisle and district between 300 and 400 (*Workington Star,* 28 July 1944, 6; *Penrith Observer,* 25 July 1944, 3; and *Carlisle Journal,* 1 August 1944, 1).
15 *West Cumberland Times,* 19 July 1944, 2.
16 A. Allport, *Browned Off and Bloody-Minded: The British Soldier Goes to War, 1939-1945* (New Haven and London, 2015), 32.
17 *West Cumberland Times,* 19 July 1944, 1 and 2.
18 J.F. Dow and M. A. Brown, *Evacuation to Westmorland from Home and Europe 1939-1945* (Kendal, 1946), 35 and 36.
19 Boud, *Great Exodus,* 149.
20 Ibid., 35.
21 *West Cumberland Times,* 22 July 1944, 5.
22 Whitehaven Archives, SUDC/6/1/2Z/4, Government Evacuation Scheme Minute Book. Unless otherwise indicated, the evidence in this and the following four paragraphs is drawn from this document.
23 RVS Archive (Devizes, Wiltshire), Cockermouth Urban District NR, July 1944.
24 Kendal Archives, Ev/2/1a.
25 Kendal Archives, WDSO 92/1-2, report of 1 November 1944.
26 *Workington Star,* 7 July 1944, 6.
27 *North-Western Evening Mail,* 13 July 1944, 5; *Barrow News,* 22 July 1944, 4; *Westmorland Gazette,* 26 August 1944, 5.
28 *Barrow Guardian,* 12 August, 1944, 2.
29 *North-Western Evening Mail,* 15 July 1944, 1.
30 *Barrow News,* 15 July 1944, 4.
31 Ibid.
32 *Barrow Guardian,* 22 July 1944, 4.
33 *Barrow Guardian,* 22 July 1944, 4; 5 August 1944, 5; and 2 September 1944, 5.
34 Kendal Archives, WDSO 92/1-2, WVS Annual Report, 1 November 1944, p. 4; *Whitehaven News,* 5 October 1944, 6.
35 *North-Western Evening Mail,* 8 August 1944, 2 and 4; 10 August, 1; 11 August, 2; *Barrow Guardian,* 26 August 1944, 2.
36 *Cumberland News,* 15 July 1944, 6.
37 *West Cumberland Times,* 19 July 1944, 2.
38 *Penrith Observer,* 25 July 1944, 2.
39 MOA, DR no. 2845, July-August 1944; and FR 2189, p. 16, Report on Flying Bomb Evacuation, December 1944.
40 Dow and Brown, *Evacuation* (1946), 33.
41 Ibid., 37.
42 Ibid., 35; Kendal Archives, WDSO 92/1-2, 'Interim Report on Evacuation by Miss Woodall, Social Worker', 21 July 1944.
43 *Carlisle Journal,* 22 September 1944, 1.
44 *Westmorland Gazette,* 23 September 1944, 5.
45 *Westmorland Gazette,* 16 September 1944, 5; *Workington Star,* 15 September 1944, 2.
46 *Penrith Observer, 19* September 1944, 3. Vehicle-lighting restrictions were still significant. Headlights on cars were still restricted but side-lights could be used if covered with one thickness of tissue paper and bicycle lamps could be used free of restriction. (*Westmorland Gazette,* 16 September 1944, 5.)
47 *Workington Star,* 15 September 1944, 2.
48 *Cumberland and Westmorland Herald,* 14 October 1944, 5.

49 *Carlisle Journal*, 8 September 1944, 5.
50 *Penrith Observer*, 19 September 1944, 3.
51 *Westmorland Gazette*, 4 November 1944, 5. In point of fact Mrs Hornyold-Strickland and Lady Reading held rather different views. The Home Office extended the WVS official role for two years after the end of hostilities in Europe though many members did resign. The private WVS charity (WRVS from the 1960s) long outlived both of these strong women as an organisation focused on the elderly and known in particular for delivery of 'meals on wheels'. In the spring of 2013 the WRVS was rebranded as the Royal Voluntary Service (RVS), open to members of both genders and with a mandate to serve the isolated elderly.
52 *Westmorland Gazette*, 2 December 1944, 5. Many were pleased to see the mayoress, Mrs. Pennington, take part in this small ceremonial leave-taking since her strenuous work as deputy WVS organiser for Westmorland had led to what might now be called a nervous breakdown, which left her unable to assist in the July evacuations. (Kendal Archives, WVS, Westmorland Monthly Narrative Report, June and July 1944.)
53 *Westmorland Gazette*, 2 December 1944, 5; *Whitehaven News*, 7 December 1944, 3.

Chapter 8
Personal Struggles

> 'Life became uncertain, depressing, harrowing [in later 1944]. We carried on as usual, but the war weighed more and more heavily on our minds.' (A Member of the Canadian Women's Army Corps in England.)[1]

War was bound to bring to some people desperation and misery. Cumbrians, while relatively safe at home,* did die in combat, mostly on or near battlefields abroad, on land, at sea, or in the air. Other servicemen, many of them only temporarily based in the county, died from accidents, which could happen anywhere, such as at training airfields. Wartime flying accidents were commonplace, resulting in large numbers of deaths of men in uniform. Some 3,000 men were killed while participating in the British Commonwealth Air Training Plan; the weather at these bases in Canada was often as foul as it could be in Cumbria.[2]

During the first half of the war deaths of local men in combat were numerically modest. Thereafter things changed, and many more sons and young husbands and fathers in the forces were being killed. From around mid-1943 newspapers in Cumberland and Westmorland regularly reported the growing numbers of casualties of local servicemen. Often these reports were accompanied by the man's photograph and a few biographical details. During the six months between early June and the end of November 1944, around 100 of these casualties were reported with their photos in the

---

* An official compilation of civilian war deaths (TNA, HO 198/245) lists a total of thirty-one deaths in Cumberland between 1940 and 1944 – the most lethal incident was at Maryport on 21 July 1940 when seven or eight were killed – and fifteen in Westmorland, all but two of these in 1941-42. So around twice as many people were killed in Barrow during six nights of bombing in April/May 1941 as were killed in Cumberland and Westmorland during all of the war.

Exceptionally, eleven people were killed on the night of 16-17 April 1941 at Cooper House, Selside, six miles north of Kendal, when it suffered a direct hit by a German bomb that was probably jettisoned by the plane's crew after attacking Barrow-in-Furness. (See www.bbc.uk/history/ww2peopleswar/stories/16/a6317516.shtml). The fact that such stray bombs occasionally *did* fall – and stories about the consequences would have spread with ease – must have fuelled lots of regional anxiety. Details of the Selside tragedy were allowed to be published, and most of the victims were identified, though the place was not. To allay anxiety, the local report observed that 'the chance of a direct hit must have been one in a million'. (*Westmorland Gazette*, 19 April 1941, 5.)

Westmorland Gazette, and more were reported without a photo. During the same half-year the *Cumberland and Westmorland Herald* gave details of some 85 deaths of local men in uniform. By then it was rare for an issue of a weekly paper not to carry news of at least one local serviceman's death. The families of these men were often well known in their communities, and the grim news would have circulated widely.

Bereavement, then, must have been felt in thousands of Cumbrian households, but it was rarely documented. Usually you can only imagine what a bereaved person's feelings must have been, such as the young woman in Carlisle who, early in the war – and the press reported her loss – cancelled her wedding when it was learned that her fiancé's submarine was reported missing and presumed lost. (Such tragedies were not yet commonplace.)[3] People who lost loved ones may not have grieved in silence, but they mostly grieved outside public notice. On 27 July 1943 (*NLW*, p. 245) Nella Last wrote of the shock felt on hearing of the death of one of her fellow WVS members in Barrow, who was only 50 years old. 'She never really recovered from the loss of her idolised RAF son. She never said much, never apparently "grieved", but she grew curiously "old". For the weeks she held out hope she looked feverishly bright and confident and then a light seemed to go out in her eyes.' The distress of the bereaved was often constrained by reticence.[4] It is not hard, though, sometimes to read between the lines. 'A neighbour has lost her son, a Lieutenant in the Army, and only 22', wrote Mrs. Last on 24 December 1941 (*NLW*, p. 176). 'This is their second son to go and their third and last boy is an air pilot. He went to school with Cliff [Nella's younger son, in the army]. It looked so sad to see the military escort standing there, mostly lads themselves, and I think of all the boys going – going with all their bright hope and ambitions unfulfilled.'

A similar feeling came upon her on 19 August 1943 (*DONL*, p. 205). 'Two women have sat side by side for four years at [the WVS] Centre sewing at bandages. One has lost two sons at sea – and now learns that her airman son has to be "presumed dead." The other one's three sons work in the [Ship] Yard – have good jobs. The daughter of 28 is "reserved" as she is considered necessary as a secretary to a boss in the Yard. The other woman's daughter had to join the WAAF.' Wartime contingencies meant misery for some women, relief for others. Pure chance played a big role. Nella herself was deeply upset on 7 May 1941 (*NLW*, p. 137) when she was told of a young married woman she knew who had just been killed in the blitz on Barrow, the unlucky victim of a direct hit on Hawcoat Road. 'Kathie Thompson, the gayest, sweetest and most loveable of all the nice young things that came and went when the boys [her sons] were home, the loveliest little bride I think I've ever seen, only three months ago, and only 21 now.' Nella commiserated with Kathie's grim-looking brother, who had just disclosed the bad news. Then there were losses which, though less severe, were hardly minor. She spoke on 4 May 1941 (*NLW*, p. 132) of new neighbours: 'They were bombed out at Harrow and then again at Liverpool and the little boy has such a stutter and his mother said it came on after the raid in London.'

Thus, arbitrarily, did war affect families in different ways. Mrs Last once reflected on this (19 August 1943, *NLW*, p. 249). 'My heart aches. Even in that small circle [of WVS workers], the bravery and courage, the "going on" when only sons have been killed, when letters don't come, when their boys are taught to fight like savages if they are Commandos, when they are trained and trained and *trained*, for bodies to be made to endure, to go kill other women's lads, to wipe all the light from other mothers' faces.' There was no way that sacrifices were or could be shared equally. War was bound to heighten a sense of life's capriciousness. With its high stakes, war tended to make the unfairness of life seem doubly unfair. At a dance in Windermere in August 1941 a young woman spent time with a 25-year-old engineer from Bradford, who was on holiday. His elder brother had been killed in the war. He felt 'the family had lost its only intelligent member and it wasn't very cheerful for him to hear all his mother's complaints all day'. This diarist thought the man 'Appeared very much affected by his brother's death and a run of bad luck; was very conscious of the war-muddle and seemed dazed by it. Said he didn't know who suffered more, the men a long way from home or the women left alone.'[5]

Only infrequently was personal grief portrayed in detail. One of these occasions happened in Barrow on Boxing Day 1941 (*DONL*, p. 129), when Nella Last, working at the WVS canteen, noticed 'One lad [who] seemed so dreadfully ill and dazed and his two pals had a "protecting" air towards him. One of them came back to the counter for more tea and told me that he had just got in from Hull where he had been to the "funeral of his family." To my look of surprise he whispered hurriedly "his father and mother and brother and sister were all killed when a bomb fell at 11.30 in the morning on their house, and it was his father's first week on nights for over a year and he was asleep!'[6] Almost two months later, on 20 February 1942 (MOA), she spoke with this soldier at the canteen – he was one of the regulars. 'He is such a nice lad and I rather worry about him – he seems to be going downhill.... For a time he looked the same but now there is a "big-eyed" look about his thinner face and he has really maddening fidgety tricks like tapping with his spoon in his cup all the time or lightly kicking the counter front. He never sits down and drinks cup after cup of tea – one girl asked him if he has a hollow leg!' She suggested he take a nerve tonic. 'He said "I'm not going near that Medical Officer again if I can help it. I'm not ill you know, and I know it as well, so why should he say what he did?"' The doctor had accused him of 'lead swinging' – that is, shirking, or malingering.

Many residents of Cumbria, even if they rarely encountered bombing alerts, had friends and loved ones elsewhere who were not so fortunate. These ties gave them cause for worry. Manchester, Liverpool and Glasgow (all heavily blitzed) were not that far away, and evacuees from Tyneside were kept abreast of the perils there. On 16 November 1940 Nella Last (*NLW*, pp. 80-81) remarked that

> Barrow is plunged in gloom over the terrible Coventry bombings [which killed some 570 people] for it's a town where many Barrow people have moved to in times of bad trade. I have many friends and old neighbours there and also a cousin and his wife and no word as to their safety or otherwise has yet come through. At Spark Bridge there was the same feeling of unease for several people had sons and daughters who had gone to work in Coventry. One woman was very upset for she had refused to let her daughter come home to have her second baby. There was some trouble when she came to have her first baby and the mother said she was tired of being "put on" and daughter had plenty of money to pay for attention. The poor woman was distraught as she remembered her daughter's words about the flat she occupied "in the shadow of the Cathedral" [which now lay in ruins].

There was joy in Spark Bridge a few days later when it was learned that the pregnant daughter was safe and planning to return north for her delivery.

* * * *

One of the first detailed accounts of an individual's wartime ordeals appeared in the *Westmorland Gazette*, 16 December 1939, p. 7. It gave a vivid sense of war's potential for chaos and personal suffering, though little of this had by then affected Britons. Nineteen-year-old Priscilla Pritchard from Ulverston had been employed since July 1938 as a companion to a British lady in Warsaw. 'The day before war was declared officially,' said Miss Pritchard, 'the Germans dropped chocolates from aeroplanes which were poisoned, and I myself saw children die who picked them up and ate them. I wanted to get back home, and so on 5 September I booked a ticket and got a train at Warsaw for Riga and my passports and everything were in good order. The train went 50 miles in three days. We had no food or water. Many passengers ate raw potatoes, grass or whatever could be found in the fields.' On the third day the train was destroyed by German bombing, leaving the passengers to their own devices. For several days she sought help in nearby towns, unsuccessfully, and had several close calls in and around Brizsce. Once she got a lift from two Polish officers. As they reached Lwow "'the Germans entered, so we ran right into them. When they saw the officers' uniforms they started to shoot, but we turned the car and started to go back again. I sat on the floor of the car, which was being riddled with bullets through the windscreen and the driver had also to sit on the floor and steer as well as he could from there, but we got away from the Germans.'" Subsequent encounters at gun-point with Russian soldiers prolonged her perils.

In due course, after days on the run, she escaped on a cattle train, got first to Vilna and later to Kovno, where the British consul arranged for her to travel via Riga, Stockholm, Oslo and Bergen to England and her grandmother's cottage at Jenny Hill, Ulverston, where she was then living. This lengthy narrative, occupying a full column of the newspaper, was, in part, testimony to the novelty of such brushes with death in late 1939 and the importance then attached to encounters with violence which, a few months later, would be seen as much less remarkable, even normal.

Some of the distress of wartime was linked to efforts to keep families together in the face of pressures splitting them apart. Families craved solidarity and security, and often were failing to find them. Loved ones were separated from one another. Intimate relations became harder to sustain. Vulnerable individuals were left to fend for themselves. Illnesses took a toll – perhaps a husband who had been invalided out of the forces had to spend time in hospital.[7] Children sent from home were sometimes deprived of adequate care and nurturing. Wartime circumstances drove husbands and wives in different directions. Personal plans were routinely in jeopardy and readily sabotaged by unwelcome events. The sort of sheer bad luck that had always loomed over life (notably over the lives of labouring people) became even more pronounced in the face of the vagaries of a national struggle for survival.

Mothers coping on their own were particularly at risk. Nella Last met one, a regular soldier's wife, in Barrow on 21 March 1941 (MOA). Her shoes were broken and she was in search of hand-me-down clothes for herself and six children, all under eight, with a seventh on the way. 'She seemed surprised there was no "charity or help" in Barrow for people like her [though she had just discovered the WVS] and said she had had her babies "all over the place" – one in India – and she had *always* had somewhere to go for *everything* and a place to "go to get it over in".' Nella wondered about her background but did not press for details. 'I did not want her to think I wanted to pry into her private affairs for the price of a bundle of cast-off clothes but when I saw her and her two children it struck me afresh how wrong things were all round.' Then there was the soldier's widow with four children whose trials were mentioned at a meeting on 18 February 1943 of Whitehaven's Emergency Committee for Social Services. She had been mistakenly classed as a single woman, which meant that her children were unable to get free milk and vitamins.[8] Such hard luck must have occurred again and again. Many women were vulnerable. Things could easily go wrong in their lives, even more so in wartime.

* * * *

Evacuation was one cause of anxiety, though only occasionally can we read the words of a worried mother. One such instance is a letter written in early March 1941 to the authorities in Penrith by a Mrs. Cruikshanks at 6 Ravensworth Terrace in South Shields. 'Will you please help us', she wrote, 'by trying to find us a billet in Penrith or near? I have three children evacuated there. They have been there seventeen months and I have four children at home. My husband is away for the duration of the war. My nerves are bad with the air raids. I would like to be near where the other three children are, or somewhere in Cumberland.... Please try and help us by finding me a billet for me and my four children.'[9] (Since Penrith was already packed with evacuees, this would have been very hard to do.) Much later in the war an evacuated mother from West Ham, billeted in Cockermouth, was appealing to the town clerk (20 November 1944) for approval for her mother, a pensioner, to stay with her. 'My husband has had to bring my mother down to me because her nerves are so bad and without that I've had so much trouble with my baby since I've been here. He's been under Doctor Goven all the time.'[10] The loss of the security of 'home' and family could be exacerbated in various ways.

In March and April 1943 the Cockermouth Rural District Council investigated the living conditions of many of its evacuees; all were named and their circumstances remarked on.[11] Here are a few cases. A woman from Newcastle with two children was billeted in Braithwaite and had 'Domestic difficulties with husband'. A Mrs. Wood from Portsmouth with one child, also billeted in Braithwaite, had a husband in the navy: 'Home bombed and given up. Furniture stored at 5s per week.' Other evacuated women whose homes had survived still paid the rent for them. 'Husband in Asylum. Public Assistance Case': these were the details given for a woman with three children from South Shields who was billeted in Gilcrux. As for a Mrs Smith from Coventry who was then billeted in Great Clifton (she was originally from there), it was reported that her husband was killed in an air raid, 'and home and all furniture destroyed. Only income now is 17s 6d per week widow's pension and 9s per week disability allowance owing to personal injury in air raid.' She was billeted with her mother, 'an aged widow', and 'their financial position is not very good'.

A letter of 13 March 1944 from Florence Dounard in Brighton, searching for a billet in Cockermouth, was rather desperate in tone. She had five children, fifteen to one-and-a-half years of age. Her thirteen-year-old daughter 'has not attended school for over six months with air raid nerves – she is still under the doctor. Also another girl age eleven has had pneumonia and pleurisy twice through sleeping in the Morrison shelter and I am under the doctor for nervous disability. He has advised me to get off the coast as soon as possible.' Mrs. Dounard had more bad news to convey.

> I have had my father killed in this last raid and just about feel at the end of my tether. My husband is serving in the Royal Navy – has been in for four years. Also my brother in the Services. I know it is a big worry for you Sir to help everybody that applys to you but if only you could I don't mind were it is as long as I can get my children and myself out of here and see them smile and look happy again. I do hope you are not offended with me for writing. Please let the urgency of my appeal be the excuse for my writing you. If you can help me you will have my sincere gratitude always, also my husband's, because he always wanted me to get out of here after our first bombed out.[12]

Residents accommodating or pressed to accommodate evacuees might have their own issues to ponder. On 17 July 1944, a few days after an evacuated woman and her two young children had been billeted on a woman living at Rosemary Cottage in Keswick, she lodged a protest. The rooms the billetees were occupying, she said, 'were set aside for my parents-in-law, now living at 24 Fell View, Cockermouth', for they had been given notice to leave by the end of August. 'They have no private means, being entirely dependent on my husband for maintenance. Their case is extremely hard, as they lost all they possessed in Prague; we had to save them from France after the fall. And the flat we had for them in London they were bombed out of, and have since been living at the address given. As a result of this their state of health is very poor, my father-in-law having had a slight stroke within the last fortnight.' She, too, was struggling with ill health and had been advised to undergo surgery. 'I am quite desperate as I have to take them into my house and also now without room for them.'[13] While some pleas of illness as grounds for not taking in evacuees were concocted, hers has the ring of truth.

Billeting evacuees was bound to be more of a challenge for some households than others. 'Could you please let my evacuee, Mrs. Crumpton, and her three children have a condemned house', wrote Wilhelmina Thompson, 24 Grasmoor Avenue, Cockermouth on 29 September 1944, 'as I am expecting my husband home from abroad shortly. Mrs. Crumpton and her children are occupying my husband's bedroom, and I will need it. As Mrs. Crumpton is an expecting mother, I shouldn't like to ask her to go, without having any place to go to.' Mrs. Crumpton wrote independently, asking for a condemned house, 'otherwise I shall have to go home' (where, presumably, she felt she would be at risk).[14] Since Mrs. Thompson appears to have had five children of her own, her domestic responsibilities were indeed heavy. Another letter, undated, from a Mr. Stephenson at 40 Windmill Lane, Cockermouth, probably from around mid-summer 1944, testifies to some of the strains of wartime living arrangements. He was asking that new billets be found for the mother and two children billeted in his house. 'My wife', he said,

> is in a very bad state of nerve trouble and is now under the doctor, and he has ordered her to have complete rest, but this she can't get as she has our own three children to attend to and I am not always there for to give any help as I get up at half past three in the morning for to start off for work. Above all this one of these young children cries out at night which is putting a big strain on me through loss of sleep as I am a coal miner. My job is very essential these days and I am beginning to lose work through the want of sleep, and if you need any further information as to my wife's health I wish you to communicate with Dr. Larson.

There must have been other families like the Stephensons, who were barely hanging on and under constant strain, but whose plight was never documented. And then there were people – usually women – who lacked family support. We can never know how common such insecurities were. Moreover, hardships were bound to vary in severity, perhaps over time, perhaps depending on whether or not outside assistance was available. In some cases the WVS played a helpful role. In the late summer of 1941 Kendal's WVS 'had a most grateful visit from the Kendal woman whom we had helped with advice and much correspondence to get an allowance from the military authorities for her illegitimate child by a prisoner of war'. In November 1942 they were helping 'a poor evacuee mother with correspondence about her daughter and grandchildren who are trying to get back from Belgium via Lisbon'; they had also advised a German woman married to a British seaman 'both as to behaviour and billets (she is frequently drunk and then threatens to commit suicide and becomes anti-British!)'. The following month they were dealing with 'a special request from York WVS for billets for the Italian wife of a Middle East soldier who wants to bring her children to the Lake District, having been originally bombed out of London'.[15]

WVS reports mentioned several instances of aid rendered. 'At the moment we are dealing with a pathetic case. A mother and her small children just arrived in this country from Bombay with no possessions, and hardly any clothes. We are doing all we can for them.' The woman was expecting and had 'not heard from her husband for ages' (Westmorland, NR March 1943). In late 1942 a 'worried soldier' stationed in the North of Scotland 'asked us to visit his wife and children living in Kendal. Mrs. Pennington [deputy organiser of the WVS] found they were in a very poor condition, having been bombed out of their home, and the wife had not known where to turn. We were able to put her in touch with the proper Authorities'. Several soldiers' wives were helped 'with their various problems' and Mrs. Pennington 'was called upon to visit a farmer near Kendal whose wife was very ill and had been rushed to hospital. An arrangement was made whereby the children could be looked after in the mother's absence.' (Kendal WVS, NR December 1942.)

The following summer it was said that 'Various problems of a domestic nature with servicemen's wives continue to crop up, and we do our best to help and advise' ((Kendal WVS, NR August 1943; also September 1943). Wartime separations were bound to be seriously unsettling for some women on their own, many of them young and unfamiliar with the ways of the world. Kendal's WVS report for January 1944 touched on this issue: 'Problems are arising particularly with regard to young married women with husbands serving abroad, and work is being done along with the Probation Officer and other people interested in social welfare'. A specific case was cited two months later: a serviceman returned from overseas 'to find his son so out of hand that he asked Mrs. Pennington to support his request for a compassionate posting nearer to home' (Kendal WVS, NR March 1944).

⋆ ⋆ ⋆ ⋆

Spouses and lovers torn apart was a prominent reality of wartime. On 22 January 1941 (*NLW*, pp. 96-97) Nella Last received at her home a mother and daughter, the latter of whom had

> married her soldier sweetheart and ... has spent her brief married life living near wherever he was stationed – and now he has gone "overseas" for two years! She is a tall, handsome "brooding" kind of girl – only 22 – and today her beauty was clouded and dimmed.... My heart ached so for her, and for all the other unhappy girls like her.... As I showed them to door she turned to me in hall and said "Isn't life odd, Mrs. Last. Bob and I adored each other and longed passionately for a child, and no signs, and we were married nearly a year. If I'd been a soldier's 'pick-up' I'd have had a baby in my arms by now." Mrs. Holt, her mother, flushed scarlet and said "Laura, you shock me when you talk like that," and I felt sorrier still for the girl. If she cannot talk and say whatever she likes to her own mother and find understanding and sympathy, where can she do so?

A sadder case appears in Mrs. Last's diary for 3 April 1941 (*NLW*, p. 114). The 'adored daughter' of one of her fellow WVS members had recently had a baby, nearly eight months after the father had gone east. They had not been able to marry, and now the young mother was in bad shape, ashamed for the '"disgrace" she had brought on her mother. She has no interest in her baby or its father's frantic loving letters that the girl's mother says would "melt stone".'

War threw up evidence of everyday human misery that might otherwise not have been documented. The assiduousness of wartime reporting, public 'intrusiveness' into private lives at a time of national emergency,[16] and better-than-usual record-keeping tended to draw marginal and many working-class people into the mainstream of social observation. As more people were shaken out of their sheltered circumstances, poor living conditions and domestic abuse were more likely to be witnessed close-up than they had been before the war.[17] The wartime press was probably more inclined to write about domestic distress, such as the 'almost unbelievable poverty' of some of the Tyneside households that in 1939 sent evacuees to Carlisle, or the evacuated woman with five children who was struggling to survive on 30s a week 'and one bag of coal', her 'husband ill in the home town and unable to contribute'.[18] Bad housing was more frequently exposed, for housing had become a major matter of public concern. Public health and nutrition – bleak in some places – came to be more widely discussed as inner-city children were evacuated and put in the care of better-off strangers. Other basic necessities, such as durable footwear, had to be dealt with by policy-makers, as bare feet and flimsy shoes were ill-suited to muddy country lanes, and as Wellington boots came to be regarded, reasonably enough, as essential to normal life in most rural areas (but rubber was scarce).

The increase of letter-writing in wartime, as more families were split up and friends scattered about, meant that life's problems were more likely to get written about, for often people could no longer speak face-to-face about the incidents of everyday life. One of these assiduous letter-writers was a housewife in her early thirties, Evelyn Harwood, whose husband, Ernest Harwood (b. 1910), had been in the forces since October 1940. They remained apart for most of the war, and for her these were years of loneliness and worry. On 23 March 1944, from her home at 10 Mint Street in Kendal, she wrote him a letter that testified to the sort of gloom that must have sometimes seeped into many house-bound women's minds:

> Here, it is miserably dull. Jeanne [their daughter] has a nasty cold. Was crying with earache last night, but is not away from school. The child next door has scalded her arm. A child of 18 months was being nursed upon the mother's knee before the fire when the woman reached up to take a cigarette from the shelf. In doing so she dropped the child onto the fire. Now the child, in Manchester Hospital, will be blind for life. Kendal is a sorry place at the

> moment. A soldier of 21 or so accidentally shot himself whilst out rabbiting. A fellow you probably know, Freeman of Windermere Road, worked at Solicitors (Thompsons, I believe, but not sure), bailed out of his plane into the sea and was drowned. Now for scandal. A woman had been going around with a married man. Heard her husband was coming home on leave, so took a hundred or so aspirins and now lies in Kendal County [Hospital]. What a world.[19]

This was not the first marital tragedy she had written about. The previous year, on 23 July 1943, she mentioned a man in the RAF, 'just landed home on leave', who 'found his wife was dead. Had illegal operation performed right before he was expected home. Died right away. Mrs Stavert (husband prisoner of war in Germany) is charged with murder, not manslaughter. Both parties [aged 29] have two children. Now what makes it even worse to my mind is that, according to husband, she was an excellent wife and mother before in contact with a certain party frequenting the Town Hall dancing. It makes me feel very sad'.** Months later, on 30 October 1944, she was able to entertain Ernest with another, though less distressing (reputed) scandal. 'I heard a very funny story, supposedly true. A woman having acquired a child during her husband's absence abroad, bribed her next door neighbour to take the child until the husband departed again. Unfortunately the neighbour "spilled the beans" so the wife said "Well, I too will spill the beans and shew you who is the father", thereupon calling upon the neighbour's husband. Priceless!' Such tales, whether true or false or highly embroidered, seem to have enjoyed a wide currency during the second half of the war.

Cases of marital infidelity sometimes did draw in the WVS, which had an interest in overseeing the welfare (broadly defined) of members of the forces – indeed their well-being became one of the WVS's main missions. The WVS report from Westmorland in March 1943 indicated that its second-in-command had dealt with 'several cases of illegitimate children born to wives whose husbands are prisoners of war or in the Far East' and in some instances

** Gladys Stavert claimed that her desire was 'to help her neighbour' (*Westmorland Gazette*, 24 July 1943, 5), who was in distress and begging for help. At her trial in Carlisle in October, where she pleaded guilty, the chief constable of Kendal spoke in favour of a mitigated penalty. Up to the time when her husband was taken prisoner at Dunkirk, he said, 'she had been a hard-working and contented woman, willing to give her neighbours a helping hand. Since the capture of her husband she had frequented public houses, neglected her children, and associated with men principally from the Forces. Since the commencement of this case, however, her conduct had greatly improved, and there was no doubt, in his mind, that she was repentant, and had realised her foolishness.' She was sentenced to three years in prison. (*Westmorland Gazette*, 16 October 1943, 5.)

'she has got the grandparents to take charge of the legitimate children and had their allowances transferred by the Military Authorities.' Some cases were trying – and time-consuming. In December 1941 (WVS NR) Westmorland's county organiser told of 'a difficult case' involving 'the wife of a military transport policeman, who followed her husband up here – she herself being pregnant and already having one child – as she knew he was fooling with another woman. She came to us for help, is quite ill and threatened suicide'. At this point the deputy organiser and mayoress, Mrs. Pennington, who was also in charge of billeting in Kendal, 'offered to tackle the "other woman", whom she caught actually with the man; put the fear of the Lord into the girl, whom she knew was happily married but the husband away; and *that* girl is not playing the fool any more. But the soldier was still being beastly to his wife so we got hold of his Commanding Officer, who came to see us and then sent for the man, whom Mrs. P. lectured again and extracted a promise that he would see his wife and come to terms and stop drinking, which he promised his officer he'd do.' (Such interventions in private lives were not uncommon, especially when some sort of public issue was involved, such as finding housing.) 'If he behaves', she concluded, 'we'll get the wife properly billeted here and then arrange for her confinement. But if the man won't be decent we shall advise her to go back to her parents. He has already given her scabies, and we hope nothing worse!'

Prolonged separation – not just for months but frequently years – was bound to put acute strain on many marriages. These stresses were thoughtfully discussed at the time in a short book by Kenneth Howard, *Sex Problems of the Returning Soldier* (Manchester 1945). While young marriages could usually survive a few months of being apart, two years or more of separation were a challenge to many couples. The strains endured by Kendal's Mrs Harwood, with two children and usually an evacuee or lodger as well and separated from her husband for most of the war, are manifest in her voluminous correspondence. These strains must have been commonplace. On 2 October 1941 a single woman in her early twenties, living near Ulverston, met a young lieutenant in the Signals whom she knew, and the subject of separation came up. 'This young friend said "It's so easy to forget that one is married [as he was] because home seems at the other end of the world". He makes rash promises to his wife about not seeing other women but of course he just does see them. Women stay so horribly faithful and expect too much from their men. They forget how deathly boring a serviceman's life is.'[20]

Perhaps after three more years of war this observer's confidence in women's fidelity would have waned. A woman who spent most of the war in Carlisle and rarely saw her naval husband recalled that 'there were lovers all over the place. In fact everybody was taking lovers [not, one presumes, to be taken literally]. Me and all the women round me were taking lovers. Polish officers were in great demand. It was just happening, and that was the beginning of the end of my first marriage'.[21]

Ruptured relationships, some a product (at least in part) of wartime strains, were occasionally reported in the press. One such case was heard in the late summer of 1943 at the Carlisle Police Court. The husband, Thomas Thompson, a 31-year-old army sergeant from Patterdale, had been serving for over two years in the 8th Army, mainly in the Middle East. 'During his absence Mrs. [Lily] Thompson [aged 29] gave birth to another child. Mrs. Thompson wrote a confession to her husband. He refused to forgive her and came home on compassionate leave.' He had the children taken from her and placed with his married sister in Carlisle; his wife appealed to have them back, partly on the grounds that they were to be raised as Roman Catholics, not Protestants. Court testimony indicated that 'she had worked at the Post Office and for the Ribble Bus Company. She admitted that she went to dances and had drinks with girl friends. Asked if she "consorted" with soldiers and airmen, she replied that she had had acquaintance with only two men.' While she was at work, her two daughters, aged six and three, stayed at home with Mrs. Thompson's mother, father and married sister, and two social workers testified that this household was properly maintained and the children 'well brought up and tidy'. Sergeant Thompson, however, raised what seems to have been a key objection: that she had adequate financial means and did not need to go out to work. 'The Government had decided', according to his counsel, 'that the best national service for a soldier's wife with young children was in her home.' The court unanimously ruled in favour of the husband, granting him custody of the children, 'the mother to have access to them once a month'. Here, then, was a case in which a straying wife was accorded little sympathy, and found her children taken from her.[22]

Other cases exposed the sorts of strains that could affect younger couples – strains that might have existed anyway, but were exacerbated by the circumstances of wartime. On 23 March 1943 (*NLW*, 236-37) Nella Last had a talk in Barrow with a middle-aged woman who was in great distress. Her 23-year old daughter, a partying WREN whose husband had been a POW since Dunkirk, was pregnant. The young woman's 'story is that she "knows nothing about it – it must have happened when she was 'tight' some time – all the parties she goes to there is "everything to drink".' Her naval friends had easy access to alcohol. Her father was calling her a slut, her mother didn't know what to believe, or what if anything should be told to her daughter's husband. Nella advised her to be supportive, not punitive. Then there was Ivor Sandford Reeves, a man serving in the Royal Electrical and Mechanical Engineers, who had married in Patterdale in 1936, lived in Penrith before the war, fathered two children, and gone into the forces in 1940. Four years later he was filing for divorce. 'After he went into the Forces his wife struck up a friendship with a man working in the district. In July, 1941, he spent a leave with his wife's people. The man called every other day' – and sometime later, presumably while he was away on service, she went to live with him. Reeves was granted a divorce,[23] as were many servicemen in the mid-1940s.

Each breakdown must have had its own distinctive features. The previous year, 1943, John Harrison, a private in the Border Regiment, had cut off his wife's maintenance allowance, to which she was entitled, and for this she brought him to court in Penrith. They had married in 1938. His defence was that 'he had begun divorce proceedings against his wife and stopped his wife's allowance on military legal advice. He alleged that his wife had been unfaithful and that he found a man in her bedroom.' When doubt was cast on his evidence to justify a divorce, he replied that 'I have the evidence of my own eyes and my brother's evidence that she has been in public-houses with soldiers. I had also her sister's evidence but she withdrew it.' His charge of adultery was judged to be inadequately substantiated and he was ordered to pay his wife £1 per week, which supplemented the £2 she was earning on her own.[24] A year later Mrs Freda Cloke (aged 21) of Shap appealed for a maintenance order for herself and baby against her husband, Robert Henry Cloke (aged 22), an instrument fitter in the Royal Naval Air Service. They had been married a year and not lived together for some eight months. He suspected her of adultery, which she denied – incriminating letters to her had been intercepted by his mother. She only admitted that she had danced most of one evening 'at a hunt ball at Orton with a trooper of the 7th Hussars whom she had not met previously' – and given these suspicions he had arranged for the Admiralty to stop her weekly allowance of 49s 3d. The three-person police court ordered him to pay her 10s a week and another 5s for 'her' (she claimed 'their') child. No explanation was offered for this verdict, though the report concluded by noting that 'the Chairman expressed the hope that these two young people, only on the threshold of married life, would endeavour to "make it up"'.[25] Perhaps they – and other couples in similar circumstances – did succeed in doing this, when, post-war, they were able to live together under the same roof, in more or less 'normal' shared conditions.

As the war was nearing its end, it is not surprising that marital breakdowns became more talked about and certainly more common.[26] Kendal's WVS reported in February 1945 'a spate of welfare cases to deal with – broken homes owing to unfaithful wives chiefly. In one case Mrs. Pennington was able to patch up a peace and husband and wife are together again, but in another case where the returning soldier found his wife with an Italian prisoner the home has been broken up and the children are in an Institution. In yet another case we were able to arrange for an illegitimate child to be looked after by another relative when the husband came home from the

Far East.' Evidence of this sort is a reminder of the insecurities and lack of stability endured by many children, not all of them evacuees. Such family tensions must often have persisted for years, perhaps as portrayed in Melvyn Bragg's highly realistic novel, *The Soldier's Return* (1999), which is set in Wigton immediate post-war.

On at least one occasion the WVS was instrumental in facilitating sexual intercourse. In July 1943 Kendal's very active Mrs. Pennington was called upon to look into the circumstances 'of a soldier in the Middle East who wanted leave on compassionate ground as he and his wife were approaching middle age and both longed for a child. They had been married for some time and had no children. The Commanding Officer wished the matter to be investigated, and Mrs. Pennington was asked to obtain the wife's consent, and the Doctor's assurance that this was a genuine case. This she managed to do.' (Kendal WVS, NR July 1943.)[27] Here was one of many instances in which private intimacies became matters of semi-public knowledge.

Then were the numerous people – mainly women – who by the later months of the war were worn out and (it seems) increasingly prone to illness. For many women by this time feeling fit was probably exceptional, not the norm. There are routine references in sources from 1944 and sometimes earlier, to women's health failing under wartime stresses, and to the need to take leave from work or be granted some appropriate respite. In the summer of 1944 one man who refused to billet a woman with two children defended himself (plausibly) on the grounds that his wife was too sick to cope with evacuees. 'Her illness was due to voluntary work,' he claimed. 'She had an accident while assisting in camouflage work; it affected her heart and set off blood pressure.'[28] One other example can stand for many. 'I have recommended one of our hardest workers for a rest cure in a Red Cross hostel,' wrote Westmorland's WVS county organiser in her report for January 1945. 'Miss Law is typical of many of our WVS helpers. She is nearly 70 and has a very tiny income, lives in uncomfortable lodgings, and has worked most faithfully in our British Restaurants and now a school canteen ever since she started. She badly needs a rest and change which may save her from a serious breakdown. So we hope her application, countersigned by the County Medical Officer and the ARP Controller, will be successful.' It was, and Miss Law was granted three weeks' rest at a home in Nantwich (Westmorland WVS, NR February 1945).

Finally, the occasional personal mishap carried a comic twist, or at least a touch of levity. On 21 September 1944 James Garnett, the organiser (unpaid) of the Zion Rest Centre in Kendal, wrote to the social welfare officer at Westmorland County Hall. In the course of his recent work with evacuees from the V1 missiles attacking London, he had sustained an injury, which he described in some detail. 'On the evening of the 11 July several complaints were made, both by the evacuees and our Rest Centre helpers, that the biscuits served for the reception meal [supplied by the Ministry of Food] were too hard and indigestible and altogether unsuitable for consumption by mothers and young children. In order to test these complaints, I decided to sample one of the biscuits, but the result was very unfortunate from my point of view, although it fully justified the complaint.' He then recounted his misfortune. 'An upper denture of mine, containing three false teeth, could not stand the extreme hardness of the biscuit and the roof and two of the teeth were split and the whole structure weakened in consequence. I had worn this denture for several years but it was still in good condition and giving excellent service.'

Understandably, he sought professional help. 'Upon taking the denture to my dentist, he explained it was impossible to repair it as the structure had been wrecked, and I have been obliged to have a completely new denture, the cost of which is £4 4s 0d [i.e., 4 guineas] as shown by the accompanying receipted account.' (This was no trivial sum; it was roughly the standard weekly wage of a semi-skilled labourer – though Mr. Garnett was undoubtedly middle class.) Since this 'unfortunate happening occurred during the proper execution of my duty as Rest Centre Organiser', he felt he ought not to be personally out-of-pocket, and 'I shall be happy to learn that you can arrange for me to be compensated for the expense incurred'. His request was duly granted, with the approval of the clerk to Westmorland County Council.[29]

Notes and References

1 D. Gregory, *How I Won the War for the Allies: One Sassy Canadian Soldier's Story* (Vancouver, 2014), 116.

2 T. Cook, *The Necessary War: Canadians Fighting the Second World War 1939-1943, Volume One* (Toronto, 2014), 165.

3 *Cumberland News*, 20 January 1940, 6.

4 On 1 August 1945 the organiser for the Women's Voluntary Services in Thursby, Cumberland summed up in an upbeat manner her members' accomplishments since 1939 and concluded by expressing her thanks to them, without whose help (she was planning to say), 'I could not have carried on this last year, for as you know my home life has been very disturbed and saddened [she had struck out the preceding nine words from her text]. I have been passing through a very trying period in my home life....' She did not state the exact nature of her loss, since most of her listeners would have known what it was, and a degree of stoicism was expected of people sorrowing over losses. (Carlisle Archives, DX/1576/29.)

5 MOA, Diarist no. 5290, 13 August 1941.

6 While German bombing largely ceased after May 1941, Hull was an exception. It endured significant raids in August and September of that year.(T. Geraghty, *A North-East Coast Town, Ordeal and Triumph: The Story of Kingston upon Hull in the 1939-1945 Great War* [Howden, 2002; first published 1951], Appendix).

7 This is a theme of one woman's reminiscences, who lived and worked in Carlisle and was separated from her husband for four years, as presented in J. Thistlethwaite, *Cumbria: The War Years – Lake District Life during the 1940s* (Kendal, 1997), 56-61.

8 Whitehaven Archives, DH/154/1/1.
9 Carlisle Archives, SUDP/1A/Box 16, papers on Penrith evacuees and evacuation. The bombing of the North East was particularly severe in February-April 1941 (J.Gardiner, *The Blitz: The British Under Attack* [London, 2010], 283-84; and M. Hill and J Alexander, *The Blitz on Britain* [Croxley Green, 2010], 155, 173, and 178). Air raids during the war on Newcastle alone killed some 140 people and left hundreds homeless, mostly during these months in 1941.
10 Whitehaven Archives, SDUC/1/3/199.
11 Carlisle Archives, SRDC/1/3/2/23.
12 Whitehaven Archives, SUDC/1/3/282, evacuation correspondence 1939-1944, file 2.
13 Carlisle Archives, SUDK/1/3/1/83, E2 (b), a file of miscellaneous papers on evacuation.
14 These two documents and the following letter are all found in the Whitehaven Archives, SDUC/1/3/119, on evacuation 1939-1945.
15 Kendal Archives, WDSO 92/1-2, Kendal WVS Narrative Report for September 1941 and Westmorland WVS Narrative Reports for November 1942 and December 1942.
16 To illustrate: on one occasion the police in Kendal asked the town's WVS Organiser, Mrs. Hornyold-Strickland, 'to visit a German woman, unhappily billeted, married to a British sailor [perhaps the same woman mentioned above]. I found that owing to loneliness she was drinking and getting into loose company. Luckily I have been able to billet her in a friendly home and am keeping an eye on her.' (Kendal Archives, WDSO92/1-2, January 1942.)
17 One young evacuated girl's precocious sexuality in 1942 gave rise to much local concern and revealed family circumstances that suggested, at the least, negligence and drunkenness on the part of her father, and perhaps worse (it was reported that she sometimes slept with him). The distinctive wartime features of this case were related to billeting and parental separation, quite normal in the early 1940s, for the father was employed in Workington and probably had a girlfriend while the mother was still at home in South Shields with three other children. The case is described in unusual detail: Carlisle Archives, SRDC/1/3/2/31.
18 *Carlisle Journal*, 3 November 1939, 1.
19 Imperial War Museum, Documents.16878.
20 MOA, Diarist no 5290.
21 Reminiscences of Pauline Crabbe, in M. Nicholson, *What Did You Do in the War, Mummy? Women in World War II* (Bridgend, 2010; first published 1995), 1. By contrast, right after her husband was called up, early in the war, 'I was quite shattered at being left. I'd had no preparation for it. In fact I had never been alone before.' (39) She saw her subsequent affairs as 'linked with a feeling of unexpected freedom. ...My freedom came when I actually earned my own money. Not that it was a lot, but I decided how it was spent.' (41)
22 *Cumberland and Westmorland Herald*, 4 September 1943, 1. Courts may have been particularly unsympathetic to soldiers' wives who were seen as neglecting their children: *West Cumberland Times*, 29 June 1940, 7.
23 *Cumberland and Westmorland Herald*, 14 October 1944, 3.
24 *Cumberland and Westmorland Herald*, 23 October 1943, 1.
25 *Cumberland and Westmorland Herald*, 9 December 1944, 6.
26 This subject is handled sensitively in A. Allport, *Demobbed: Coming Home after the Second World War* (New Haven and London, 2009), 89-94.
27 This was in fact deemed by the Army a legitimate reason for applying for compassionate home leave: S. Ferguson and H. Fitzgerald, *Studies in the Social Services* (HMSO, 1954), 19n, a volume in the *History of the Second World War: United Kingdom Civil Series*, ed. Keith Hancock.
28 *Carlisle Journal*, 5 September 1944, 1.
29 Kendal Archives, WC/C9, Bag 1, file 1/1, 'Miscellaneous Correspondence'.

Fig. 5. Wartime parade in Kendal *(Kendal Library)*

Fig. 6a. Canning fruit *(Kendal Library)*

Fig. 6b. Land girl feeding poultry *(Lakeland Museum)*

Fig. 7. Women's Land Army doing timber work at Elterwater *(Kendal Library)*

Fig. 8. Barrow Island victory party, May 1945 *(Barrow Archive Centre)*

Chapter 9
Peace

> 'There will be no spectacular change to sweep things away on V.E. Day – or as the song says, "when the lights go on again all over the world".' (Nella Last, 4 May 1945, *NLW*, p. 266)

> 'The peace will have greater and more difficult problems than ever war had.' (Nella Last, 11 May 1945, *DONL*, p. 212)

The actual ending of the war in Europe (8 May) and the war in the Far East (15 August) must have been accompanied by many intense emotions. The newspapers did their best to convey people's sense of relief and joy and to report their displays of revelry and celebration.

Much that happened in Cumbria was similar to what happened throughout Britain. These included bonfires, fireworks, floodlighting and illuminations, services of thanksgiving, bell-ringing, band performances – the Risehow and Gillhead Collieries Band performed in Flimby[1] – community singing, parades, lots of flags, abundant streamers and bunting, with almost everywhere a focus on outdoor parties and games for children. On 8 May 'until the early hours of the next day the streets of Kendal were alive with people'. Dancing in the street outside the town hall was briefly halted as the press photographer raised his camera. At Kirkby Lonsdale 'the gaily decorated Drill Hall was the scene of a victory dance at night, for which the Return Home Fund committee was responsible'. At Milnthorpe 'the youngsters collected material for a bonfire alongside which the effigy of Hitler, well stuffed with sawdust, was burned with evident satisfaction'.[2] Burning effigies of the defeated dictators was standard fare. In Penrith the buzzer at the gas works, 'silent for so long, came into action to host the V signal'. In the evening soldiers arrived in town to join the celebrations. The following day 'hundreds of children scrambled for coppers thrown by the crowd of civilians and soldiers. The crush was so great among the open-air dancers that it was practically impossible to move'.[3] Appleby's VE festivities included a football match between the National Fire Service and the Express Dairy.[4] At Whitehaven's hospital 'one of the most imposing victory signs in the town was to be found, for blazoning from the roof was a brilliantly lighted read, white, and blue "V", with the word "Victory", and the victory sign stretched between the two arms of the letter'.[5] Ships in the harbour 'were flaunting all their signal flags', as were those at Maryport.[6]

Most communities of any size organised victory festivities – and for VJ Day in August as well (though often less extravagantly). Everywhere ordinary folk were celebrated, at events sometimes planned months in advance; soldiers and their families were honoured and war heroes and POWS applauded. Nella Last thought that 'the poorer more demonstrative people in little streets' were particularly inclined to arrange communal parties in Barrow (*DONL*, 11 May 1945). The very young and the very old were often given a treat of some kind (Fig. 8), something that had been all too rare in wartime. The general mood was less to mourn the past and more to voice hopes for the future. Cumbrians, many singing and dancing, were encouraged to look ahead. The future rested in the hands of the young, and most communities focused on them, as well as honouring the adults who had helped win the war. In Penrith 300 lucky children had a particularly memorable experience when they were taken by coach to Allonby on the Solway, where some of them saw the sea for the first time. This special excursion had been arranged to replace the earlier VE Day celebration that had been spoiled by foul weather and was now effectively a VJ outing.[7]

Nationwide, there are probably hundreds if not thousands of surviving personal accounts of VE Day, each with its own distinctive character. One description from Cumbria is found in a letter written on 9 May 1945 by Barbara Miller-Jones in Bowness to her husband in the army. (He was about to return home.) It gives a good sense of one woman's feelings about the day, blending routine with specialness.[8] She began by wondering how her 'dearest Rod' had celebrated victory, and then spoke of her own 8 May.

> We started off in typical fashion with a good old drizzle – very warm – and we all felt flat and lethargic after the sudden change of weather. I almost felt depressed in the morning – it all seemed so difficult to realise and yet I knew it was just because I was here, cut off from all the excitement and rejoicing. I felt much better in the afternoon when the sun came out and we heard Winston do his stuff at 3.00. Did you hear it? We all sat in the window and listened to him, Angela [her daughter, b. July 1939] too. I wanted her to hear it just in case she can remember later. Then we heard the bells all over the county and the ships all hooting and buzzing in the Mersey [broadcast on the radio]and I began to feel quite elated.

Then Barbara and her young daughter visited friends for tea and sat outside. 'It was very hot and sunny and beautiful and we enjoyed it.' In the evening, 'after we'd heard the King and all the rest, we heard guns and noises and went out to look and to my delight I could hear shouting and singing in Bowness and they were sending off Verey lights – pink and yellow and green. It was *something* at last in the way of celebration.' She and her father watched, 'standing on the edge of the lawn – it was very warm and lovely scented air'. Then she woke Angela to watch too and she 'loved it of course' and 'was thrilled with it all. We eventually got to bed about 2 feeling a little bit more convinced that the war was over!' The following afternoon, after a morning of cleaning, cooking and receiving visitors, 'I took Angela down to the village green where there were sports and music and flags and crowds, soldiers and WAAFs and most of A's little friends and some of mine. So that was quite a success. Angela loved watching the sack race and the three-legged race.' That evening 'we listened to the programmes about the celebrations in London, and Winston's priceless ride round on the top of a police car with Richard Dimbleby following behind with his mike. There was a marvellous "Victory Variety", all the good people together.' (Barbara was reunited with her husband on 28 May.)

⋆ ⋆ ⋆ ⋆

The ending of armed conflict, at different times in different theatres of combat, brought consequences in Cumbria that were similar to those in other regions. These included the return of POWs, whose arrival home received lots of newspaper attention. Virtually every issue for several weeks reported the return of prisoners, often with individual details concerning their family background, previous employment, and perhaps future plans. Many of the earliest returnees were men, often members of the Border Regiment, who had been captive since Dunkirk.[9] Others came home from the Far East, frequently from Burma. Readers of these reports in sparsely-populated Westmorland and Cumberland often knew individual POWs and other returning soldiers and thus, reckoned newspaper editors, would be anxious to learn their stories. Page after page tell tales of their dreadful experiences at the hands of (in particular) the Japanese, but also of their gratitude for gifts from home that, they said, helped to pull them through. As one officer who spent nearly five years in enemy hands declared, 'Had it not been for the work of the Red Cross many prisoners would not have returned to this country'.[10] On 20 January 1945 the *Westmorland Gazette* (p. 5) devoted extensive coverage to a Kendal contingent of men returning from the Far East and noted that some had visited the paper's offices, anxious to talk about the Burma campaign though not about personal hardships, preferring to 'remember only the more happy days in that land of swamp and jungle'. One man told the paper that 'Kendalians as far as humanly possible kept together' and reinforced each other's commitment to returning home; this theme recurs in other reports – and no doubt was what local readers wanted to hear. Another prominent theme was the breadth of world experience that many of these men were bringing home with them. The soldier quoted above had served in France,

Egypt, Syria, Libya and India before being posted to Burma. At the other end of the spectrum were the men imprisoned by the Germans as early as 1940, some of them, presumably, on their first military mission.

Cumbrian veterans were given enthusiastic homecomings as well as some practical aid. In Penrith the Troops Entertainment Committee, which over the previous five years had provided pleasure to troops posted in the town, now hosted a social and dinner for the town's POWs.[11] Such gestures were repeated across an appreciative county. Practical demonstrations of gratitude appeared in the form of what were often termed 'Welcome Home' funds to assist POWs and other returning military men to reintegrate into Cumbrian society.[12] While the specifics varied, these funds were meant to provide financial aid until men found jobs, suitable housing, and appropriate social and medical support.

All this was well and good, but some soldiers had their own personal goals, including getting married. 'He'll wed the girl who waited for him,' declared headline of an article about the return of an Egremont man who had endured three years of near-starvation in a Japanese prison camp.[13] More often routine marriage announcements identified the groom as a veteran and where he had served or been a prisoner. At other times the press recounted meetings of Cumbrians serving abroad or special efforts to reunite kith and kin, as when an RAF sergeant from Kendal, when serving in India, was granted permission to travel 1,000 miles to see his son in Rangoon.[14] Such human interest stories were meat and drink for the local press.

* * * *

Most people had expected the war to end months before it actually did. Enemy resistance was formidable in the winter of 1944-45, and many more men were to die before hostilities ended.[15] Still, with victory appearing probable, much more thought could be given – and certainly was given – to imagining and planning for life in a post-war world. Sustained discussion about Britain's future had actually emerged around the middle of the war. A major stimulant was the publication in December 1942 of the Beveridge Report, which laid out the framework for a welfare state. The report attracted widespread and largely favourable attention, and, for the rest of the war, proposals for social reform and a better British society were regularly in circulation. These future-oriented outlooks were helped by the allied victories in late 1942 and early 1943, which strengthened the view that the corner had been turned and the nation would eventually emerge victorious – people became more confident of saying this – but with much rebuilding to be done. This rebuilding was often broadly interpreted. In 1943 and 1944 the Cumbrian press was full of stories about plans for a reinvigorated post-war society. In later 1944 the *West Cumberland Times* ran a series of articles on this very topic.

One almost universally discussed need was housing. While destruction from bombing had been limited almost entirely to Barrow, few doubted that Cumbria had significant housing needs. Some of its people lacked the barest of conveniences – no running water, electricity or gas heating, much less indoor lavatories. Standards, then, were in many places low. Virtually no new houses had been built since 1940, and in the meantime some had fallen into disrepair. Supply was clearly inadequate and demand was bound to increase, including from men soon to be demobilised and wanting to resettle. Action was urgently required.

Well before hostilities ceased, local authorities were planning to meet anticipated post-war needs. In January 1943 Carlisle City Council appointed a special committee to consider post-war planning – it included two female members, presumably to represent those with lots of everyday expertise on the subject.[16] It was generally agreed that the first call on any reconstruction funds should be 'the housing of the people', which would include clearing and replacing slum dwellings.[17] Some months later the Penrith Urban District Council purchased the Scaws Estate to meet the town's housing needs and hired a town-planning consultant to advise on layout and design.[18] At the end of 1944 a conference of Cumberland local authorities agreed on the importance of building houses and of achieving high standards and proper planning. Unanimously a number of recommendations were passed 'designed to speed up post-war housing programmes'.[19] In October 1943 Kendal's Housing Committee voted to ask for 144 houses, but not before one alderman said the town could do with 1,000, arguing that there were already 244 unfit houses in Kendal and there would be many more before the war was over.[20]

In Kendal and elsewhere it was recognised that new housing should be attentive to demographic changes, and to the desires of young couples – many of the men were war veterans – looking to live in an adequately-appointed house of their own (and not with parents or in-laws). But times were hard. Workington's plight was desperate. Here was an economically depressed area that had actually built 1,500 new houses between 1919 and 1939 and still had a waiting list of some 1,500 applicants. Local authorities anticipated that more dwellings would be unfit for habitation by war's end – substandard, even condemned, houses in Cumbria had been sometimes used to accommodate evacuees. The Workington Housing Committee thought that nothing less than a 'new Workington' was needed, involving some 4,000 additional homes over twenty years – there were about 7,000 houses in 1944. It thought that the old Workington 'was a terrible example of lack of planning', and hoped that future plans would reflect changing needs such as smaller flats for smaller families as well as provision for schools, parks, pubs and community centres. It would take 'the best brains that Workington can obtain and the most careful consideration on the part of the Council'. The committee concluded optimistically that Workington could be transformed into 'a town not only convenient and healthy to live in but good to look upon'.[21]

None of these concerns was misguided. Agricultural housing was so inadequate that even in the midst of a war the government approved the construction of a limited number of farm cottages to help ensure that the people growing the nation's food had a place to sleep. Permits were approved to erect a small number of dwellings for farm workers, who were essential to the wartime stress on increased tillage as opposed to grazing.[22] Almost everywhere housing was a big issue which would loom even larger with the return of peace – it featured prominently in Melvyn Bragg's realistic novel, *The Soldier's Return* (1999), set in post-war Wigton. There were serious obstacles: building labourers and material resources were in short supply. Stories of desperation got into print. On 28 September 1945 (p. 1) the *Carlisle Journal* told how a family of five, unable to find a house, was living in a makeshift tent, covered with sacking and canvas and 'pieces of rusty, corrugated iron'. With no heat or other amenities, it was not surprising that a three-year-old had been taken to hospital. After reporting a few more harrowing details, the paper was able to add that this struggling family was at or near the top of the housing list.[23]

Throughout Cumbria there was active and vigorous debate concerning future housing. It was deplorable that horrible buildings should be found in 'such a glorious land as England'.[24] New ideas circulated, and there was much talk about, and usually support for, 'temporary' houses – that is, 'prefabs', which, though small, came with modern amenities and promised to be comfortable. One report predicted that 'Barrow could have 550 houses in six months' if pre-fabricated houses were applied for.[25] It was generally agreed that one of the best 'welcome-homes' a soldier could have would be a good roof to put over his and his family's heads.[26]

* * * *

Many other issues were raised with regard to post-war conditions. These included agriculture, tourism, transportation, and industrial renewal. Would those employed in government works (most of them war-related) be laid off?[27] This, indeed, was a national issue: on 3 April 1945 an editorial in *The Times* (p. 5) referred to the 'the unchallengeable necessity of preventing a return of unemployment to the former distressed areas when the present war activity declines'. This clearly applied to Barrow and much of West Cumberland. What changes in farming practice would be needed, with the winding down of wartime controls? Peace was expected to be challenging, but also to afford opportunities for creative renewal. New teachers would have to be recruited and trained, and the 1944 Education Act would have to be implemented constructively at the local level. Some towns were keen to attract new industries. Innovative approaches with possible economic benefits were more likely to get a hearing in the mid-1940s than they would have been before the war, though tourism was probably one sector that was more tightly wedded to the preservation of tradition.[28]

There is abundant evidence of forward thinking. During the last year of hostilities the *Carlisle Journal* carried numerous stories that looked ahead to future needs and desires – on farms, in industry, for recreation, in educational reform. In early 1945 a comprehensive 70-page plan for the revival of industry in West Cumberland was drawn up and circulated; a couple of months later the Cumberland County Council was discussing the ways in which wartime factories could be retooled for post-war use.[29] The West Cumberland plan was full of specifics, including recommendations to foster a 'successful small market gardening industry to provide vegetables and fruit for the [proposed] cannery, and in reviving the local woollen textile industry which has almost disappeared. The establishment of local woollen and rayon industries would tend to help a number of other smaller industries, such as the manufacture of buttons, textile trimmings, etc., as well as tailoring. All of these have already been established in the area.' Maryport was said already to have the second largest button factory in Britain.[30] A plan for Whitehaven called for the development of light industries.[31] Everyone was concerned to keep Cumberland's industrial unemployment to a minimum – the county had been hit particularly hard during the 1930s.[32] The West Cumberland munitions workers sent a resolution to the President of the Board of Trade asking for assurances that they, with their proven abilities as first-class workers, 'shall not be allowed to fall into unemployment' and that Cumbrians returning from the forces would find suitable jobs – they mentioned 'the deplorable amount of unemployment between 1918 and 1939'.[33] Proposals for improvements in cultural facilities were also in the air. On the lighter though still commercial side of life, a proposed renovation of Her Majesty's Theatre in Carlisle would permit an increased capacity from 1,000 to 1,600 people. This would make it more attractive as a venue for touring companies.[34]

There were signs that careers for women were gaining legitimacy, along with sympathy for their ambitions for a higher education. Waged-labour for women had of necessity been widely accepted in wartime, and some plans for post-war Cumbria assumed that many of them would continue in the industrial workforce. Some girls would, and should, go to university, declared the dean of Carlisle at a prize-giving ceremony at the Red Gables School in December 1944. 'They were unfortunately placed at Carlisle in having no University near them. In that respect the north-west was the most lonely part of England.' He endorsed young women's educational ambitions. 'The parents' sacrifice in sending a girl to a University was well worth making providing they had evidence that their girl was likely to profit' from these studies. And some, he was sure, would later enter the business world and bring to it 'a more humane outlook on life'.[35]

* * * *

Peace had very different meanings for different people. For those who had lost loved ones – a son or husband or boyfriend or fiancé or grandson – celebration was bound to be muted. Women whose husbands were still away and in uniform in mid-1945 were likely to feel anxious and lonely, even as hostilities had ended or were about to end. For the men in the forces who had survived, many were delighted to return to a version of their pre-war lives and to get on with things; others felt let down after the intensity of battlefield experiences, with their occasionally thrilling and heroic moments, and (for some) their first experience of exercising real authority. Adjusting to peace was bound to pose challenges. Many overworked women welcomed the relaxation of some constraints, especially married women with significant household duties (though most rationing remained in force). Other women regretted a certain loss of purpose and camaraderie, as their services ceased to be needed. Nella Last in Barrow often spoke of the pleasures she found in volunteering, and of being liberated from the pre-war tyranny of perpetual housework and a fussy husband. The imminent closure of the WVS canteen left a hole in her life. "Won't we miss working at this canteen?" remarked one of her fellow WVS members on 1 June 1945. "I never remember a Friday yet we did not laugh and see something interesting or meet someone different to talk to." Here was testimony – which was repeated again and again – to the stimulating and broadening dimensions of life on the Home Front, in a part of Britain that vigorously supported the war effort but was largely spared its destructiveness.

Was there, though, a risk that some welcome wartime services, such as those for young children, would be shut down? 'Many mothers', according to the *Carlisle Journal* of 13 February 1945 (p. 3), 'some of them war-widows, who know that they will need to go out to work, are becoming alarmed about the prospects for the future. Is all the good work of the wartime nurseries to cease, or is it to be extended so that in peace-time the nursery will enable the mother to work if she wishes or needs to do so, and will give her more leisure for social and political life or to take part in educational and cultural activity?' Here was a question with a very modern ring. It was soon clear that the answer would be, resoundingly, to end these services.

The desire to return to a sort of normality was very strong. Pre-war pleasures started to be restored (at least in part). Spaces that had been out-of-bounds for security reasons during the war were again accessible for walkers and holiday-makers. Some hotels that had been appropriated for public purposes now had room for tourists. Societies that had not been functioning 'for the duration' resumed their activities, and thus, as one paper put it, 'we have got back agricultural shows, sports and other events held amid pastoral scenery'.[36] The Penrith Association Football Club, which had suspended operations in 1939, was planning for a 1945-46 season, albeit recognising that it might take a while to become competitive.[37] The Windermere sheep dog trials on Applethwaite Common were held for the first time in five years.[38] The steamships on Lake Windermere were running again.[39] Petrol (albeit rationed) became available for private motoring. During the August Bank Holiday period in 1945 at Grange-over-Sands it was said that 'Motor traffic was heavy. One of the most popular enjoyments was the motor coach ride into the Lake District. It was estimated that coaches from Morecambe one evening took nearly 400 people to Grange.' Around Kirkby Lonsdale 'Traffic on the roads was the heaviest of the year'.[40] As restraints on travel were eased, people were eager to spread their wings in beautiful surroundings.

Also of note was the ending of the constant appeals for money in support of worthy wartime causes. The final meeting in July of Kendal's Civic Committee of the Red Cross Penny-a-Week Fund recorded that since 1941 it had collected £14,228 by means of 'house-to-house collections, weekly deductions from wage-packets, collections taken in shops, hotels, etc., and many successful social functions'. Employees of 59 firms had been making regular contributions.[41] This was high-profile and hard-to-avoid fund-raising. (Much of the money had been spent on parcels for POWs.) Now the Red Cross had enough money in the bank for current requirements, and further appeals were to end. Other signs of a return to normality included the standing-down ceremonies and breaking-up parties that were commonplace for all sorts of wartime organisations in 1944-45 (ARP, Home Guard, some branches of the WVS), leaving tens of thousands of people, most of them volunteers, with time to spend in other ways.

* * * *

The ending of war had some distinctive implications for Cumbria. One of these issues was the preservation and protection of its remarkable landscape. The war had not been entirely kind to the Lake District. Military training, munitions works and other usages of property by the forces had left some regions badly scarred, compared with their pre-war state. Now there was a keen commitment to restore the land, as much as possible, to its earlier state and bring in rigorous measures to protect it in the future.

The Friends of the Lake District led this campaign for environmental protection. During the years before the war they, the Council for the Preservation of Rural England and others had begun efforts to have the Lake District designated a national park.[42] With the return of peace, this lobbying was renewed, and newspapers began to carry lots of reports of discussions of landscape and heritage protection. The many places of beauty, according to these activists, needed to be preserved. These priorities were also boosted by pragmatic considerations. The hospitality industry and local Chambers of Commerce enthusiastically endorsed the idea of environmental protection, seeing these initiatives as a promising aspect of Cumbria's post-war development.[43] The region's three county councils formed a joint committee which supported parks designation as part of its overall proposals for town and country planning.[44]

Local support for preservation was not, however, unconditional. Honouring through public policy a Wordsworthian appreciation of Lakeland's untamed natural beauty, accessible to all, was one thing, but this was not Cumbrians' only priority. Others included the urgent need for improvements in rural living standards and the desire for good secure jobs, especially in long-depressed industrial districts. Parks, it was said, should not undermine economic developments that were likely to boost prosperity. There was also a thread of distrust of national organisations and fear of their possible intrusiveness into local life. During the war the national government had routinely interfered with, and overridden, local authorities, and there were fears that such interventions would continue, to the disadvantage of local interests. Referring to the Friends of the Lake District, the editor of the *West Cumberland Times* highlighted these issues in a long editorial entitled 'If they are real friends of Lakeland they will consult' and later headed the letters-to-the-editor column 'Save Us from our "Friends"'.[45] Tension over what to do with the housing at the decommissioned Calgarth seaplane factory site was another sign of clashing priorities: environmentalists wanted to see the promised-to-be-temporary buildings demolished, others wanted to preserve them – however roughly built, they were better equipped than many rural dwellings – in an effort to ease the housing shortage. (In 1954 the Friends of the Lake District got their wish, and they were finally torn down.)[46]

A few families felt that the land and its values should be visibly associated with those who had died in defence of the nation. This was a way of honouring young lives lost. One propertied family gave 300 acres near Skelwith to the National Trust – two fell farms set high and adjoining Tarn Hows – in memory of their son, Captain Philip Scott.[47] The donated property included magnificent views – 'a panorama of all the highest hills including Scafell' – and was added to surrounding land already owned by the National Trust or protected by covenant. The two farms had houses said to be 'typical of the district', one of them full of old oak partitioning itself worthy of preservation. A family from Cheshire had erected a mountain bridge 'at a lovely spot' above Stonethwaite across a beck that had been often admired by their late son, 'a keen lover of the fells'. 'He'd have been well pleased,' thought a fellow walker who had been involved with the project.[48] Other gifts were unconnected with the honouring of some named individual. The Lake District Federation of the Ramblers' Association raised money to replace a bridge over the River Derwent that had been swept away at the foot of Sour Milk Ghyll. This was their first independent action undertaken to protect the rights of walkers. It was later reported that the Association wanted to erect a plaque stating that the bridge had been given to the National Trust in 'appreciation of all those who have sacrificed so much in the Second World War to preserve our freedom'.[49] Gifts like these, to the National Trust or some other body committed to environmental protection, was, as the *Cumberland and Westmorland Herald* for 3 March 1945 (p. 3) put it, 'a very appropriate way of enshrining the memories of those who have laid down their lives'.

These diverse efforts for preservation were part of the background to the passage in December 1949 of the National Parks and Access to the Countryside Act, which officially initiated a process that would see the creation of many new parks and Areas of Outstanding Natural Beauty, among them in 1951 the Lake District National Park.[50]

* * * *

As war was ending, some Cumbrians were attending to the social welfare of people outside the North West. Among them were those abroad, including members of the British forces and, most notably, those who had been, or were being, liberated from Nazi oppression. Many of the comforts produced in Cumbria in 1944 and 1945 were intended for suffering people in Europe. Thousands of Cumbrian knitters were kept busy for the sake of this mission, which was done in addition to their work for men in the forces. It was reported on 1 November 1944 that Westmorland's WVS had already sent 5,600 knitted vests to the 'liberated countries',[51] and efforts of this sort continued throughout the following year. On 17 May 1945 Nella Last was in Ulverston and 'saw a good idea': 'A notice asked for *clean* blackouts to be made up into pinafores for the children in occupied countries on the Continent' (MOA). In the spring of 1945 rosehip syrup was being flown to France 'for Polish children deported by the Germans for work in the fields of France'.[52] During these weeks groups of Dutch children, weakened from their gruelling experiences during the preceding winter, were being brought to Cumbria for short stays to aid their rehabilitation.[53] Later that summer some 300 Jewish orphans were flown to Crosby aerodrome, outside Carlisle, brought to Troutbeck Bridge, near Ambleside, and given refuge there for several months.[54]

Another expression of welfare directed to outsiders was the 're-homing scheme' by which household goods were collected to send to people in the South East whose homes had been seriously damaged by raids in 1944, if not earlier, and who were lacking many of the basic necessities of life. Those whose lives had been unscathed by bombing were asked to assist those less fortunate to get back on their feet. Such outreach would help 'to lessen the inequality of sacrifice war has demanded of them'.[55] Collections of cash and household furnishings – kitchen utensils, crockery, curtains, pillow cushions, and the like – for distressed people in Kent and elsewhere in the South were organised in Whitehaven and nearby districts and in Workington, usually by the WVS.[56] The donations included loads of china, kitchen ware, and furniture.[57] Recently blitzed areas received 23 large crates of goods from Workington in March.[58] Carlisle adopted Croydon as its southern beneficiary. During February members of the Boys' Brigade, in uniform, were making door-to-door collections for household goods, under WVS supervision, and by late April Carlisle had sent three lorry loads of household articles there and collected £441 for appropriate purchases.[59]

Kendal's WVS was active in support of Camberwell in South London and in May canvassed vigorously for donations. Mrs Hornyold-Strickland, the town and county WVS organiser, had already visited London before launching the appeal for help. 'There will not be a great response', she thought, 'as everyone has had evacuees for six years and their household goods are worn out, but having seen the destruction in Camberwell, Mrs Pennington and myself will do our best to get as much as we can' (Kendal WVS, NR April 1945). The appeal was publicised in the press. Salvage stewards with their vans and loudspeakers campaigned most evenings for a fortnight, and by later June 1945, 53 tons of goods had been collected in Westmorland and almost £340 raised, two-thirds of which had been spent locally on items for Camberwell.[60] 'So much money was collected', according to Mrs Hornyold-Strickland, 'that we have been able to buy many new and really useful articles, specially pots and pans and floor coverings. I have encouraged each Centre Organiser, where the local shops had sufficient supplies not to run too short, to buy the goods on the spot, and this has helped to make the scheme more popular' (Westmorland WVS, NR May 1945).

These gifts were gratefully received by London's residents. 'Camberwell has a remarkably good friend in the county of Westmorland,' declared the *South London Observer* on 15 June 1945 (p. 1). Nine van loads of goods had arrived from Kendal at the WVS Centre on Peckham Road. Staff there were still busy distributing the donations – 'Their work has increased recently, owing to the return of many evacuated families.' As it happened, a WVS member from Kendal – she had lived there for most of the war as an evacuee – observed some of this distribution. 'There was a system of points in force by which a woman was given so many to spend on goods on one particular day and could come back later to receive more, and I was told this worked perfectly. The women I saw all seemed immensely grateful and each one chose the goods she wanted most.'[61] Camberwell had also been adopted through this re-homing scheme by Bury in Lancashire, where an audience had been told of the bomb damage to the borough 'and the conditions under which the population had had to live during the war'.[62] This gift-giving was probably the last explicitly war-related instance of the North West rendering aid to the injured South East.

One reality at the end of the war that had implications for everyone everywhere was the atomic bomb. This extraordinary weapon was bound to generate discussion, whether of appreciation or alarm. 'Everywhere men and women are talking of the Atomic Bomb,' according to the editor of the *Barrow Guardian*, 11 August 1945 (p. 4). 'The importance of the discovery cannot be exaggerated, and there can be nothing but thankfulness that it was not the Axis scientists who made it. ...It is certain that the end of the Japanese war will be hastened. This is the justification for the use of so formidable an instrument.' The destructiveness of the second world war of the twentieth century seemed bad enough; now, in future conflicts, unlimited mass destruction seemed possible. These perils were acknowledged by this newspaper and others. There was so much uncertainty – even more than there had been before the destruction of Hiroshima and Nagasaki. 'The war is over,' wrote the *Penrith Observer* on 21 August (p. 2), 'and for that we are unfeignedly thankful. But whether the end of war marks the beginning of peace is a thing we are none of us clear about.' What about the future of civilisation? 'We think that mankind's very existence is threatened by the latest weapons of war. An improved rocket, an atomic bomb with even more deadly power, and mankind might vanish from this earth, or perhaps exist in conditions too terrible to envisage.'[63] Nella Last voiced similar misgivings – she said on 8 August 1945 that a conversation with a neighbour had 'a very Wellsian turn' (*NLW*, 293). 'This atomic bomb business is so dreadful. Was it something like this that happened when Atlantis disappeared under the sea, and the Age of Mythology began?' Still, two days later, after the second atomic bomb had been dropped and with the prospect that Japan would sue for peace, she thought that 'Perhaps it's as well that dreadful bomb *was* used' (*NLW*, 294).

Peace had come, after almost six years of hardship and (for some Cumbrians) agony, but could such brutal warfare – in the future possibly suicidal warfare – realistically be kept at bay? The terms of human existence had been suddenly transformed. 'Mankind has now unravelled one of Nature's secrets,' thought the *Cumberland News* of 7 August 1945 (p. 3). 'On how the knowledge is used hangs the future of mankind.'

Notes and References

1 *West Cumberland Times*, 12 May 1945, 8.
2 Evidence in the *Westmorland Gazette*, 10 May 1945, 5.
3 *Cumberland and Westmorland Herald*, 12 May 1945, 1.
4 Ibid.
5 *Whitehaven News*, 10 May 1945, 5.
6 Ibid; *West Cumberland Times*, 12 May 1945, 8.
7 *Cumberland and Westmorland Herald*, 1 September 1945, 6.
8 We are very grateful to Lisa Bell, Barbara's younger daughter, for permission to quote from her mother's letter (see Chap. 7, 118-19).
9 *Cumberland and Westmorland Herald*, 17 March 1945, 1 and 24 March 1945, 1.
10 *Cumberland and Westmorland Herald*, 9 June 1945, 3.
11 *Cumberland and Westmorland Herald*, 26 May 1945, 1 and 16 June 1945, 1.
12 For example, *Westmorland Gazette*, 6 January 1945, 3; *Workington Star*, 23 March 1945, 5; *Cumberland and Westmorland Herald*, 18 August 1945, 3.
13 *West Cumberland Times*, 11 April 1945, 2.
14 *Westmorland Gazette*, 21 July 1945, 8.
15 The sole significant German threat to the British home front from September 1944 until March 1945, was the V-2 ballistic missile, which killed several hundred civilians around the country – 378 struck the extra-metropolitan area of Essex alone (P. Rusiecki, *Under Fire: Essex and the Second World War* [Hatfield, 2015], 274). None fell in Cumbria, though the V-2 attacks kept a few evacuees there longer than they would otherwise have stayed.
16 'It is often said that it is the women who should have a say in the planning of a house', according to the *Barrow Guardian*, 22 November 1941 (p. 2), 'and this is justified, for it is the woman who has to work in it and keep it clean'. The writer condemned jerry-built houses, which were not unusual before 1939.
17 *Carlisle Journal*, 15 January 1943, 3.
18 *Cumberland and Westmorland Herald*, 29 July 1944, 1. The subsequent plans for this estate, involving twenty temporary houses to begin with, seemed well thought through, with due attention for such amenities as playing fields, allotments, a shopping centre, tennis courts and a bowling green (*Cumberland and Westmorland Herald*, 16 June 1945, 1 and 5).
19 *Whitehaven News*, 14 December 1944, 3.
20 *Westmorland Gazette*, 16 October 1943, 5.
21 *Workington Star*, 21 July 1944, 7.
22 *Westmorland Gazette*, 13 March 1943, 5.
23 Earlier that month a man admitted to stealing coal from a railway embankment as his family had no heat in their tent. The NSPCC had tried but failed to find them a home. It was said that a local doctor saw the children and 'wept at their plight'. (*Carlisle Journal*, 18 September 1945, 1.)
24 *Workington Star*, 12 January 1945, 7.
25 *North-Western Evening Mail*, 11 April 1945, p. 4; also issue of 3 July 1945, 4.
26 *Carlisle Journal*, 29 May 1945, 1.
27 *Whitehaven News*, 24 May 1945, 4.
28 This conservatism was central to 'Catering for the Tourist – and the Native', by Brendan Bernard Williams, in the *West Cumbrian Times*, 26 May 1945, 7.
29 *Carlisle Journal*, 27 February 1945, 1 and 4 May 1945, 3; also *West Cumberland Times*, 10 January 1945, 2 and *Workington Star*, 25 March 1945, 3.
30 *Whitehaven News*, 5 October 1944, 6.
31 *Whitehaven News*, 10 May 1945, 5.
32 For example, Ibid.; *Whitehaven News*, 22 March 1945, 3 and 5 and 29 March 1945, 3; *Carlisle Journal*, 9 October 1945, 1.

33 *Whitehaven News*, 12 April 1945, 6.
34 *Carlisle Journal*, 6 April 1945, 1.
35 *Carlisle Journal*, 8 December 1944, 1.
36 *Westmorland Gazette*, 11 August 1945, 4.
37 *Cumberland and Westmorland Herald*, 18 August 1945, 3.
38 *Cumberland and Westmorland Herald*, 18 August 1945, 1.
39 *Westmorland Gazette*, 21 July 1945, 8; 4 August 1945, 5; 8 September 1945, 4.
40 *Westmorland Gazette*, 11 August 1945, 5.
41 *Westmorland Gazette*, 21 July 1945, 5.
42 John Cousins, *Friends of the Lake District: The Early Years* (Lancaster, 2009), Chap. 7.
43 *Westmorland Gazette*, 25 August 1945, 4.
44 *Whitehaven News*, 17 May 1945, 4.
45 *West Cumberland Times*, 14 April 1945, 7 and 28 April 1945, 7. Rebuttals of these criticisms from H.H. Symonds, the hon. secretary of the Friends of the Lake District, were printed in the issues of 21 April 1945, 7 and 31 May 1945, 5.
46 Cousins, *Friends of the Lake District*, 111-13.
47 *Cumberland and Westmorland Herald*, 3 March 1945, 5.
48 *Cumberland and Westmorland Herald*, 20 January 1945, 5.
49 *West Cumberland Times*, 7 April 1945, 2.
50 Cousins, *Friends of the Lake District*, 128.
51 Kendal Archives, WDSO 92/1-2, WVS Annual Report, 1 November 1944.
52 *Penrith Observer*, 12 June 1945, 1.
53 *Penrith Observer*, 1 May 1945, 1; *Westmorland Gazette*, 14 July 1945, 5 and 28 July 1945, 10.
54 *Whitehaven News*, 16 August 1945, 5; *Carlisle Journal*, 17 August 1945,1; *From Auschwitz to Ambleside: The Story of 300 Child Holocaust Survivors and the Community that Welcomed Them* (Another Space Publishing, 2015).
55 *Whitehaven News*, 7 December 1944, 5.
56 Ibid.; *Whitehaven News*, 15 February 1945, 2; *Workington Star*, 9 February 1945, 8.
57 *Whitehaven News*, 8 February 1945, 4.
58 *Workington Star*, 30 March 1945, 6.
59 *Carlisle Journal*, 27 February 1945, and 27 April 1945, 1. The nationwide character of this scheme is discussed in our *Women at the Ready*, 276-84.
60 *Westmorland Gazette*, 19 May 1945, 4 and 5; Kendal WVS, NR May 1945; *Westmorland Gazette*, 30 June 1945, 6; Westmorland WVS, NR June 1945.
61 K. Rhodes, *December Brings Me Roses: A Book of Memories* (London, 1950), 103.
62 *South London Observer*, 15 June 1945, 1.
63 Similar sentiments were expressed in the *Cumberland and Westmorland Herald*, 11 August 1945, 5 and in part of a Methodist sermon reported at length in the issue of 1 September 1945, 3.

Epilogue

The Second World War continues to be seen as one of the great moments of British history – and with reason. The survival of a sovereign Britain in 1940-41 was pivotal to modern world history. The nation hung together, muted many differences, and weathered the storm. There is a danger, though, that these years are romanticised, and peopled with an excess of heroes and heroines and exemplary self-sacrifice. This romance is largely a product of hindsight and victory, and a taken-for-granted nationalism. Emotional tugs can be distorting. As George Orwell once remarked (in April 1945), 'To study any subject scientifically one needs a detached attitude, which is obviously harder when one's own interests or emotions are involved.'[1] To be triumphant in this war was and has been deeply gratifying. Defeat would have been unbearable.

The stakes were high and people's responses were all over the map. Daily life in wartime Cumbria was dominated by ordinary people, some of them perhaps not especially admirable, but most of them probably trying to do their best in extraordinary circumstances, responding to the need for some personal sacrifice, hoping to rise to the occasion – some may not have aspired to rise very far – and enjoying a degree of success in their efforts. These extraordinary circumstances establish the war as a constant magnet for the attention of later generations, for, unlike peace-time, it forced millions of people out of their routines, their zones of comfort and predictability, and made them summon up unknown resources, perform unfamiliar acts, reconsider some assumptions, and face facts they had never before had to face. Of course, those who succeeded tend to be the best documented and thus the best remembered.

Many histories of the war have recounted shared national experiences, which to some extent did exist. Who, for example, whatever their social class and wherever they lived, could evade the blackout and its associated fears and annoyances? Who, aside from a very few political heavyweights, could ignore the inconveniences and discomforts of wartime transportation? Who, whatever their station in life, could expect to eat a banana? And what citizen who enjoyed dancing had far to look to satisfy his or her pleasure? Most wartime recreations were inexpensive. Even the rich, with their still well-stocked wardrobes, felt the pressure of austerity and largely abandoned their customary extravagances of dress. Death, too, was an equalizer: war was as likely to cut down the son of a landed gentleman as the son of a lorry-driver or shopkeeper. These were the facts of war that placed everyone in more-or-less the same boat. They were elements of an abrupt shift towards a social levelling that was widely acknowledged (and later regretted by many traditionalists).

Almost everyone experienced war both intimately, in solitude or with one or two others, and in the public realm. The former experiences, in their immediacy, are less well documented, mainly because most people were not writers. Those who were revealed the sorts of thoughts and feelings that must have been commonplace, in part because of the unfamiliarity of so much of what was being seen and heard. Take, for example, the words of a young man who lived in Flimby. A little after 2 p.m. on 10 February 1943 he was waiting for a bus into nearby Maryport, when a bomb disposal squad appeared to deal with a section of the minefield on the shore. After the first explosion, 'Shrapnel tinkles on roofs and a piece lands on the grass by the bus-stop. Three other mines explode. Am glad to see the 2.30 bus arrive. A man taking his greyhound for a trial on Workington dog-track holds its head as the mines are exploded.'[2] Here was a local expression of national realities. At such times ordinary civilian life and wartime perils intersected. This must have happened a lot – and in many parts of Britain. On 25 March 1943, Nella Last reported that 'crowds of soldiers have been about in the street – and played "invasion" in all the bombed houses about and the officers have yelled orders and shots have been fired' (*DONL*, p. 149). Her 1930s estate was, temporarily, a mock battleground. A few weeks later, after a Sunday walk near Barrow's coast (MOA, 2 May), she wrote of the view of imposing Black Combe and 'the Irish sea sparkling and glittering across the fields. Larks sang so loudly and sweetly, not silenced by the constant roar of planes, and seemed louder and sweeter when *they* had gone. ...I looked at the ugly Nissen huts [accommodating soldiers] – at the training planes overhead – and at the gorse, so brave and gay. I felt "There will be golden gorse and larks when all the ugliness of huts and torn-up country roads is past and when khaki is not general wear". I'd a queer sadness on me somehow that not even the sunshine could dispel.'

Many experiences were heavily dependent on the peculiarities of place and position and the ways in which war altered the established patterns of life in a specific locale. Eighty per cent of the British population lived outside London, which has attracted the lion's share of historians' attention, and this majority has commonly taken a back seat in wartime histories. Local particulars were always important. Most people's experiences were coloured by whether or not troops or other uniformed services were nearby; whether they lived on or near the coast – indeed, which coast (the south and east were more hazardous); whether the threat of air raids was high or low; whether local shops were reliably or erratically stocked; the special needs of the strangers in their midst; and what the weight was of, say, farming or munitions manufacturing in the local economy. Our reconstruction of life in wartime Cumbria has tried to highlight these particulars, and show (we hope) how details really mattered. Not only did the Lake District and nearby regions have their own distinctive war; individual Cumbrian families encountered war differently, and felt its impact in all sorts of ways, sometimes heavily, sometimes lightly.

Most Cumbrians were fully aware of this diversity. There was, for example, resentment (often proclaimed) of the objective fact that some people benefitted from wartime much more than others, especially financially; that the sharing of sacrifices was more evident in public rhetoric than in actual practice; and that some people were getting a much softer ride than others – regarding the putting up of strangers, for example.* On one occasion a housewife in Workington who was heading for a cake queue was overheard suggesting that 'all confectioners' shops be closed, the sugar distributed etc. to housewives for home baking and the girls etc. of the shops put into munitions'.[3] Grumbling of this sort, which was widespread and often linked to feelings of pessimism or frustrated impatience, could be offset by private contentment. 'It was lovely strolling along in the cool twilight,' wrote Nella Last about the evening of Sunday, 14 March 1943 (MOA), after she and her husband returned from the pictures in Barrow. 'The moon is so bright tonight and all is so calm and peaceful. It's so hard to think of fear and death, cruelty and suffering.'

But whatever the perceptions of fairness and unfairness and the episodic moods of gloom, the demands of wartime were frequently in some sense galvanising, imposing upon individuals a marked intensity. As the war persisted, this feeling often came to be accompanied or even replaced by weariness and stoical endurance, bolstered by a confidence in eventual victory. The moods of almost six years of war were anything but stable. And by war's end, few people, excepting the most conservative, thought that social life in Cumbria could be returned to its traditional pre-war patterns. War had exposed social ills that could no longer (most agreed) be tolerated or excused. Social planning gained a lot of legitimacy from the planning necessitated by war. Full employment, for example, came to be expected, not just hoped for.

* Perhaps the group with the most compelling grounds for grievances were the coal miners, who from May 1941 were prohibited from leaving their arduous and poorly-paying jobs in the pits to pursue better paid employment elsewhere. This industrial bondage was deeply resented. On the positive side, their earnings were increased substantially in the second half of the war. (O. Wood, *West Cumberland Coal 1600-1982/3* 1988, 224 and 239-41.) Objectively, many married women with dependent children whose husbands were in the forces also had good reason for unhappiness, since the money each received from her man's pay was usually less – often much less – than his pre-war wages, and this reduced income could be all or almost all her family had to live on.

And inadequate housing was almost universally acknowledged throughout Cumbria to be a problem demanding active attention and lots of financial investment.

The aftermath of 1945 is another story, which certainly deserves to be written. The post-war years posed challenges for a proud and victorious but nearly bankrupted nation. Our goal has been to reconstruct the realities of the war years, to highlight the experiences of those who lived then in Cumbria and to reveal something about the specific character of their wartime lives. We favour (shall we call it) factual solidity. These specifics, gathered from many witnesses and commentators, have been woven together to produce what we hope is a rich tapestry of testimony. It is this grounded solidity, driven by particular questions and highlighting major themes, that is central to our portrait of Cumbria in wartime.

Notes and References

1 G. Orwell, *Essays*, ed. J. Carey (London, 2002), 855.
2 MOA, DR no. 2845, January 1943.
3 MOA, Diarist no. 5226, 15 April 1943.

Appendix: Evacuated Students and their Schools in Wartime Cumbria

Given the prominence of several of the schools evacuated to Cumbria, it is not surprising that some of their experiences are reasonably well documented. Probably the best documented was the Newcastle Royal Grammar School, which spent five years, until September 1944, in Penrith. The most socially prominent was Roedean, known to some as 'the girls' Eton',[1] whose students spent the war years in Keswick. Schools large and small, elite and ordinary, were evacuated to Cumbria for years or just a term or two, and in the process they made an impact on this rural and beautiful part of the land for which their elders were fighting. Sometimes their reminiscences of Cumbria were later collected and put into print.*

For most of these schools getting to Cumbria was a major enterprise. While, decades later, the years students spent in Cumbria became a part of legend for some of the longest-staying schools and the focus of a few reunions, at the time relocation was sometimes an occasion of dispute among masters, board members, and parents. To move to Cumbria may have been a farsighted, if forced, decision to protect the young; but almost always it was something of a logistical nightmare. Roedean was located on a cliff on the Sussex coast, which both made it a target and ensured that it would be requisitioned by the military. In the early months of the war the school was a reception centre for the Francis Holland School from London. In May 1940 fascinated students could see hospital ships bringing back injured soldiers from Dunkirk. In the following month, with Britain facing the prospect of invasion, a contingent of the school crossed the ocean to Nova Scotia – later they were mocked for their dreadful Canadian accents, but perhaps benefitted from their more lavish North American diets; and at the same time senior students were evacuated to Oxford to take their exams undisturbed.

---

* This appendix is based on a variety of sources, notably W. Furness, ed., *The Centenary History of Rossall School* (Aldershot, 1945); D. Leinster-Mackay, *Alleyn's and Rossall Schools: The Second World War, Experience and Status* (Leeds, 1990); J. Moore, ed., *Memories of Roedean: The First Hundred Years* (Seaford, East Sussex, 1998); G. Palliser, *Evacuation: A personal account of the Newcastle Royal Grammar School in Penrith, Cumberland, during the years from 1939 to 1944* (Newcastle upon Tyne, 1979); B. Wilkinson, ed., *A Safe Haven: Evacuees in Keswick, 1939-1945* (Carlisle,2010); D. Winterbottom, *The Tide Flows On: A History of Rossall School* (Rossall School, 2006); D. E. De Zouche, *Roedean School: 1885-1955* (Brighton, 1955, printed for private circulation); and E. M. Rees, *A History of Huyton College* (Liverpool, 1985), 67-73.

In due course, following a period of negotiations, Roedean's 260 girls and their gear arrived in September 1940 in Keswick, population around 5,000, and occupied the Keswick Hotel (its headquarters), Milfield Hotel and the Shu-le-Crow guest house. The equipment moved to Keswick included many pianos – even though the school later borrowed local residents' instruments as well for their students to practise on. In addition, school supplies, beds, and even chamber pots made the move, and classes were held in locations across town, including the waiting rooms of the town's railway station and a garage at the back of the Keswick Hotel for the art studio. The Newcastle Royal Grammar School transported to Penrith books and microscopes, projectors, and workbenches for its physics and chemistry laboratories.

Perhaps, on a day-to-day basis, those who saw the most of the Newcastle Royal Grammar scholars were the students of Penrith's Queen Elizabeth Grammar School, which shared buildings and sports facilities and some activities with the Newcastle boys. The author of a 1963 history of the Penrith school noted that some of the friendships formed during the war 'continued over the years'. The two schools maintained their cordial relations after the war and in 1948 the Newcastle school presented its Penrith counterpart with a carved oak table and chairs to commemorate their shared wartime years.[2] Old boys' reunions and events involving the two schools continued to take place in Penrith for decades after the end of the war, and the Newcastle school placed a plaque of appreciation in Penrith's town hall, where it can still be seen. This was regarded as a highly successful evacuation, institutionally and for most individuals.[3] And it is worth recalling that not only did these grammar school boys come to Cumbria with, for the most part, good manners, financial means (compared to most official evacuees), and refined (to some ears) accents, but also they were well monitored by teachers and other authority figures who were usually able to sort out with a minimum of fuss problems of, say, billeting, homesickness, petty delinquency, or vandalism. These adults, if not always their charges, knew that the reputation of a renowned school was at stake – and there were also concerned parents and benefactors to be listened to and occasionally mollified.

Sometimes government requisitioning of school property came as a complete shock. Rossall School, an Anglican boarding school on the Fylde coast north of Blackpool, was advised to leave at short notice and, amazingly, the head was able to move the school in only 24 days to Naworth Castle, near the small market town of Brampton in Cumberland, with the support of the Countess of Carlisle, while the junior school was located at a nearby country estate, Kirkinton Hall. This evacuation, reportedly greeted by the students in at least a spirit of adventure, was to be short-lived. The fun of living in a castle faded quickly when the drains proved to be the likely source of a 'virulent streptococcal infection'. The influential Lord Derby persuaded the government to shift the Ministry of Pensions staff to another location near Blackpool. It was said, nonetheless, that a season in the Lake District did more benefit than harm and bonded the school together 'as never before' (Winterbottom, *Rossall School*, 97-100).

What did these 'foreigners' think of their new Cumbrian surroundings? Their experiences, understandably, were almost as varied as the individuals they were, but there are a few common threads. For many it was, initially at least, quite an adventure, in beautiful locations that offered more freedom than was the norm at a tightly managed public school. Classrooms were often improvised and activities scattered in buildings across small Cumbrian towns, which of course meant that students in their distinctive uniforms became a familiar sight tramping through the streets. 'It was fun, and crazy –not really like school', recalled one former Roedean student, while another loved the relative freedom and the beauty of the fells. They had been 'so penned in at Brighton that walks and bicycle rides were a great joy'. Skating on the lake and walking and cycling in the fells made her year in Keswick the happiest of her school years recorded another. (*Memories of Roedean*, 80.) In Penrith, one boy's first letter home concluded with a request to have his bike sent up, as other boys had already had theirs sent. Everywhere students spent a great deal of time outdoors, both on their own and on organised rambles with their teachers or volunteers. The children of a much more modest Liverpool orphanage were even more enchanted with their evacuation. Their final destination, Hawes End on Derwent Water was, according to one former resident, 'the nicest place we had ever lived' (*A Safe Haven*, 136). Like their fellows from classier institutions, these children commonly remembered their main pastime as climbing the fells.

Harsh weather offered both opportunities and discomforts. Cancellation of afternoon games because fields were frozen caused teachers to improvise. Boys could not be left to their own devices. So for the Royal Grammar School in Penrith 'sledging' was arranged for the younger students on the golf course. Older children skated – the young Roedean women who returned from Canada had developed some proficiency. But there was a downside too. The hotel in which the Roedean girls were placed was never meant for winter use and tales of frozen wash basins and sleeping in cloaks and heavy sweaters abounded. One former Roedean student, Daphne Hoare, recalls that she spent her first term 'sharing a room with three other girls on the top floor of the [Keswick] hotel. Your room and room-mates changed each term. It was a tough life with no central heating. In the bitter winters we muffled ourselves in our long woollen cloaks and wore mittens in class but still suffered from chilblains' (*A Safe Haven*, 151). In Penrith, the Newcastle Grammar School boys and their masters endured outside loos which had to be tepidly warmed by primus stoves and, in the staff bedroom at least, hot water bottles left under the bed were partially frozen by night.[4]

While many grammar school students and teachers from Newcastle were lodged in common accommodation, usually hostels, others, particularly in the early months, were billeted.[5] Their experiences were enormously varied. Few of the Royal Newcastle Grammar School billetees stayed in the same location over the five years. In the early months visiting parents stirred the pot by complaining about their children's billets – this was before petrol restrictions kept them away. There were sometimes real problems – bedwetting, children sleeping three to a bed, no proper space to do homework, etc. One lad recalled having an unexpected religious education while lodging with observant Methodists who took him to Sunday school three times on Sundays and a few other times during the week. Occasionally life-long friendships were made either at the billet or via shared classes and games with other schools.

The arts figured in the lives of some school evacuees, who put on musical and theatrical performances to which local residents were enthusiastically invited and who also experienced performances put on by others. Did the eminent actress Prunella Scales hone some of her skills in the Lake District? She attended the pre-war Eastbourne-based Moira House School in its wartime home at the Ferry Hotel at Windermere.[6] Art, music, and theatre thrived in the Lake District and many schools made special efforts to use their students' talents and enthusiasms to connect with local residents. From scattered press reports it seems that they were largely successful.

Evacuation had taken these students away from war, but some of them did their best to serve in it. They formed ARP groups and trained for first aid or related skills. But most important was the significant work many students performed in harvesting Britain's crucial arable crops. The Newcastle Royal Grammar School was particularly prominent over its five years' residence in supplying boys and young men to lift potatoes and other crops. The government urged parents (not always successfully) to leave their children in reception areas during school breaks. When they did, teachers felt obliged to keep the students busy. Local farmers were pleased to get help, and the boys sometimes earned a little and were satisfactorily supervised – and no doubt were admirably tired and well-exercised at the end of a working day. It was a beneficial arrangement for all parties, which was frequently lauded in the press. It was also one of the numerous signs of the positive linkage between the young visitors and their Cumbrian hosts, which still survive in a few (now very few) memories.

Notes and References

1 *Cumberland and Westmorland Herald*, 13 July 1940, 2.
2 J. Jackson, *The History of the Queen Elizabeth Grammar School, Penrith* (Penrith, 1963), 156-57.
3 B. Mains and A. Tuck, eds., *Royal Grammar School, Newcastle upon Tyne: A History of the School in its Community* (Stocksfield, Northumberland, 1986), 205-06.
4 Palliser, *Evacuation* (1979), 20-22.
5 Ibid., 33-43.
6 I. L. Muir, *The Ferry Inn on Windermere* (Kirkby Stephen, 2011), 320.

Index